PIGEON ON THE WING

The Diary of a Political Prisoner

By

Tim Burton

Copyright © 2019 by Timothy M. Burton

All rights reserved. This book or any portion thereof may not be reproduced or used in any manner whatsoever without the express written permission of the publisher except for the use of brief quotations in a book review.

Printed in the United Kingdom
First Printing, 2019

ISBN: 9781705625798

All enquiries to the author:
Email tim@counterjihadwarrior.com
Website www.counterjihadwarrior.com

DEDICATION

*This book is dedicated to all those who have lost their lives
or liberty through the baleful and pernicious effects of political correctness,
multiculturalism and 'diversity'.
May your sacrifices not have been in vain.*

Timothy M. Burton – November 2019

CONTENTS

ABOUT THE AUTHOR i
DISCLAIMER iii
ACKNOWLEDGMENTS v
FOREWORD 1
PREFACE 3
INTRODUCTION 5
ESSAYS - WHEN IS HARASSMENT NOT HARASSMENT? 7

CHAPTER 1 Judgment Day 10
CHAPTER 2 The Descent 17
CHAPTER 3 Brief Encounter 23
CHAPTER 4 Journey to Thameside 29
CHAPTER 5 The Lions' Den 35
CHAPTER 6 The Cell 41
CHAPTER 7 The Pigeon has Landed 47
CHAPTER 8 Ground Zero 53
CHAPTER 9 Prophet of Doom 59
CHAPTER 10 The Pigeon Awakens 65
CHAPTER 11 Pigeon on the Wing 71
CHAPTER 12 The Pigeon and Religion 77
CHAPTER 13 Background to the Birmingham Taqiyya Trial 83
CHAPTER 14 Showdown in Birmingham – Part 1 of 2 89
CHAPTER 15 Showdown in Birmingham – Part 2 of 2 95
CHAPTER 16 The Revenge of Fizzy Mendacious 103
CHAPTER 17 The Southwark Crown Court Trial – Part 1 113
CHAPTER 18 The Southwark Crown Court Trial – Part 2 119
CHAPTER 19 The Southwark Crown Court Trial – Part 3 125
CHAPTER 20 The Southwark Crown Court Trial – Part 4 132
CHAPTER 21 The Southwark Crown Court Trial – Part 5 138
CHAPTER 22 Pigeon on a Sunday 145
CHAPTER 23 Assessment Time 151
CHAPTER 24 A New Wing for the Pigeon 159

CHAPTER 25 The Kettle 167
CHAPTER 26 Visitors 175
CHAPTER 27 Release of the Pigeon 184
CHAPTER 28 A Year of Probation 193

APPENDIX: Essays from the Dark Side 201
   What should we do about the Muslims living among us? (Part 1) 202
   What should we do about the Muslims living among us? (Part 2) 208
   Why Islam should not be considered as a religion under UK law 215
   The Problematic Definition of Islamophobia (Part 1, 2 & 3) 220

ABOUT THE AUTHOR

Tim Burton has studied Political Islam since 2001 and has written numerous articles on the subject for local and international publications.

He was Radio Officer for the political party Liberty GB in 2014 when a prominent Muslim claimed to be offended with his writings, and he was taken to court on a charge of Racially Aggravated Harassment.

Tim won that case, which became known as the Birmingham Taqiyya Trial, highlighting as it did the doctrine of deceit within Islam.

Tim stood as Member for Parliament for Birmingham (Ladywood) in the 2015 General Election, standing on the Liberty GB ticket of 'Stop Islamisation' (which some say was a brave thing to do in that part of Birmingham). He lost by a whisker against the Labour incumbent, Shabana Mahmoud (where 1 whisker = 26,228 votes).

The same prominent Muslim that Tim won his case against in

2014 declared himself to be offended again by Tim's writings in 2016 and this time Tim was convicted of Religiously Aggravated Harassment and sentenced to twelve weeks in Her Majesty's Prison, Thameside.

They do say that 'everyone has a book in them', and *Pigeon on the Wing* is Tim's first published work.

He lives in Sutton Coldfield in the West Midlands, and his hobbies include the Japanese martial art of Aikido, in which he holds a Dan grade (black belt) certification.

DISCLAIMER

This work depicts actual events in the life of the author as truthfully as recollection permits and/or can be verified by research. Occasionally, dialogue consistent with the character or nature of the person speaking has been supplemented. All persons within are actual individuals; there are no composite characters. The names of some individuals and organisations have been changed to respect their privacy.

References are provided for informational purposes only and do not constitute endorsement of any websites or other sources. Readers should be aware that the websites listed in this book may change.

The author shall not be held liable or responsible to any person or entity with respect to any loss, or physical, psychological, emotional, financial, or commercial damages, including, but not limited to, special, incidental, consequential or other damages caused, or alleged to have been caused, directly or indirectly, by the information contained herein.

ACKNOWLEDGMENTS

During the course of this book I have drawn upon the writings of many prominent individuals within the counter-jihad movement. People such as Robert Spencer, who runs the website Jihad Watch, and Bill Warner, who runs the website CSPI (Centre for the Study of Political Islam) have been instrumental in providing clarification on a subject which some people may find is a difficult subject to fully comprehend – the malignant nature of Political Islam and its implications for all of us non-Muslims.

In Chapter 9, I refer specifically to Prophet of Doom – an online publication by Craig Winn – and extracts are quoted (with kind permission) from the introduction to the book.

I have drawn upon the work of Graham Senior-Milne (again, with kind permission) for my essay on 'Why Islam should not be considered a religion under UK law', and many thanks are due to Dr. Peter Hammond for the permission to draw on extracts from his book *Slavery, Terrorism and Islam* – which I have included in Chapter 28.

In the appendix at the back of the book, I have drawn upon, adapted, and modified documents (with kind permission) from the Citizen Warrior website for my two essays on 'What should we do about the Muslims living among us?'

Referring to my series of essays on 'The Problematic Definition of "Islamophobia"' – I have drawn extensively (with kind permission) from a document of the same name published by the International Civil Liberties Alliance in September 2013.

Finally, I would like to acknowledge the contribution of Fizzy Mendacious OBE and his band of merry men from Grievance Mongers UK, without whose sheer arrogance, bloody-mindedness, fraudulent misrepresentation, grievance-mongering, mendacity, opportunism, over-sensitivity, pompousness, petulant whining, pigheadedness, sense of entitlement, spitefulness, 'Taqiyya' and a tendency to throw tantrums to rival the 'terrible twos' whenever and wherever the most minor obstacles are encountered, this book would never have been written.

Timothy M. Burton – November 2019

FOREWORD

This is a book that should be read by every single person who cares about freedom of speech not only in the UK, but also in every democracy throughout the Western world.

It is much more than simply the journey of one man through the labyrinthine twists and turns of the British legal system; and much more than simply a chronicle of the injustice meted out to a man of principle who stood up for what he believed was right.

It is a story of the gradual understanding that not everything that we have been told by our political elites, the British Establishment and the mainstream media is true; and how the process of uncovering the truth leads the author to some very unpleasant realisations.

How is it, for example, that we seem to have become mired in political correctness – a system of thinking that permeates everything we do and everywhere we go in our society? When did it become *verboten* to discuss certain topics, even among friends, because offence might be taken somewhere or by somebody with an axe to grind?

More importantly, what has political correctness done to our ability to defend ourselves against external forces which are most definitely not working in our best interests? For example, who decided that the characteristics of an ideology founded fourteen hundred years ago in the Arabian Desert should supplant our perfectly good Judaeo-Christian morals, ethics, and traditions – values that have served us admirably for two millennia and have arguably led to the most advanced civilisation that mankind has ever known?

Why is it that the slightest criticism of this barbaric, totalitarian, supremacist ideology is enough to land otherwise law-abiding citizens in jail, or worse, when that ideology is inferior in almost every single characteristic that is measurable, and inferior also in terms of the ways in which we interact with each other and with the world at large?

In short, why do we allow this state of affairs to continue when a little logical reasoning and critical analysis would lead to the inevitable conclusion that we are in danger of losing everything of value that we would pass on to our children and grandchildren?

If you care about our freedom of speech, then I implore you to read this book, and when you do, just like Saul on his way to Damascus, the scales will fall from your eyes.

PREFACE

The idea for this book came about while I was serving at Her Majesty's pleasure in HMP Thameside in 2017. Over the previous decade or so I had written a series of highly critical articles and essays about politics in general, and about Political Islam in particular. These articles and essays had been published on a variety of international websites and blogs throughout Europe, Canada, Australia and the United States.

My writings had clearly upset some prominent people – I was memorably described as 'the worst "Islamophobe" ever' by Mohammed Ansar on Twitter in 2013 – and my entirely justified criticism of a prominent Muslim member of the British Establishment during the same year led to a charge of Racially Aggravated Harassment in the Birmingham Magistrates' Court in 2014. The case turned on the definition of 'Taqiyya' – an Islamic doctrine which allows Muslims to lie with a clear conscience to non-Muslims, even under oath in a British court of law, if it furthers the cause of Islam.

I had a very capable expert witness at that time to testify on my behalf, and I won that case, but the same prominent Muslim two years later saw his chance to exact revenge following an exchange of emails between his organisation and myself, when he claimed to have been threatened, alarmed, intimidated and distressed by my mocking words – and this time the judge and the jury fell for his side of the story – hook, line and sinker.

This time I had been charged with Religiously Aggravated Harassment, and once again the case turned on the definition of 'Taqiyya', but this time I was unable to bring my expert witness to testify on my behalf, as he had sadly passed away the previous year.

Although I was subsequently found guilty by the jury – and although I'm fairly sure that the fact that the jury foreman was Muslim didn't have anything to do with the outcome – I had thought it unlikely that I would end up serving a custodial sentence. But the judge clearly wanted to make an example of me, and so I was duly dispatched to HMP Thameside to serve six weeks of a twelve-week sentence behind bars.

The story of my time in prison – which I have endeavoured to present in a light-hearted manner so as not to overly depress the reader – is interspersed with a series of essays which I hope will shed some light on some of the relevant concepts and issues that were behind my prosecution, conviction, sentence and subsequent incarceration.

INTRODUCTION

The first few chapters of this book reflect my feelings on my becoming part of the prison system, together with a detailed description of what it was like to be taken to HMP Thameside, via the subterranean maze that runs under the Inner London Crown Court, and the wheezing, asthmatic diesel vans that transport the various convicts, remand prisoners, old lags and ne'er-do-wells like myself around the prison system.

There then follows some background information to put my current experience into context. This includes what led me to investigate the subject of Political Islam, and my subsequent realisation that what I had been led to believe for most of my life (by our political elites, the British Establishment and the mainstream media) was largely untrue.

The story of my original trial at Birmingham Magistrates' Court in 2014 is told using an essay that I wrote at the time – which was just as well, as the official record made by the clerk of the court seems to have mysteriously disappeared from the public domain.

My subsequent trial at Southwark Crown Court in 2017 is also elaborated upon in some detail – and although a transcript of those proceedings is available to the general public, I felt that the cost of obtaining a copy for use in my book would be prohibitive, so once again I have endeavoured to provide as much detail as I can from my own recollections so that I can do justice to the complexity of the proceedings.

The last few chapters of my book describe my experiences over the following six weeks of a twelve-week sentence, and my subsequent release and probationary period. I have interspersed some of my own essays between chapters in order to add context to what some people may find is a difficult subject to fully comprehend – the nature of Political Islam and its implications for all of us non-Muslims.

Due to the fact that these essays were each originally designed to be read stand-alone, there may be a certain amount of repetition, for which I apologise in advance.

I hope that through reading this book, the reader will come to appreciate the dire threat posed by Political Islam and will be inspired to do whatever he or she may be able to do in order to make sure that the future of our civilisation and our way of life is secured for our children and grandchildren.

Essays from the Dark Side

When is Harassment not Harassment?

When it's on Social Media

April 2014 – I was thinking this week about the whole concept of 'harassment' as it applies to communications sent via email or social media. I have to declare an interest, of course, since someone not a million miles away from me is shortly due up before the beak in Birmingham Magistrates' Court to face a harassment charge. This is as a result of an exchange of online communications between the head honcho of the nest of vipers that is Grievance Mongers UK, and my good self, Timothy Martin Burton, currently residing in the Royal Town of Sutton Coldfield in the West Midlands.

Now, in order to prove a charge of harassment under English law, it is not sufficient to rely solely on a 'course of conduct'. A course of conduct merely means a series of two or more actions which are deemed to be related for the purposes of the charge.

There must also be an element of behaviour that causes alarm or distress (or is likely to cause alarm or distress in the mind of any reasonable person) or behaviour of a threatening or intimidating nature. Let's explore this behaviour in more detail.

Back in the days before we had the Internet, it was necessary to seek out your target for harassment purposes, maybe by finding out his telephone number or his home address or his place of work, and either bombard him with telephone calls and letters, or accost him in person and wag your finger vigorously under his nose while telling him exactly what you thought of him in no uncertain terms.

Now that is genuine, good old British harassment good and

proper, that is – genuine copper-bottomed gold-plated harassment with the Assayer's '100% Pure Harassment Mark' hall-marked into the side of it. The reason that it is harassment is because your target can't easily walk away from it without suffering some material or psychological inconvenience.

If you are bombarding him with phone calls, for example, he can try not answering the telephone, but then he might miss that all-important call from the President of the Bank of Swaziland whose uncle had suddenly died and unexpectedly left a large amount of funds unclaimed, 50% of which would be immediately available to him for the up-front cost of a small advance fee.

Equally, if you are bombarding him with snail mail, you might induce a certain psychological anxiety in your target as he attempts to sort through his mail with a view to distinguishing your vitriol-filled missives from that all-important letter from Littlewoods telling him that he was this week's lucky pools winner.

And of course, if you accost him on his doorstep, or in the street, or at his place of work, although he could in theory turn tail and run away, or thump you on the nose if he thought you were being particularly obnoxious, neither of these courses of action would be particularly becoming for a man who had been awarded the OBE for distinguished services to the community in the face of unremitting 'Islamophobia' by legions of fascist, racist, extremist, hateful and intolerant right-wing knuckle-dragging bigots.

However, if you are communicating with someone via email or Twitter, I contend that the concept of 'harassment' cannot possibly exist. The manufacturers of the email and Twitter software platforms, in their infinite wisdom, foresaw the possibility that one or more of their users might decide to be mean to some of their other users and start sending emails or tweets of a distinctly unfriendly nature. These emails or tweets might range from the mild 'I don't like you very much' to the not-so-mild 'I know where you live and I am coming round tonight with a chainsaw to hack off the heads of your entire family.'

But with the click of a mouse on the Block button, the potential for harassment has been eliminated at a stroke. All past, present and future communications are deleted from your purview; and peace and harmony are immediately restored. (Unless of course the perpetrator in question does in fact come round to your house that night and slaughter your entire family with a chainsaw, in which case you may have some redress under the existing laws without having to resort to complaining about online harassment.)

Of course, there is always the possibility that you might not want the sender of the email or tweet in question to cease his communications to you. You might (forgive me for plucking a purely hypothetical example out of the ether) want him to continue sending his emails or tweets in the hope that one or more of them might be suitable for your online 'hate crime' database, which you just happen to be compiling for your organisation in the hope that you can persuade the holders of the Government purse-strings to release hundreds of thousands of pounds worth of tax-payers money to you.

In which case, it's not really harassment at all, now is it?

CHAPTER 1

Judgment Day

'Twelve weeks.'

The words hung in the air like a malevolent mist on a winter's day.

I looked up from my reverie. I had been thinking about my soon-to-be-undertaken journey home from Courtroom 4 of the Inner London Crown Court – a journey which I had intended should take place later that morning. The words of the sentencing judge had rudely interrupted my train of thought, and I became aware that various people in the courtroom had turned their heads, and were looking at me keenly, as if to observe my reaction.

It was an unwelcome intrusion. In my mind, I was already halfway between London and Birmingham, having settled back in a comfortable chair on a Virgin Inter-City train. I had been just about to contemplate – if such a word may be permitted under the circumstances – one of Virgin Rail's refined and delicate cheese and onion sandwiches.

I had also been considering the allocation of some of my meagre funds on a pot of Virgin Rail's similarly refined and delicate Earl Grey tea – for although I wouldn't normally partake of such a beverage on such a journey, there would be some cause for celebration to commemorate my lucky escape from the slavering maw of the British legal system, and Earl Grey tea would seem at that moment to be just the ticket.

'Twelve weeks.'

I frowned slightly. Perhaps I had misheard the judge. After all, there was no way I was going to prison, was there?

There was no way the judge would sentence a sixty-four-year-old man with a heart condition and a previously unblemished record (that would be me) to a term of imprisonment, merely for sending a well-deserved handful of jocular, non-threatening emails as a tongue-in-cheek response to a job advertisement for a case-worker.

There was no way, even if those emails had been directed to an organisation run by a fraudulent, mendacious, grievance-mongering Taqiyya-artist with previous form for vexatious litigation.

There was no way, even if that fraudulent, mendacious, grievance-mongering Taqiyya-artist happened to be a member of the British Establishment with an OBE after his name.

I had been assured of this on several occasions by various respected and experienced members of the legal profession over the previous three or four weeks. I specifically recall the words of one particular solicitor as he leaned back in his creaking office chair and perused my case notes:

'You don't have to worry, Mr. Burton. You may have been, unjustly in my view, convicted of a charge of harassment, but there was never any suggestion of violent or threatening behaviour, and even though political correctness is all-pervasive throughout the British legal system these days, no judge is likely to follow through with a custodial sentence under such circumstances. It's not as if there was any intent to cause alarm, distress or intimidation with your emails – in my opinion, most reasonable people would interpret it as merely a light-hearted attempt by you to employ mockery and satire in the face of pomposity and arrogance.'

So, surely I had misheard the judge. But the faces in the courtroom continued to observe me keenly.

'Twelve weeks.'

I looked around the courtroom. The room was momentarily quiet, although the low hum of an air conditioner could just be discerned in the background.

At the far end of the court, directly in front of me and elevated on a platform, was the bench on which the judge sat. He was around fifty years of age, bewigged and bespectacled – with the demeanour of a wise old owl who has decided that a change of appearance is well overdue, and who has decided to spend the day rummaging through the oddments box at the local costume hire shop.

The 'bench', for those who do not know, is more of an elongated desk, stretching from side to side in the courtroom, behind which justice is dispensed by one or more magistrates – or judges in this instance, as we were in a Crown Court rather than a Magistrates' Court.

The bench was embellished with the logo of the Inner London Crown Court (the lion and the unicorn alongside the shield and crown) and plainly designed to intimidate all those unfortunate enough – such as myself – to land in the dock.

I had always supposed that at least three judges are needed at any one trial in case two of them fall asleep after a strenuous lunchtime session at the Boot & Flogger wine bar in the nearby Borough Market. However, as it was only 10:30 in the morning on this particular day – Friday 28 April 2017 – the decision had obviously been taken that one judge would be sufficient.

The judge at the Inner London Crown Court

To my left was the press gallery – which was reserved for the assorted conglomeration of singularly ill-favoured weasels representing the British mainstream media in court that morning.

These so-called journalists had occasionally glanced at me as they busily scribbled away in their notebooks or made notes on their laptop computers.

To my right was the jury bench, which was vacant. (Today was merely a Hearing for Sentence, rather than the full trial which had taken place four weeks previously, and the jury members were no longer required for this particular stage of the justice process.)

Towards the back of the court were some more benches, presumably for members of the public, which also appeared to be vacant. I found this to be odd, as I had met some of my supporters that morning prior to entering the courtroom. Where were they?

I later found that my supporters had been escorted to seats hidden from my view by a wooden panel at the side of the dock. Why this was, I couldn't say. Perhaps the judge was worried that at my command, my supporters would rise up en masse and lay waste to the courtroom.

The judge needn't have worried. Mindful of the fate that had befallen William Wallace, (another firebrand revolutionary of an earlier age) I had exercised a certain degree of forethought, and had left instructions that any pike-staffs, pitchforks and torches were to be left outside in the care of the courtroom security staff.

In front of me, in the well of the court, bewigged and cloaked in black silk gowns, and with all the self-important airs that one comes to associate with such members of the legal profession, were the prosecution and defence lawyers, together with the clerk of the court and the usher. They were the ones who had turned from their benches to look at me in the dock as the judge finished speaking.

The dock was a self-contained area behind a series of overlapping sheets of armour-plated glass between me and the rest of the courtroom – these days there is nothing left to chance in a Crown Court, I can tell you. I dare say that after a sufficient number of burglars, rapists or serial killers had flown into a rage after sentencing, leapt over the dock barrier and attempted to throttle the presiding judge with their bare hands, the decision would have been taken to employ some extra security.

Back in the good old days, criminals were no doubt much better behaved at the time of sentencing. 'Jeremiah Hardcastle, I hereby sentence you to a severe flogging and life imprisonment with starvation rations and hard labour in a penal colony in Australia for the heinous crime of stealing a loaf of bread from Old Mother Perkins' bakery in Pudding Lane on 24 December 1867.'

'Thank you, Your Honour. You're very fair, so you are, and it's no more than I deserve. I'm so sorry to have troubled the court with my petty misdemeanours. I realise that trying to feed my starving family on Christmas Eve can never be an excuse for breaking the law. Just have the dock officer affix the manacles to my wrists and the ball and chain to my ankles, and I'll make my own way down to the cells to await my 500 lashes and subsequent transportation to Van Diemen's Land.'

Still, times change, and good manners – especially among the criminal fraternity – have regrettably deteriorated. So there I was, behind enough sheets of armour-plated glass to stop a Challenger tank. Or at least, I assumed there would be enough. There's never a Challenger tank around when you want to borrow one to test out your theory.

I was accompanied by a bored-looking dock officer dressed in a crumpled and down-at-heel uniform, sitting at a wooden table on the right-hand side of the dock. He had the kind of five o'clock shadow one associates with a tramp who has recently run out of Gillette razor-blades but who has not yet sunk low enough to part-exchange his prized bottle of methylated spirits for a chance to improve his appearance.

Every now and again he would look up from his half-completed Sun newspaper crossword to take a cursory interest in the proceedings. He seemed friendly enough, having offered me a biscuit and a glass of water at the start of the sentencing hearing, but I wasn't about to engage him in conversation, as by now I was listening intently to the words of the judge as I began to realise that perhaps I wasn't going home later that morning after all.

'Twelve weeks. And there will be a victim surcharge of eighty pounds.'

Eighty pounds? EIGHTY POUNDS? That was real money the judge was talking about. Not only that, but unless I was very much mistaken in the matter, it was my money he was referring to. What a cheek, I thought. Talk about adding insult to injury.

And what was all this about a 'victim surcharge'? There hadn't even been a victim; merely a pompous, arrogant, mendacious grievance-mongering Taqiyya-artist milking the situation for all that it was worth. This particular mendacious grievance-mongering Taqiyya-artist had sought to paint himself as a model of rectitude and pillar of the community, and one, moreover, who had been cruelly maligned, distressed, alarmed, intimidated, and unfairly harassed by a fascist, racist, bigoted, hateful and intolerant, right-wing knuckle-dragging 'Islamophobe' (that would be me, apparently) – and the court had swallowed his version of events hook, line and sinker.

To add further insult to injury, the judge continued his sentencing remarks with some sweeping generalisations concerning not only myself, but also my 'associates', inferring that we had collectively 'conducted a campaign to tar all Muslims as Islamists'. (This was later to result in a formal complaint made against the judge, as my 'associates' had not been charged with any offence and no evidence was put before the court concerning their conduct. Given that the judge's remarks might be read by actual Muslim extremists who might try and target us as a result, and given that there were some 25,000 jihadists currently walking the streets of our country, as estimated by our police and intelligence services at the time, he should have been aware that he had no business making unsupported claims of that nature that were not relevant to the matter before the court and that could have very serious repercussions.

The sentencing remarks were reported in the mainstream media, and various counter-jihad publications picked up on it, but the formal complaint was never properly looked into or investigated. Not that this was a matter of great surprise to me, as you will see.)

The judge looked up from his notes and asked me if I had anything to say. I thought for a moment. I could have said a great deal about the enormous injustice that had just been perpetrated on me, but I sensed that it would achieve very little under the circumstances. 'No,' I said, and that was that.

Beside me, the dock officer stirred slightly and regarded me with interest, with a look on his face similar to that of a well-fed Labrador who perhaps would have been quite happy reclining in front of a coal fire for the rest of the day, but was now anticipating a run around the local park in pursuit of his favourite ball.

He put aside his newspaper with the half-completed crossword and rose to his feet. Brushing the biscuit crumbs from the front of his uniform, he examined a set of keys that hung from his belt on a steel chain. He selected one of the keys and approached the two doors at the back of the dock.

The door on the left, I knew led to freedom (for that was the way I had come in), but the door on the right that I presumed led to the cells underneath the court might as well have had a sign on it reading 'Abandon Hope, all ye who enter here.'

He opened the door on the right and beckoned me towards it.

CHAPTER 2

The Descent

I picked up my black Mil-Tec rucksack from the chair next to where I had been sitting, and made my way through the door on the right at the back of the dock, pausing at the top of a flight of some thirty or forty concrete steps that spiralled down to the cells beneath. Behind me, I could hear the dock officer locking the door with an air of finality. This was it.

I turned towards him and he indicated that I should descend the flight of steps, so I did so, not without some trepidation. He followed me down the steps, remaining about two steps behind. As I stepped off the bottom step and into the middle of a brightly lit corridor stretching for at least fifty yards in each direction, two burly uniformed prison officers were there to greet me.

'Well, well, what have we here?' said the first prison officer. He was a tall, well-built man in his forties, swarthy and dark-haired, and surprisingly genial in his manner. His words echoed off the walls of the corridor like those of an overly enthusiastic demon receptionist welcoming a newcomer to Hades.

'This is Timothy Burton – he'll be joining us for twelve weeks,' said the dock officer, a little too smugly for my liking.

It has to be said that I wasn't really sure exactly what to expect at this point, perhaps a water-boarding session or a stretch on a medieval rack followed by the attachment of some electrical jump leads to the more sensitive parts of my anatomy, but his words alleviated my fears, at least to the extent that I could feel a sense of calm starting to descend upon me.

Underneath the Inner London Crown Court

It's an odd thing, but at times of extreme stress I sometimes find that I am almost able to detach myself from my body and view the situation as a dispassionate observer. It's difficult to say where this ability came from – I certainly don't remember being able to call on it when I was a child – but I don't think it would be unreasonable to put this down to my training in Japanese martial arts and meditation over the last thirty years. The Japanese call this sensation 'no-mind' and with extensive practice it allows one to accept what is inevitable and to make the most of one's situation, without wasting mental energy on ineffective strategies such as panic and anxiety.

The second prison officer examined his clipboard. 'Timothy Burton? Tim Burton? Not Tim Burton the famous film director? What's a toff like you doing here?' He was younger than the first man, with wispy hair, a light complexion and accompanied by a disposition that was at least as equally genial as his colleague.

Hearing his words, I was rather taken aback. It's not often that I am referred to as a 'toff'. I checked myself to see whether, perhaps in a fit of absent-mindedness while getting dressed that morning, I had clothed myself in some accoutrements that would have justified such a description, perhaps a top hat, or a monocle, white spats and a mahogany cane, but no, I was simply dressed in my dark blue suit, black shoes and the shirt and tie which I had donned for the occasion in a gesture of respect for the court.

(I was surprised to find out later that many defendants turned up for court somewhat less well-turned-out, if not downright scruffy and unkempt. Call me old-fashioned, but I can't help but feel that such a devil-may-care approach to sartorial matters under such circumstances would not assist their chances of achieving a favourable outcome in front of the judge.

Then again, I had just been handed a sentence of twelve weeks by this particular judge, so perhaps my theory concerning the appropriate dress to wear at court was not altogether as infallible as I might have first thought.)

'No, not that Tim Burton,' I said. 'I should be so lucky.'

The first prison officer indicated that I should stretch my arms out so that I could be thoroughly searched, patted down and screened with a metal-detecting wand, which emitted an unnerving screech as it hovered over my jacket pocket.

'There's nothing in your pockets that you shouldn't have, is there?' asked the first prison officer. *Busted!* I thought, as I was relieved of my house keys, nail clippers, wallet, Casio digital wristwatch and mobile phone, all of which were placed in a large polythene bag which had (ominously) already been labelled with my name.

That was odd, I thought. It was almost as if they had been expecting me.

The second prison officer spoke again. 'Follow me and we'll get you processed.' He turned and led the way down the corridor to a room on the left, where a lady prison officer sat at a desk with a computer, intently tapping away on the keyboard as if her life depended on it.

'It's Timothy Burton, Miss.' He motioned to me that I should relinquish my rucksack. I sat down at the side of the desk as he started to unpack all my worldly possessions, or at least those I had brought with me that morning. Not that I had brought a great deal, anticipating as I had that I would by now be on my way home, but all the same, it was an odd feeling to see my rucksack being pulled apart in such a way by the hands of a stranger.

'Don't worry, we'll keep this safe for you,' he said, gesturing to the now empty rucksack and the surprisingly large pile of my belongings that were piled up on the desk. Had I really brought all that with me? How many pairs of socks did I need anyway? And what on earth was I thinking of when I packed two toothbrushes?

'Although,' the officer added, 'we'll have to confiscate these food items.' He pulled out of the pile of belongings a Marks & Spencer chicken and bacon sandwich, together with a couple of Yorkie raisin and biscuit chocolate bars (that I had kept in my rucksack in case of an unexpected dearth of supplies on the anticipated Virgin Inter-City train journey later that morning) and placed them on a separate shelf, no doubt in order to subject them to a detailed forensic examination later. You can't be too careful when it comes to Marks & Spencer sandwiches.

The lady prison officer studied the computer screen and then turned to me. 'First time in prison, is it, Mr. Burton? Let's see – you'll be going to HMP Thameside. Don't worry, it's an OK nick. And you've been given twelve weeks, which means you'll be out in six.'

She made it sound like a walk in the park. I hadn't even had it on my radar that there might be such a thing as an 'OK nick'. As far as I was concerned, although UK prisons might on the face of it be run to certain standards, driven by health and safety rules and the need to keep suicides to a minimum, they were still universally tough places where the weak were preyed on by the strong and the law of the jungle prevailed.

'I'll need to confirm a few details,' she continued, and proceeded to question me about every aspect of my existence since I was about five years old, entering my answers onto her computer.

Was I allergic to anything? (Not unless you count my sporadic outbreaks of hay fever.) Did I have an alcohol or drugs dependency? (Not unless you count my heart medications.)

As far as those were concerned, I could very well be said to be dependent, on the grounds that if I didn't take them every day then my forthcoming sojourn at Her Majesty's pleasure might be unexpectedly curtailed, and not in a good way.

Did I have any diagnosed mental illness? How about an undiagnosed mental illness? Was I a member of a particular religious affiliation? I fought back the urge to say that I was either a Satanist or a Jedi Knight – neither of which would have been true, anyway – but I had sensed that this might not be the right time to reveal my religious affiliations or indeed, the lack of them.

Having been convicted and sentenced for harassment (with a

'religiously aggravated' component due to my use of the word 'Taqiyya' in my email communications), I felt that it might be advisable to play down the 'religiously aggravated' aspect of my conviction in the event of my unexpectedly encountering any Islamic religious fanatics. I was aware that there were likely to be a fair number of such people within the confines of Her Majesty's prisons, and there was no sense in looking for trouble – or antagonising people unnecessarily – at such an early stage.

Also, I had no wish to end up in a straitjacket. My sense of humour is not for everyone.

A laser printer in the corner of the office burst into life, and disgorged a single sheet of paper. 'Sign here,' said the lady prison officer. It looked like a disclaimer, presumably to be brought out and flourished if I met with an untimely death while in custody. Should I sign it? I signed.

After this initial interrogation I was led to a holding cell. For those of you unaccustomed to the delights of the subterranean residences of the Inner London Crown Court, this was an enclosed space of about twelve feet by twelve feet with a concrete floor, a ceiling with a fluorescent light set into it under a vandal-proof cover, brick walls painted with a faded shade of duck egg blue, and a concrete bench along one wall.

There were no windows. I made a mental note to request some Vitamin D supplements at the earliest opportunity. I had no wish to be released back into the outside world only to die horribly from rickets. Actually that wasn't quite true. At that moment I would have cheerfully put up with the prospect of an excruciating death from rickets if it meant I could have been released there and then.

I also noticed that there appeared to be a distinct lack of en-suite facilities. To be fair, I hadn't been expecting a combined shower and bath arrangement, even though it would have been very welcome after the traumatic events of earlier that morning.

I hadn't even been expecting an ornamental wash-basin, perhaps with some miniature sachets of eau-de-Cologne marked 'With Compliments of the Inner London Crown Court – we hope you enjoy your stay, come back and visit us again soon.' But at the very least I would have expected some basic plumbing in the event of my wishing to powder my nose.

I decided that I would make time to speak to the Howard League for Prison Reform on the subject whenever I next had the opportunity.

'There you go, Mr. Burton. Sing out if you need anything.' There was a sound of creaking hinges as the thick steel door slammed shut behind me, a series of clunks and clicks as the key turned in the lock, and for the first time since sentence had been passed earlier that morning, I was utterly alone.

CHAPTER 3

Brief Encounter

The door had been securely locked, and I was now alone in the holding cell underneath the Inner London Crown Court. At that time it must have been about half past eleven in the morning, and I wondered whether I might be moved straight away to the 'OK nick' that was HMP Thameside, or whether I was going to be in this holding cell for a long stay.

I sat down on the hard concrete bench provided and contemplated the separation from the outside world, thinking that I might as well look on the bright side – I hadn't as yet been handcuffed, and I hadn't as yet been forced into one of those trendy bright orange jumpsuits which I understand are all the rage with the inmates of Guantanamo Bay. (Orange is not at all my favourite colour when it comes to sartorial matters.)

I was still wearing my dark blue suit and black shoes – although I had been instructed to remove my tie, which with my pile of belongings had been unceremoniously thrust into another large heavy duty polythene bag with my name on it. I supposed that – disclaimer or not – they didn't want the inconvenience of the paperwork in the event that I was to strangle myself in a paroxysm of despair before they had had the chance to dispatch me to HMP Thameside.

However, after around thirty minutes, the cell hatch snapped open and yet another cheerful face appeared. I swear that they must select prison officers for their cheerfulness. I suppose that the average prison officer must face the prospect of an awful lot of disgruntled convicts, a category that I was fast in danger of joining, insofar that I was now most definitely a convict and could be said to be in the initial stages of being somewhat disgruntled.

Or at least, even if I was not in the final stages of the disgruntlement process at this time, I was certainly a long way from being completely gruntled.

'You want some lunch?' said Mr. Cheerful.

'Uh – yes please,' said I, not wanting to subject Mr. Cheerful to too much trouble on my behalf. For all I knew, Mr. Cheerful might hold the keys that would make a difference between a pleasant stay in the holding cells, or a one-way trip to the water-boarding suite complete with a set of electrically operated testicular agitation devices.

'What do you want?' he asked.

I hadn't realised there was a choice. For a moment I thought about asking for the menu – I rather fancied selecting the mushrooms fried in garlic, followed by a medium-rare Chateaubriand steak and a bottle of Moet & Chandon's finest champagne, but in the end I said, 'Uh – what have you got?'

'Lasagne,' said Mr. Cheerful, in a tone that suggested that I was extremely lucky to have visited the premises on this particular day when this particular item happened to be on the menu.

'Lasagne? Is that it?'

'That's it, I'm afraid. Although you can have two portions if you want.' I was obviously looking under-nourished. Either that or they had over-ordered on the lasagne in anticipation of a large consignment of Italian malefactors arriving, perhaps following the recent outbreak of ice-cream wars on the streets of London.

(I love the phrase 'ice-cream wars'. It conjures up a picture of Italian ice-cream vendors facing off against each other on the streets, armed only with fistfuls of chocolate Cornettos and bottles of strawberry sauce. 'Mamma Mia, it's-a Luigi. Hey Luigi, you on-a my patch. Take-a that!')

Never having been one to look a gift horse in the mouth, I said, 'OK then – two portions would be great.' And to be fair, when the two portions arrived in a microwaved plastic dish, they were absolutely delicious. Not five-star Ritz hotel delicious maybe, but delicious enough for a starving, newly convicted reprobate like myself who has just seen his last sandwiches and chocolate disappear in a metaphorical puff of smoke over the horizon for the foreseeable future.

The next few hours passed slowly, and I found myself engaging in any number of mentally distracting activities – counting the number of bricks in each wall of my cell, trying to gauge the length of the corridor outside by the footfall of the prison officers, listening to the incessant complaints of the man in the cell next to mine – 'So why can't I have another cigarette then? You screws are all the same. You're infringing my human rights! I want to speak to my lawyer.'

I was just starting to think that maybe they had forgotten about me and that I was destined to spend the next six weeks on a diet of truculent chain-smoking neighbours, lasagne and brick-counting, when there was the clunking of a key in the lock, the door opened and Mr. Cheerful appeared again.

'Your brief's here.'

Now, I can't say that I was terribly impressed with my brief (defence lawyer). She had demonstrated remarkable incompetence during my trial, committing all sorts of cardinal errors that a barrister with twenty years' experience should never have committed.

I later found out that the highlight of her career was defending the welfare of a bunch of scrofulous rabbits. (This is actually true, a factoid that I subsequently gleaned from the website of her Chambers in King's Bench Walk, a supposedly prestigious firm of barristers in London.)

I don't think she had prepared herself adequately for the defence of an actual human being, let alone a concerned patriot like me. Prior to the trial, she hadn't even bothered to read my specially prepared defence notes, an omission which had more than likely contributed to my current situation.

'How are you doing?' she said as she walked into my cell, motioning to Mr. Cheerful that he should wait outside. She sat down on the concrete bench next to me. I could smell her perfume, straight out of Coco Chanel's Come Hither Bunny Lover range of fragrances.

I paused for a moment before considering my reply. One the one hand, it was possible that she might be able to assist me over the course of the next few months if some further legal difficulties should arise following my conviction and sentence. On the other hand, I was strongly disposed towards the notion of beating her to death with a shovel and burying her mutilated remains deep in some swampy marshland just outside Birmingham. I decided that discretion was the better part of valour, and in any case, there were no gardening implements within reach, which was probably just as well.

'I can't complain,' I said, 'the room service is very good, although I'm a little perplexed at why I'm down here in the first place. You assured me that there was no way the judge would hand down a custodial sentence given that I was of previous good character, that it was a non-violent offence and that I was suffering from a serious heart condition.'

'Yes, well, the judge wasn't really in your corner from the start,' she breezed. (This was true enough. I have seen cornered rats that were more in my corner than that judge was.) 'But you could have done worse than to have been assigned to HMP Thameside, by all accounts.'

I found out later that HMP Thameside is (according to its website) a Category B private prison for adult males in the West Thamesmead area of the Royal Borough of Greenwich, South-East London. It currently has the capacity to hold 1,232 convicted and remand prisoners. So far so good, you might think. You can almost sense the unspoken presence of the allocated five-star Trip Advisor rating.

A Category B prison is just one step down from a maximum security Category A prison such as Belmarsh, which is reserved for terrorists, murderers and serial rapists. Just the place for a decrepit old geezer like me with a dodgy ticker convicted of sending half a dozen jocular and non-threatening emails to a mendacious grievance-mongering Taqiyya-artist, you might say.

The website goes on to say – 'the regime at Thameside Prison combines work, education, vocational training, as well as accredited "addressing offending behaviour" programmes, and prisoner health and other appropriate interventions.'

I noticed that there is no reference on its website to hard physical labour or sewing mailbags. These are activities which – I was to later discover – are nowadays generally frowned upon by most of the more enlightened prison directors and senior prison staff (although I'm sure there are a few unreconstructed dinosaurs – members of staff who hanker after the good old days with treadmills and the like.)

HMP Belmarsh (above and adjacent to Thameside in the photograph) is a Category A maximum security prison

Indeed, there were no references to treadmills either, although these days I dare say that even the most unpleasant experiences are sugar-coated on prison websites. Such as – (with regard to treadmills) 'We aim to provide the very best for our customers, such as our bespoke invigorating continuous walking experience which has been proven to improve the circulation and to prevent atrophy of the leg muscles of our guests during their stay with us.'

I glanced at my defence barrister. She was working up a certain level of enthusiasm concerning my prospects. I hesitate to use the term 'waxing lyrical', but it wouldn't have surprised me if she was earning commission from my board and lodging over the next six weeks. I half expected her to reach into her briefcase and brandish a holiday-style brochure for me to peruse on my way to this luxurious establishment.

'You might not even have to do the full six weeks,' she continued, 'if you keep your head down and do as you're told, you should be out in next to no time. In fact, if you volunteer for some of the prison jobs in the library, or the laundry room, or handing out meals in the canteen, you could be eligible for home detention with an ankle tag after as little as three days.'

This was a fiction, as I was to find out. A fiction, a lie, no doubt designed to distract my attention away from the discussion of her dismal performance in court during my trial. I dare say that she had encountered several such tricky situations in her legal career, if her unprofessional and slapdash approach to my personal circumstances was anything to go by.

Oh, how easily are the newly convicted taken in by such falsehoods. Nevertheless, as much as I was aggrieved by my circumstances and the part that she had played in enabling those circumstances to come about, I felt that as politeness and courtesy cost nothing, I should at least acknowledge her meagre efforts. Revenge, after all, is a dish best served cold.

She rose from the concrete bench and filed her papers back into her briefcase. I could see that she was looking forward to heading home to a life of comfort, luxury and presumably unlimited erotic sessions of no-holds-barred rabbit fondling, whilst I was to languish for the next six weeks in an environment that might hold no end of trials and tribulations.

She exited the holding cell with what she obviously considered to be a friendly smile, and the cell door was closed and locked once more.

However, two hours later, the door of the holding cell was unlocked again – and I was about to start my journey from the Inner London Crown Court to HMP Thameside.

CHAPTER 4

Journey to Thameside

The two genial prison officers from the corridor entered the holding cell. They were almost apologetic. 'Rules,' said the first officer. 'You're on your way to the nick, but we have to cuff you now. You don't mind, do you? We're going to be entering a Double Cuff area.'

I was about to leave the confines of the holding cells for the journey in a prison van from Inner London Crown Court to HMP Thameside. Words seemed superfluous, so I extended my wrists and submitted to the adorning of heavy metal in the manner of one who actually had a choice in the matter. A 'Double Cuff' area meant that not only did you have to have your own wrists hand-cuffed; you had to have a wrist cuffed to the wrist of a prison officer as well.

I looked at the cuffs. They were not exactly the style I would have chosen had I been in the bondage department of the Ann Summers retail outlet. I would have chosen a set with a soft and furry covering of faux leopard skin (and preferably with a separate set of keys that I could have used to unlock the cuffs while the officers' backs were turned.)

But at least the blood supply through my wrists was unrestricted and the officers seemed genuinely concerned for my wellbeing. We exited the holding cell in a semi-dignified manner with me being concerned mostly with not tripping over my own feet after six hours of inactivity.

The second officer draped my jacket over my cuffed wrists, which I thought was a touching gesture in the unlikely event of us running into a sizable collection of paparazzi en route to the van destined to transport me to my new home at HMP Thameside. I would not have wanted the impression to be given – at least not on the front page of the Times or the Daily Mail – that I was accompanying these genial souls for any reason other than of my own volition.

I was led through the winding corridors underneath the Inner London Crown Court and up several flights of concrete steps to a courtyard in which three or four white prison vans were standing. I blinked at the intensity of the afternoon sun as we entered the courtyard, and I could see and hear the small birds chirping in the trees surrounding the high walls.

For those of you who are unfamiliar with prison vans, imagine a large horse-box with individual compartments for up to six prisoners, three on each side, each with just enough room to sit down, each securely locked with an armour-plated door and a small, square, heavily smoked, armour-plated glass window to the outside world.

The driver and an auxiliary prison officer are in the front of the van, which is totally isolated from the rear of the van containing the prisoners, save for radio communication between them and a third prison officer supervising the human cargo.

There were five of us prisoners in the courtyard, all apparently scheduled for HMP Thameside. I surveyed my fellow passengers. There were two gangly teenagers who seemed to immediately recognise each other and burst into animated conversation – 'Hey! Where have you been? Weren't you at Chelmsford nick in 2014?'

There was a scruffy, downtrodden-looking white-haired man with a cadaverous complexion, who must have been in his seventies, who didn't seem to be inclined to communicate with the rest of us at all.

Finally there was a dignified black gentleman who was about the same age as myself, who regarded me gravely as we boarded the van, and gave me a slight nod as if to say – 'We are on the same path together, and we had better make the most of it.' It was the unspoken bond between two fellow travellers whose lives happen to cross – as ships pass in the night.

At this point I should say that if I refer to individuals during the course of this book as black or white, or indeed of any other colour or hue, it is not because of racism. It is not because I wish to make a point about some races having characteristics that are positive or negative in respect to other races. I subscribe to the notion that we are all equal in the sight of God, even if our idea of God may vary from person to person, and indeed, some of us might say that there is no God at all.

However, when one is introduced to someone for the first time, one makes an instant assessment or judgment based on observations made at that time. Such observations may include body language, manner of speech and facial expression as well as the colour of their skin and complexion.

Such assessments and judgments are made during the course of a split second, and are usually entirely outside of one's conscious control at that time. It is a fact that most people, including myself, make irrational judgments from time to time, and wherever possible I try to seek out the causes of irrationality and to address them in a logical and consistent manner.

I am sure that most people do this, which is why it annoys me so much that we are frequently accused of racism when all we are trying to do is to acknowledge that there are differences, as well as similarities between individuals.

As you may have discerned, I have a propensity for elaborating on philosophical and political themes for the edification of my audience at every opportunity. Some of my acquaintances refer to it as incoherent rambling, which I consider to be unkind. I am merely attempting to enlighten my fellow man, although I have occasionally felt that the experience is (present company excluded, of course) akin to casting pearls before swine.

Anyway, there we were, locked into our individual compartments, uncuffed and left to our own devices as the van started up and we began our journey across London, exiting through the gates of the Inner London Crown Court and travelling along the A2 to HMP Thameside, which, as I have said, was located in West Thamesmead, just across the River Thames from London City Airport. I could hear the two teenagers in the back of the van still swapping war stories through the armour-plated doors from their time in Chelmsford prison in 2014. From the other two prisoners there was silence.

An array of wheezing, asthmatic G4S prison vans taking a well-deserved break

I looked out of the window to my left at the outside world and regarded the cars, buses, cycles and motorcycles keeping pace with us along the London roads. Every now and again I attempted to make eye contact with someone on the outside who was still free, only to realise that they couldn't possibly see me behind the heavily smoked, armour-plated glass.

I imagined them going about their daily lives, having breakfast with their partners, going to work, having lunch, coming home to their families, having dinner, perhaps going out to the pictures, to the theatre, to a night-club, meeting friends with never a thought as to how they might react if they had their liberty taken away from them.

As the prison van trundled along, we passed people sitting in small, friendly groups at tables in outside pavement cafés, sometimes friends chatting quietly on the street, sometimes lovers walking hand-in-hand without a care in the world.

And there was I, locked in a claustrophobic space in a converted horsebox without even the possibility of reaching out to another human being and exchanging conversation or pleasantries, let alone articulating my innermost thoughts.

I could feel that this line of thought was not going to lead me to a 'happy place', and so I turned my attention away from the outside world and started to think about what it would be like to arrive at a prison like HMP Thameside. All I knew about it was that it was an 'OK nick' according to the lady prison officer I had met earlier that morning in the maze of corridors underneath the Inner London Crown Court.

From that simple phrase I imagined that it could be anything between a Geoffrey Archer-style open prison (like Ford prison near Arundel) where prisoners could come and go as they please, to something like the notorious Evin prison in Tehran, where it would be touch-and-go as to whether you would emerge with all your fingernails still attached to your fingers and your testicles still attached to the rest of your body.

I looked through the other window leading to the inside of the van, where another lady prison officer whom I judged to be in her late thirties was listening to what seemed to be the afternoon play on Radio 4 while simultaneously working her way through what looked like to be a Sun crossword.

I was intrigued. This was the second Sun crossword I had seen that day being filled in by a prison officer. Could this be significant, I asked myself? I imagined myself conducting a nationwide survey of prison officers to discern their newspaper reading and crossword habits.

Suppose that eighty per cent of prison officers confessed to completing at least one Sun crossword per week. What conclusions might one draw? That their propensity for crosswords could perhaps be explained by the recruiting and selection procedures for the UK Prison Service placing great emphasis on creativity and problem solving, and weeding out those of lesser intellectual ability?

Left-wing acquaintances of mine would probably have an alternative theory – which would be that they were mostly racist, fascist, 'Islamophobic', hateful and intolerant right-wing knuckle-dragging throwbacks for reading the Sun newspaper in the first place. Personally, I think Lefties tend to overreact to such things, but there you go.

I looked around my compartment. It was designed for someone at least twelve inches shorter than me (I am around six feet two inches in my socks) and it was difficult to get comfortable on the moulded grey plastic chair that was bolted to the floor of the compartment.

I looked in vain for any levers or buttons that would adjust my neck support, lumbar support and leg-room, things which I would consider to be standard fitting in just about any vehicle over the last decade or two, but the designers of this particular prison van seemed to have omitted such luxuries. The comfort of prisoners for transportation was obviously low on the agenda. There wasn't even a mini-bar or a button for room service, which was unconscionable, because I might be in here for absolutely ages.

My list of items for the Howard League for Penal Reform to attend to was lengthening.

The prison van continued to trundle at a leisurely pace along the urban streets, and I temporarily put aside my plans for an enterprising escape as I wondered what would lie in store for me at the other end. I didn't to have to wait long to find out.

CHAPTER 5

The Lions' Den

Despite the route being advertised as a forty-five-minute drive, as I was to later find out on Google, we encountered interminable road-works, and after what must have been the best part of two hours, the prison van turned into a large car park and pulled up at the prison entrance of HMP Thameside. The first impression of this 'OK nick' was of dark-reddish sandy-coloured brick walls of at least twenty feet in height, topped with horizontal cylinders of at least ten feet in diameter, the better to defeat enterprising inmates armed with grappling irons, or their accomplices on the outside armed with the same.

This was obviously going to be more of a challenge than I had anticipated. For the time being at least, I judged that it would be perhaps prudent to shelve my plans for becoming the second Henri Charrière (a former prisoner known as 'the Butterfly' or 'Papillon'.) Like me, he had also been wrongly convicted, but he subsequently escaped from a brutal French penal colony in the 1930s.

Besides, 'Butterfly of HMP Thameside' doesn't have quite the same ring to it, and if one aspires to escape the confinement of a high security prison and to make it into the history books, then one does at least need a cool nickname if nothing else.

Aerial view of HMP Thameside – a.k.a. the Thameside Hilton

A large solid gate set into the wall of this imposing structure slid open with a low rumbling sound to allow the prison van to drive into a 'quarantine' area. The van came to a halt, and the large solid gate slid shut again behind us. Once all the paperwork had been checked by a uniformed prison guard on the entry gate, at least as far as I could see from my vantage point inside the van, a second gate in front of the van opened and the van passed through into the main reception area from which we were required to disembark. The van stopped in front of a set of double doors and we were led out, one by one, to be processed by what appeared to be the 'welcoming committee' of HMP Thameside.

My eye was caught by a large notice affixed to the outside of the reception area, informing all and sundry that it was a very serious matter to assist a prisoner in escaping from lawful custody, and not only that, but woe betide anyone who was caught smuggling a mobile phone or any other illegal substance or contraband into the prison. Wrongdoers who were caught could expect a sentence of anything up to ten years. Quite right too, I thought. You wouldn't want to encourage any more criminals.

I was led through the double doors to what appeared to be a reception desk in front of a very busy area full of prison staff moving purposefully around. There was a mat about six feet square in front of the reception desk with two foot-shaped prints on it. 'Stand there,' growled an HMP Thameside prison officer. I regarded him with some trepidation. Gone was the geniality of the officers at the Inner London Crown Court, to be replaced by something altogether less encouraging, if not outright sinister and intimidating. He had a badge on his chest proclaiming himself to be a Senior Custody Officer.

The Senior Custody Officer referred to a sheaf of paperwork on his clipboard. The paperless society obviously hadn't reached as far as the HMP Thameside welcoming committee. Once again I was subjected to a series of questions concerning my life since I was around five years old – was I allergic to anything, did I have any diagnosed or undiagnosed medical conditions, did I have any religious affiliations – and did I have any identifying tattoos?

I did in fact have tattoos (solely on my upper arms at the time of writing). Nothing in the way of Ludo/Llandudno tattooed on the more sensitive parts of my anatomy (an old schoolboy joke, if you don't get it then ask your dad). Nothing terribly exotic, certainly compared to the numerous multicoloured tattoos of snakes, spiders' webs and death's heads over crossed motorcycle pistons that one sees all over the bodies of Birmingham citizens every day (and that's just the women).

These tattoos were from my Aikido martial art days – one was on my left bicep, spelling out the word 'Aikido' in Japanese script. The other was on my right bicep, with a far more esoteric meaning – 'Mas-akatsu-akatsu' in Japanese script. I had had them inscribed by a tattoo studio in Uttoxeter some years previously to celebrate my Aikido black belt grading.

'Mas-akatsu-akatsu' translates as either 'you cannot defeat your opponent until you first defeat yourself' or 'the only victory is self-victory' – the calligraphic symbols for victory and defeat being the same in Japanese (in the same way that the symbols for 'danger' and 'opportunity' are the same in the Chinese calligraphic script). This phrase echoes far beyond the confines of Japanese martial arts and can be construed as a metaphor for one's progress through life.

How many times have you been asked whether you can do something, and have answered, 'No, I can't do that'? Have you ever thought that perhaps your answer was dictated by the limits that you yourself imposed on your imagination? That perhaps you could do the thing that was asked of you, if only you freed your imagination from its constraints?

Such a simple concept, and yet it is so difficult for the average human being in the West to achieve. Defeating yourself in order to accomplish victory may seem very counter-intuitive, but in fact can lead to a profound and life-changing liberation of one's inner self.

I attempted to describe my Aikido tattoos to the Senior Custody Officer. He seemed unimpressed. 'We'll take some photographs of those later,' he said.

The filled-in form, with a multitude of tick-boxes on it, was placed in front of me. 'Sign here,' said the Senior Custody Officer. Should I sign it? Or should I refer it to my lawyer for perusal? I signed.

Following this interrogation, I was directed to a cubicle for the exchange of my clothes for prison-issue socks, boxer shorts, white trainers and an ensemble of tracksuit bottoms, T-shirts and jersey in a very tasteful shade of 'prison green'. It was a bit like what used to be called British Racing Green but without the accompanying aura of Formula One celebrity and the bevy of luscious bikini-clad chicks on the starting grid. All the same, the quality of the materials wasn't bad, and the trainers in particular were worthy of a five-star rating from Nike. Things were looking up.

I was then taken through an inventory of my belongings, including the plastic bag of items taken from me at the Inner London Crown Court, which had miraculously turned up at the same prison that I had. I was impressed – this was better service than one might have expected from Terminal 5 at Heathrow – where some might point out that it is not unknown for British Airways baggage handlers to send half of your luggage to Bucharest and the other half to Bangkok, while you yourself languish for four days out of a five-day holiday on the tarmac, waiting for a flight to Torremolinos.

Having signed off on the inventory of belongings, with a cheery assurance that I was almost certain to get them back at the end of my stay, I was then presented with my own Casio digital wristwatch, comb and nail clippers, which had been designated as sufficiently non-threatening for use on the prison wing. I was then taken to a desk with an enormous camera mounted on it, for the obligatory photo shoot which would form the basis for the mug-shot on my prison identity card.

It was impressed upon me that I had better take very good care of this identity card, as most of the prison services (including a regular supply of food) were going to be available only on the production of the card together with my fingerprint, which would be read into a fingerprint scanner at various stages and at various exit and entry points within the prison.

The identity card also contained a smart chip, similar to that found in a credit or debit card, which could be used in each cell to operate a basic prison-monitored intranet computer, and to control one's access to TV channels (providing your behaviour remained good enough to allow the continued use of a TV in your cell).

If you were a bad boy, then you ran the risk of all privileges, including the TV in your cell, being summarily withdrawn. I was informed that that was a big deal. It was not unknown for prisoners to become highly distraught if deprived of the viewing of regular episodes of Love Island or Jeremy Kyle. That did indeed sound serious. I resolved not to be a bad boy.

I was then escorted to what looked to be the laundry room, where I was presented with a kitbag containing clean sheets, pillowcases, pillows and a duvet. I have to say that the duvet looked a little insubstantial, and I considered asking if they had one with a higher TOG rating as I occasionally find it difficult to sleep if the ambient temperature is too low and my feet get too cold, but once again I thought it might be more prudent to keep my mouth firmly shut, at least until I had an inkling of how things worked around here.

The prison officer escorted me out of the reception area into a large courtyard and from there to a separate four-storey building with a forbidding-looking metal door, which was locked and marked with a large letter 'A'.

Behind the door marked with the letter 'A' was (perhaps unsurprisingly) 'A' wing, where all new arrivals spent the first few days for assessment by the prison staff. I was led past a communal socialising area – not unlike the interior of a McDonald's or Kentucky Fried Chicken establishment in its general ambience.

It was currently devoid of customers, and was surprisingly clean. It was filled with serried ranks of tables and chairs securely fixed to the ground (presumably to prevent unnecessary injuries in the event of unpleasant events such as a prison riot or perhaps a violent disagreement over whose turn it was to play at the communal billiards table).

The floors in A-wing were marked out as AA, AB, AC and AD. I was on AA – the ground floor. The officer stopped in front of a locked door marked AA-17.

'Welcome to your new home,' he said, with a wolfish smile. 'You'll be sharing with one other prisoner for the time being.' He inserted a key from the substantial keychain on his belt into the lock and slowly turned it anti-clockwise with an ominous series of accompanying clicks.

I entered the cell through the unlocked door. Mas-akatsu-akatsu. I was in the lions' den, and I had a feeling that over the coming weeks I would have to call on my deepest reserves in order to survive, especially if the real reason for my incarceration became known to the other prisoners.

CHAPTER 6

The Cell

As the door was locked behind me, I looked around. There was no other person in the cell at that moment, but there were all the tell-tale signs of current occupation. On one side of the cell were two hard plastic bunk beds, affixed to the cell wall. The lower of the two bunk beds contained an avocado green mattress, a sheet, a pillow and a duvet, although the bed appeared unmade, with a paperback book lying face-down on it.

There was a door-less cupboard affixed to the opposite side of the cell that contained several shelves with a handful of toiletries including shampoo and toothpaste scattered on one of the hard plastic surfaces. On the top shelf were some tea-bags and several small cartons of milk. A pile of clothes occupied one of the other shelves and a pencil and some scribbled notes lay on the desk next to the cupboard.

Also on the desk was a computer screen and keyboard, with some wires leading to a locked box secured to the wall underneath the desk. There was also a hard plastic chair and a free-standing plastic wastebasket underneath the desk. It wasn't exactly top-of-the-range furniture from IKEA, but it was functional and presumably likely to survive with minimal damage any sustained and frenzied assault from residents who might become annoyed from time to time.

The cell also contained an 'en-suite' facility. A concrete partition in one corner partially enclosed a space containing a shower, toilet and hand-basin. I was impressed. It could be said that I am easily impressed, but years of watching prison dramas and documentaries on TV had left me with the impression that the undignified practice of 'slopping out' was still the preferred method for keeping one's cell relatively uncontaminated, even in modern prisons, so this was a welcome surprise. Although any privacy one might have wished for was negated by the angle of the partition affording a clear view into the en-suite from the observation hatch set into the door. I could see that this might take some getting used to.

There was also a window, set into the far wall of the cell. It was barred (no surprises there) and the glass seemed to be at least half an inch thick. I looked out of the window into the early evening gloom and saw a heavy-duty mesh fence, topped with razor wire, security lights and cameras, running parallel with and about ten metres away from the outside wall of the cell. Beyond that was a tarmac strip wide enough for two lanes of traffic, another heavy-duty mesh fence, and then there was a perimeter wall some ten metres beyond that.

I could see that the Butterfly of HMP Thameside was likely to have his work cut out in trying to get past that lot.

Single-person cell in HMP Thameside –
to double the capacity, just add a bunk bed

From what I could see, this was a two-person cell, and given that the bottom bunk was in use, it seemed to be a reasonable assumption that the top bunk would be allocated to me. Having only just arrived,

I didn't want to cause any offence. I had no idea about cell etiquette, apart from the stories I had heard and read about cellmates being violently set upon and beaten for minor infringements such as inadvertently taking the wrong bunk, or accidentally using someone else's toothpaste or deodorant.

On that thought, I suddenly realised that I hadn't been issued with any toiletries of my own, apart from my own comb and nail clippers, and I wondered if perhaps this was a devilish prank by the prison officers to get my cellmate and I to fight to the death over a tube of Colgate's finest. No doubt they were taking bets with each other on the outcome at that very moment.

I climbed gingerly up to the top bunk – via a vertical ladder of hard plastic steps – and sat down on the avocado green plastic mattress. That way, I thought, if my cellmate should unexpectedly enter at this moment and instantly fly into a rage, perhaps because of an earlier intention that he might have had to switch bunks that very evening, I would at least have the advantage of height from which to fight him off.

I unpacked my kitbag containing the sheets, pillows, pillowcases and duvet, and set about making at least some semblance of a bed. The first thing I noticed was that the mattress was very hard. In fact, it was extremely hard. On a scale of mattress-related hardness, I put it at the level that one might feel when faced with the prospect of bedding down on a set of cobblestones for the night, perhaps after having been forcibly thrown out of the house by the wife for coming home drunk at three in the morning.

Still, there was nothing else for it, and I stretched out on the mattress with my head on the pillow, and began to study the ceiling over my bunk bed.

The ceiling was about eighteen inches above my bunk bed, and was covered in elaborate graffiti. It wasn't exactly on a par with Michelangelo's work at the Sistine Chapel, but the images and messages appeared to offer some insight into the mindset of previous residents. Religion and football featured strongly, and there were two or three anatomically correct drawings of the female form, complete with detailed explanatory wording which wouldn't have looked out of place in a medical lecture or a student gynaecologist's notebook.

As I reflected upon the extent of this wondrous variety of artwork inscribed on the ceiling, the observation hatch slid open briefly and the face of a prison officer appeared. He scanned the interior of the cell briefly, and then unlocked the door. A dark-skinned man dressed in prison greens walked in, carrying a plastic bag of what looked very much like toiletries. This turned out to be my new cell-mate. He proffered the bag up to me with a broad smile.

'Hello,' he said, with a strong West African accent. 'I think these might be for you. They should have given them to you earlier, but you know what they're like.'

At this point of course, I didn't actually know what 'they' were like at all, or even who 'they' were, but not wanting to appear ungrateful, I sat up, took the bag with my left hand, extended my right hand and said, 'Thanks. By the way, I'm Tim.'

'No worries,' he said, shaking my hand. 'My name is' – and here he gave voice to a weird, multisyllabic utterance that included some unusual clicking noises. To me it sounded completely unpronounceable.

He obviously sensed my consternation, for he gave me another broad smile and said, 'But you can call me John.'

The prison officer placed two cardboard cartons – similar in size and shape to McDonald's food boxes – on the top of the cupboard. 'You missed dinnertime,' he said to me, 'but we didn't want you to starve.' An aroma of roasted chicken and chips filled the cell. I hadn't realised that I was so hungry. Throwing caution to the wind, and completely forgetting about my defensive tactics in the face of a possibly deranged cell-mate, I clambered down from the top bunk to investigate. The prison officer left, and once again the door was locked.

It was indeed roast chicken and chips, complemented by a sizeable portion of baked beans, together with an apple and a carton of fruit juice. There was a plastic knife and fork in my bag of toiletries – and once again it was impressed upon me that I had to take care of them, because no others would be forthcoming in the event of my losing them, even in the event of encountering a freak cutlery-annihilation-related accident. I ate standing up, using the top of the cupboard as a table, as John was by now seated at the desk on the only chair in the cell, and I didn't want to inconvenience him. He was reading through the scribbles on the sheet of paper I had seen on the desk when I first walked in.

He glanced up at me. 'We'll have to find you another chair,' he said. 'I am just trying to write this letter to my brother. He has no idea I am in here. I expect he thinks I have just gone down to the shop for some cigarettes. I didn't tell him I was going to court. I thought I would be back home by now.'

You and me both, I thought.

It transpired that John had been sentenced earlier that day as well, but at a different court. He had been sentenced for stealing bicycles. Not just one or two bicycles, but dozens of them. And not just the type of bicycle that your maiden aunt would have ridden to church on a Sunday morning with a wicker basket on the front, but top-of-the-range titanium and carbon-fibre-framed bicycles with Shimano hydraulic disc brakes and Vittoria Rubino Pro tyres, each worth around £5,000.

What John didn't know about titanium and carbon-framed bicycles wasn't worth knowing, as I was to find out over time. It turned out that yuppies in the areas around the City of London and Canary Wharf would flock to work on these state-of-the-art machines and leave them locked up with chains and padlocks that had a surprising array of weaknesses. A vast criminal network had grown up around the combination of irresistible goodies and inadequate security, and John had seen his opportunity.

Unfortunately for John, the City of London Police Force was not stupid, and had set up a sting operation, leaving an unattended Boardman Elite SLR bicycle just where John might see it. He was caught red-handed cycling away from the scene by a team of undercover officers, and just as he thought he had got away from the hue and cry of the pursuit, a burly policeman about seven feet tall and with biceps the size of Bournemouth stepped out in front of him, stopped him dead in his tracks by grabbing the handlebars in a vice-like grip, and uttered the immortal words – 'You're nicked, sunshine.'

John had refused to give up the names of anyone else involved in the network, and as it wasn't his first offence, he had been sentenced to two years' imprisonment.

'So,' said John, 'what are you in for?'

I had known this question was coming, and so I had tried to prepare myself for it. I was a little reluctant to disclose the real reason behind my arriving at HMP Thameside, and whilst I knew that the prison staff would have access to my records, I had to trust that data protection laws applied and that details of my conviction would not be inappropriately divulged.

I was apprehensive for a number of reasons – one reason was that I knew that certain offences are looked on as being more objectionable than others, such as offences against women and children – and while that wasn't specifically the case with me, if it were to come out that I had been sentenced for harassment involving a Muslim, then word might reach any number of Muslim inmates with unpredictable and possibly violent consequences.

This concerned me because it was only a few months previously that a man who was sentenced to twelve months' prison in Bristol – for the heinous crime of tying bacon to a mosque door handle – had been found dead in his cell, under circumstances that at the time of writing are still unexplained.

Therefore I had decided to take the course of admitting to something less controversial. I could hardly admit to bicycle theft, as my lack of knowledge in state-of-the-art bicycle technology and the various criminal networks involved would have led the other prisoners to smell a rat.

However, it had to be something of sufficient gravity to warrant a custodial sentence, especially given that I was a sixty-four-year-old man with a serious heart condition, and under normal circumstances would have had leniency shown to him by the court.

So I had to think of something else. However, I should provide you with some relevant background information before I come to the point.

CHAPTER 7

The Pigeon has Landed

When I was a gangly fifteen-year-old teenager I used to own an air rifle, and I spent many happy hours perfecting my shooting skills in our back garden, firing pellet after pellet into a paper target pinned against a large slab of wood. I had reached the point where, with a carefully adjusted telescopic sight, I could continuously fire pellets at will into a two-centimetre diameter centre of a target over thirty metres distance. That may not sound like much of an achievement, but it is harder than it looks.

Fast forward nearly fifty years to January 2016, and I was faced with a dilemma. We had recently had solar panels installed on the roof of our house, courtesy of a Government energy-saving initiative, and the local pigeons had decided that these panels made the perfect spot for roosting. Day after day, especially in the early morning, we could hear the patter of pigeons' feet on the roof tiles as they scuttled up and down, back and forth, from the ridge tiles to the guttering.

In addition, the smell of pigeon droppings permeated the loft space, and the incessant 'coo, coo' of the pigeons was driving myself and Mrs. B (my better half) insane.

So I said to Mrs. B., 'I'll get an air rifle. Give me ten days staked out in the caravan on the front drive, and I'll give those pigeons a good old-fashioned seeing-to, *pour décourager les autres*. The pigeons will find somewhere else to roost and the problem will be solved.'

'You can't do that!' she said. 'It's cruel. Not to mention – somebody might see you and report you to the RSPCA.'

'It's not cruel at all,' I said. 'I'll aim just close enough to frighten them off. I promise I won't touch a hair on their little feathered chests. And I'll wear my ex-military camouflage outfit and balaclava to render myself inconspicuous to the neighbours. They won't suspect a thing.' But she wouldn't have it.

The next day I came home to find she had purchased an enormous lifelike plastic owl from the Internet. Well, when I say enormous, it was as if the owl had been absent-mindedly perusing the small ads in the Avian Predator section of Which? monthly magazine and had decided on a whim to embark on an Arnold Schwarzenegger body-building course which had included a special offer of a lifetime's supply of steroids and a consignment of Incredible Hulk tablets. It was a gigantic one and a half metres high.

I didn't know what effect it was likely to have on the pigeons, but by God it frightened me.

It arrived complete with a nodding, swivelling head on a spring, and I had to admit it did look quite impressive. 'I'll put this owl on the bird table in the back garden,' she said, 'and the pigeons will be so petrified at seeing such an intimidating predator, they will fly off and never come back. You are not having an air rifle.'

The owl was not quite the success we had hoped for. Quite apart from the fact that the *regular* visitors to our bird table, such as the little finches, sparrows and robins who frequented our back garden, decided that they did not want to share their bird-table with a one-and-a-half-metre-high plastic owl, the pigeons had no such sensitivities.

Day after day, the pigeons would swoop down from their vantage point on the roof of our house, settle on the bird-table, and try to engage the owl in conversation.

'Coo-coo. Lovely weather we're having for the time of year. Do you come here often? I say, old chap, would you mind if I pinched some of that birdseed? It looks delicious.'

After a few days of this, Mrs. B. handed me a lump hammer and an old metal plate on a leather strap that had once served as a dinner gong. 'Get up in the loft and make as much noise as you can to scare them off.' I dutifully complied, and spent the rest of the day giving myself a severe case of tinnitus as the sounds of the dinner gong rattled the tiles on the roof and dust started to drift down from the seams in the roofing felt. No luck. The pigeons continued to go about their business, as pigeons do, completely unruffled, which was more than could be said for me. I defy anyone to spend half-hour sessions knocking seven bells out of a dinner gong in a confined space and emerge without any hallucinatory side effects.

The following day, I came home to find that the owl had been strapped to the television aerial on the roof (using what looked to be half a roll of gaffer tape) by the handyman we had been employing to install our kitchen. 'Andy said he would do it for nothing as long as we promised to look after his wife and children if he fell off the ladder,' said Mrs. B., whose ruthless negotiating skills have become legendary throughout our neighbourhood. 'They'll be too scared to land on our roof now. You just watch.'

Still we had no success. The owl gazed balefully down at us from the TV aerial, gently nodding and swivelling its head as the wind changed, and the pigeons continued to roost as if nothing had happened.

A day or two later I found Mrs. B. downloading what I thought was music from the Internet. 'How nice,' I said, 'not another Beethoven sonata to add to your collection of classical music?'

Mrs. B. scowled at me. 'No,' she said, 'this is a recording of a peregrine falcon screeching as it searches for prey. Just go and set up the hi-fi system in the loft, will you? You have to do it by nightfall as the pigeons know that the peregrine falcon is a nocturnal hunter.'

I assumed that the pigeons probably had a better Internet connection than I did, because I didn't know anything about the predatory habits of peregrine falcons at all, and I consider myself to be fairly well-read. Still, I did as I had been instructed, and soon the screeches of a peregrine falcon were echoing around the loft. 'We'll have to leave it on all night,' said Mrs. B., 'but the pigeons will be gone by morning, just you see. And don't ask, because you are not having an air rifle.'

After the worst night's sleep of my entire life, with dreams of enormous owls rampaging around the garden and terrorising the neighbourhood, punctuated by the intermittent screeches of a horde of predatory peregrine falcons, I awoke to the pitter-patter of pigeon feet still running up and down the roof as the pigeons continued to take off and land at regular intervals. By now there were broken egg casings dropping regularly from the roof into the front garden as the pigeons had obviously decided that this was the perfect place to raise a family, and the soft squeaks of baby pigeons could be frequently heard from the loft.

We had several more nights of sleeplessness as Mrs. B. was determined to give the peregrine falcon recordings another chance, but after three days it was obvious that the pigeons weren't going anywhere. 'That's it,' said Mrs. B. as she slammed another slice of bread into the toaster at breakfast-time, 'this calls for drastic measures.'

'So I'll get the air rifle then?'

'Not on your life. I'm going to ask Andy to get up on the roof again and deploy anti-pigeon spikes around the solar panels. I've already ordered the spikes overnight from the Internet, so there's no point arguing.'

Ordering goods via the Internet overnight is Mrs. B.'s specialist subject. It is surprisingly efficient, as we have an enormous Amazon warehouse situated less than twenty miles away, and goods are usually delivered the following day. However, it also removes the opportunity for executive oversight, and usually the first time I find out about it is when I wake up the following morning.

Sure enough, the spikes arrived the next day, and I came home to see Andy securing the last few rows of spikes into place. The end result, with the spikes attached to the edges of the solar panels, looked as though a giant square hedgehog had been first run over by a steam-roller, and then nailed to the roof as a warning message in order to discourage other low-flying giant square hedgehogs.

I watched as Andy descended the ladder cautiously. I could tell that he wasn't really comfortable with heights, possibly because he was primarily a kitchen fitter, and there were not many people in our part of Birmingham who wanted a fitted kitchen installed on their roof.

The three of us stood on the front drive and looked up at the roof. 'I'd like to see the pigeon that could get under the solar panels through those spikes,' asserted Mrs. B., confidently. As the words left her mouth, a pigeon landed on the roof, regarded the spikes for a moment, flattened itself against the roof like an avian limbo-dancer, scuttled between the spikes and disappeared under the solar panels.

It's not often I see Mrs. B. speechless. I decided that the best course of action was to say nothing, a strategy which I frequently employ (with varying degrees of success) in order to keep the peace in our household. On this occasion it paid off.

Later that day she was to be found browsing the website of our local air-rifle suppliers in Tamworth. 'What do you reckon?' she said. 'Should we go for the BSA .22 or perhaps the Carbine Superlite .177 with its improved muzzle velocity? What about a Sig Sauer with a night-vision scope? On second thoughts, we probably don't need a night-vision scope, so you should save a few pounds there.'

It was nice to see that Mrs. B. was taking this seriously.

The next day I bought myself a Gehmann .22 air rifle, complete with a high-resolution telescopic sight. I'd like to say that I had done sufficient research myself to make an informed choice, but the truth is that I was a sucker for the high-octane sales patter that fell from the lips of the manager at the air-rifle dealership, and I returned home some £300 lighter, clutching the 'manager's special offer' – an all-inclusive beginners air-rifle kit which included a silencer, a telescopic sight, a soft carry-bag, a box of six-inch circular paper targets and 250 rounds of ammunition in the form of lead pellets.

'I'm not kidding, Kevin –
you should have seen that air rifle, it was this big.'

Suffice it to say that I was as good as my word, and after spending ten days staked out in the caravan on the front drive, armed with a thermos flask full of coffee and with the silenced barrel of the air rifle poking unobtrusively through the caravan skylight, the pigeons got together for urgent discussions, and had obviously decided by common consensus that the houses in the surrounding streets presented better opportunities.

For one morning, they mysteriously vanished, never to be seen again.

***

'So,' said John, 'what ARE you in prison for?'

I studied my fingernails nonchalantly. 'Oh,' I said, 'discharging a firearm and shooting pigeons within fifteen metres of the Queen's Highway.'

John considered this for a few moments. 'Pigeons?' he said, incredulously. 'Is that actually a crime?'

'Oh yes,' I said, 'and an extremely serious one as well. If it hadn't been for my dodgy ticker they would likely have thrown away the key, and I would never have seen the smiling faces of my dear grandchildren ever again.'

John looked a bit dubious, but said no more, and soon afterwards the call, 'Lights out!' reverberated around the wing. The cell was plunged into darkness and I settled back on my mattress for my first night in captivity.

CHAPTER 8

Ground Zero

I am often asked how it was that I first became interested in Islam, and what it was that led me to develop the views that I hold on the subject. At the time of writing, the majority of non-Muslims living in the United Kingdom, and indeed in most Western countries, are still unaware of – and unawakened to – the true nature of Islam, and on the date of September 10, 2001, the day before 9/11, I was one of those unaware and unawakened.

The events of September 11, 2001, had a profound effect on me, as I am sure it did on many others. I was working as a service contractor at the time – as a computer consultant in a large office where the TV news channel was on in the background. It was around a quarter to two in the afternoon (UK time), and I heard a series of exclamations from several employees present in the office as the news of the attack on the first tower filtered through to the main news networks.

I glanced up at the screen, to be presented with the most horrific video footage, including graphic scenes of people jumping from the North Tower of the World Trade Centre as the upper stories were engulfed in flames. I saw the second attack on the South Tower happen live, with the plane slicing into the building and exploding in a huge ball of fire, as the media news team cameras were by then already focused on the unfolding events.

For the rest of the afternoon, we all watched the TV in stunned disbelief as people continued to jump from the upper floors of the Twin Towers, until the buildings themselves finally collapsed, falling down one after the other, imploding and disintegrating as if in slow motion, with enormous clouds of debris billowing out across Manhattan.

I remember that for days afterwards, it was the main topic of conversation wherever I went, but nobody I knew seemed to be making the connection between the attack and the ideology of Islam itself. The US President at the time, George W. Bush, had made a point of emphasising that Islam was 'a religion of peace' and I remember wondering why he had gone to the trouble of saying that, given that I and most people I knew seemed to have no opinion of the matter one way or another on the subject of Islam.

Most of us assumed that 9/11 (as it became known) was most likely the work of a bunch of Islamic fundamentalist lunatics under the auspices of one 'Osama Bin Laden' – and after all, examples of fundamentalist lunatics exist in every religion, not just Islam. The intricate details relating to the ideology of Islam were not even on most people's radar at all, and it certainly was not on my radar at that time.

But something was niggling away at the back of my mind. This was such a terrible event, the lives of almost three thousand people snuffed out in an instant, one of the worst terrorist atrocities if not the worst in modern times, and I found myself thinking that there must be some more profound meaning behind this catastrophic destruction, that three thousand people must not have died for nothing. I also found myself thinking that maybe there was something that we in the West were not being told?

And so I started my research.

I started by trying to find out as much as I could about Osama Bin Laden – who was born to the family of a billionaire in Saudi Arabia. He studied at university in the country until 1979, when he joined Mujahideen forces in Pakistan fighting against the Soviet Union in Afghanistan. He helped to fund the Mujahideen by funnelling arms, money and fighters from the Arab world into Afghanistan, and gained popularity among many Arabs. In 1988, he formed Al-Qa'eda. He was banished from Saudi Arabia in 1992, and shifted his base to Sudan until U.S. pressure forced him to leave Sudan in 1996. After establishing a new base in Afghanistan, he declared a war against the United States, initiating a series of bombings and related attacks. He was on the American (FBI) lists of Ten Most Wanted Fugitives and Most Wanted Terrorists for his involvement in the 1998 US

Embassy bombings in Dar-es-Salaam, Tanzania and Nairobi, Kenya.

One thing that jumped out at me was the emphasis that just about every media outlet in the world at that time was focused on – that these terrible atrocities were responsibility of one particular group – Al-Qa'eda – and the implication was that if only we in the West could destroy the leadership of that organisation, the problem of global terrorism would simply disappear.

However, this wasn't what Osama Bin Laden himself was saying, as this excerpt from an October 2001 interview with Tayseer Allouni of the Al-Jazeera news channel shows:

... This matter isn't about any specific person and... is not about the Al-Qa'eda Organisation. We are the children of an Islamic Nation, with Prophet Muhammad as its leader, our Lord is one... and all the true believers are brothers. So the situation isn't like the West portrays it, that there is an 'organisation' with a specific name (such as 'al-Qa'eda') and so on. [One of our brothers] created a military base to train the young men to fight against the vicious, arrogant, brutal, terrorizing Soviet empire... this place was called 'The Base' ['Al-Qa'eda'], as in a training base, so this name grew and became. We aren't separated from this nation. We are the children of a nation, and we are an inseparable part of it, from the Far East, from the Philippines, to Indonesia, to Malaysia, to India, to Pakistan, reaching Mauritania...

So there were at least two narratives, each conflicting strongly with the other. Was Al-Qa'eda a 'fundamentalist' organisation? The translation from the Arabic 'Al-Qa'eda' translates not only to 'The Base' but also 'The Foundation' or 'The Fundament'. In which case, it made sense to neutralise the organisation itself, perhaps by assassinating its leaders and destroying its assets.

The other possibility (that nobody in Western politics, church organisations or the mainstream media wanted to address) was that because all believers (Muslims) were brothers, Al-Qa'eda was simply one manifestation of an Islamic Nation (the 'Ummah') comprising one and a half billion Muslims inescapably bound by divine command to follow the leadership of a long-dead seventh-century religious figure who had declared war – in perpetuity – on the rest of humanity.

Surely it couldn't be that? The implications would be huge – and scary.

By this time I had expanded my research to include some of the basics of Islam, including the life of Islam's Prophet Muhammad. What I had found out was not terribly encouraging – far from being a spiritual leader in the footsteps of (say) Jesus and Buddha, he was a pirate, a warlord, a ruthless murderer, a paedophile and a terrorist. And this information came not from his enemies, but from the accounts of his own contemporaries and friends.

(You might say – with friends like that, who needs enemies? But these accounts form part of the core Islamic texts that make up the ideology of Islam, and are not to be casually discounted as examples of so-called 'anti-Muslim bias' perpetrated by malicious racists and far-right-wing 'Islamophobes', as politicians and the mainstream media would have us believe.)

It was around 2003 – I had been researching the basics of Islam for about eighteen months, trying to glean as much as I could from different sources from books and on the Internet – when I was introduced to the work of Robert Spencer, who had recently founded the website Jihad Watch, and Bill Warner from the Centre for the Study of Political Islam.

All of a sudden, things started to fall into place, and I realised that everything that we were being told about the nature of Islam by our church leaders, our politicians and our mainstream media – that it was a 'religion of peace' for example – was completely and utterly false.

Not only that, but it was a falsehood on such an enormous scale as to be worthy of the term 'The Big Lie'. This was a term coined by Adolf Hitler in his book *Mein Kampf* in 1925, and expanded upon by Joseph Goebbels, Germany's Minister of Propaganda, sixteen years later in 1941.

Essentially, the concept of 'The Big Lie' is that if you make the lie big enough, and tell it often enough, then no matter how farfetched it may be, eventually a majority of people will come to believe it. This was the position with Islam.

Far from being a 'religion of peace' – as we were being told by our politicians and the mainstream media – it was a global totalitarian ideology, followed by one and a half billion people, that was implacably at war with the West, and there was essentially nothing that we in the West could say or do in relation to our domestic and foreign policy to appease it.

This realisation shocked me to the core.

I realised that Islam propounded an unremitting, uncompromising doctrine of hatred towards us in the West, not for anything that we might say or do, but for who we are. Non-Muslims, according to the Qur'an, are 'the worst of created beings' and must be ruthlessly fought with every stratagem of war – including deceit – until Islam becomes the only religion on Earth.

This deceit – 'Taqiyya' – which is at the core of the ideology of Islam and which governs the behaviour of Muslims around the world – forms a large part of the story to come, as I was to refer to it on several occasions whilst communicating with the unprincipled hyenas of Grievance Mongers UK.

While I was continuing my research, I was reminded of the scene in the 'Terminator' film, where Kyle Reese explains to Sarah Connor exactly what it is they are dealing with, and the parallel with Islam is chilling:

'Listen! And understand! That terminator is out there. It can't be bargained with! It can't be reasoned with! It doesn't feel pity, or remorse, or fear. And it absolutely will not stop, ever, until you are dead!'

Once you see and understand what the true nature of Islam is – that it is a genuinely fascist and totalitarian political ideology, far from being a 'religion of peace' – and that Muslims are instructed by means of a divine imperative to dominate the entire world – if you are a reasonable, logical person with a capacity for critical evaluation, then you have to consider the horrendous implications that this has for the rest of humanity.

It is not unreasonable to ask – how can we reconcile the presence of large numbers of Muslims living in our midst when they embrace an ideology that has the destruction of our democratic and Judaeo-Christian way of life as a primary goal on the path to an Islamic caliphate governed by Sharia?

One only has to look at the history of Islam and Jihad over the last fourteen hundred years to realise that our entire civilisation is under threat. Wherever Islam has taken hold, the result has been an unremitting catalogue of death and devastation, in a sometimes gradual, sometimes not so gradual process of Islamisation that has worked very well in favour of Islam and against the host civilisation. Why would Islam change or reform now? Why would Muslims change or reform what is considered perfect?

The answer is that it won't, and they won't. An insurmountable barrier to reformation is built into Islam, and it cannot change from within, in the way that (say) Christianity changed during its own reformation. So if Islamisation is going to be stopped, we (as non-Muslims) are the only ones who will be able to stop it. The alternative will be to lose everything decent and true that we in the West have built up over hundreds of years, and if that happens then we will bequeath a legacy of unparalleled darkness to our children and grandchildren.

CHAPTER 9

Prophet of Doom

Around this time I came across an extremely well-researched work by Craig Winn called *Prophet of Doom*. I started to see that if one looked at the Islamic scriptures in context, the narrative that emerged was a world away from what we were being told by most Muslims whenever they appeared on TV or other mainstream media outlets.

Worse still, I discovered that there is an Islamic doctrine of deceit towards non-believers that requires every single devout Muslim to lie about Islam to non-Muslims – that is, if a good impression of Islam cannot be given to non-Muslims by telling the truth. This is true even under oath in a court of law, as our secular laws are subservient to Sharia law in the eyes of a devout Muslim. His obligation to Allah supersedes any loyalty to non-Muslims or their legal institutions. If he doesn't believe this, then he is not a Muslim.

The most common word used by non-Muslims to describe this divinely-sanctioned deceit is – as I have mentioned previously – 'Taqiyya', which broadly translates to saying something that is not true, but depending on the context, 'Tawriya' (giving a false impression), 'Kitman' (lying by omission), 'Muruna' (blending in by discarding some aspects of Islam in order to advance others), and 'Darura' (a state of necessity on account of which one may omit doing something required by Sharia law or indeed may do something against Sharia law with a clean conscience), are all types of divinely-sanctioned lying and deceit.

It is what we would perhaps call anti-social behaviour if we were feeling particularly magnanimous – although it could be more accurately described as hateful, mean-spirited, mendacious and quite frankly, disgustingly offensive behaviour that should be unacceptable in any civilised society. The fact that it is used by Muslims on a daily basis to pull the wool over the eyes of non-Muslims without a second thought or any accompanying feelings of guilt, means that it represents an enormous problem for any open, trusting and tolerant Western society that is foolish enough to admit large numbers of Muslims and to treat them as equals.

This is not simply permission to lie. It was – and still is, according to mainstream Islamic schools of thought and divinely commanded by Allah himself – an obligation, mandated as an eternal doctrine, valid for all times and all places up to the Day of Judgment. It has grave implications for the innocent trust that is so often given to Muslims by non-Muslims unaware of the true nature of Islam – the same trust that is so often abused by Muslims themselves to gain an unfair advantage at the expense of non-Muslims everywhere and at every opportunity.

I will have more to say on the subject of 'Taqiyya' and other reprehensible aspects of divinely-sanctioned Islamic behaviour later in this book.

Before I conclude this chapter, I would like to quote here (with kind permission) from Craig Winn's 'Letter to the Reader' which succinctly summarises the contents of his book *Prophet of Doom* –

Islam is a caustic blend of regurgitated paganism and twisted Bible stories. Muhammad, its lone prophet, conceived his religion solely to satiate his lust for power, sex, and money. He was a terrorist. If you think these conclusions are shocking, wait until you see the evidence.

The critics of this work will claim that Prophet of Doom is offensive, racist, hatemongering, intolerant, and unnecessarily violent. I agree—but I didn't write those parts. They came directly from Islam's scriptures. If you don't like what Muhammad and Allah said, don't blame me. I'm just the messenger.

Others will say that I cherry-picked the worst of Islam to render an unfair verdict. They will charge that I took the Islamic scriptures out of context to smear Muhammad and Allah. But none of that is true. Over the course of these pages, I quote from almost every surah in the Qur'an—many are presented in their entirety. But more than that, I put each verse in the context of Muhammad's life, quoting vociferously from the Sunnah as recorded by Bukhari, Muslim, Ishaq, and Tabari—Islam's earliest and more trusted sources. I even arrange all of this material chronologically, from creation to terror.

Predicting what he called the 'Day of Doom' was Muhammad's most often repeated prophecy. While it did not occur as he foretold in 1110 A.D., it nonetheless came true. Muslims and infidels alike have been doomed by Islam. To discover why, we shall delve into the oldest surviving written evidence. These official works include the Sira, Ta'rikh, Hadith, and Qur'an. Ishaq's Sira, or biography, called Sirat Rasul Allah, provides the sole account of Muhammad's life and the formation of Islam written within 200 years of the prophet's death.

While the character, message, and deeds portrayed within its pages are the antithesis of Christ's and his disciples, the Sira's chronological presentation is similar in style to the Christian Gospels. The Ta'rikh is the oldest, most trusted, and comprehensive history of Islam's formation and Muhammad's example, called Sunnah. It was written by Tabari. His History of al-Tabari is formatted like the Bible. It begins with Islamic creation and ends with the acts of Muhammad's companions. Tabari is a compilation of Hadith quotes and Qur'an passages. As such, it provides the best skeleton upon which to flesh out the character of Muhammad and the nature of fundamental Islam.

A Hadith is an oral report from Muhammad or his companions. Muslims believe that Hadith were inspired by Allah, making them scripture. The most revered Collection was compiled in a topical arrangement by Bukhari. Allah's Book, the Qur'an, lacks context and chronology, so in order to understand it, readers are dependent upon the Sira, Ta'rikh, and Hadith.

All that can be known about Muhammad's deeds, means, motives, god, and scripture is enshrined in these books. In their pages you will see them as they saw themselves. My only point of departure from Ishaq and Tabari will be the comprehensive review of the early Meccan surahs, a period in which they had very little to say. Our paths will join again as we approach Islam's midlife crisis: the Quraysh Bargain, Satanic Verses, Night's Journey, and Pledge of Aqaba—a declaration of war against all mankind.

At this point, the Sira, Ta'rikh, and Hadith speak more clearly than the Qur'an. So that there will be no confusion, I have set passages from Islam's scriptures in bold-faced type. When quoting from the Qur'an and Hadith, I have elected to use a blended translation. No language transfers perfectly—one word to another. Five of my twelve translations of the Qur'an were combined to create the most accurate conveyance of the message possible.

However, the writing quality is so poor, the proofreaders of this manuscript suggested that I help Allah and Muhammad out by cleaning up their grammar, punctuation, and verbosity. So for clarity and readability, I have trimmed their unruly word patterns and meaningless repetitions, being careful not to alter the meaning or message of any passage. Insertions within parenthesis (like this) were added by the Arabic translators to fill in missing words or to clarify the text. Insertions within brackets [like this] represent my observations.

I have elected to present Islam's original source material in juxtaposition to my evaluation of its veracity. This format is similar to that used by the first English translators of Mein Kampf as they attempted to warn America about the dangers lurking in Hitler's manifesto. They, as I, found it necessary to hold the author accountable. A great deal was at stake then, as it is today. The last time the world was ignorant of such a hateful and violent doctrine, 55 million people died. If we don't shed our ignorance of Islam, many more will perish.

My quest to understand Islam began on the morning of September 11th 2001. I wanted to know why Muslim militants were killing us. So I went to Ground Zero for Islamic terror—Israel. The West Bank is home to more suicide bombers per capita than anywhere else on earth. I arranged to meet with the terrorists themselves. I asked members of al-Qaeda, Islamic Jihad, al-Aqsa Martyrs' Brigade, and Hamas why they were killing us. They said, 'Islam — we're following Muhammad's orders.' That adventure is recounted in Tea with Terrorists. It covers a wide range of material and serves as a companion volume, connecting fundamental Islam to terrorism.

Prophet of Doom focuses strictly on what the Islamic scriptures have to say. So, could it be? Could a prophet and a religion be responsible for today's terrorist attacks? I invested 10,000 hours in pursuit of that answer. I wish everyone had. But knowing that most are unable, I have distilled what I discovered into these pages.

Now for a word of caution: this journey of discovery is ordered chronologically. It is not prioritized by relevance. Explaining the root cause of Islamic terror is the biggest priority; yet it is not exposed until the last half of the book. I want you to know Muhammad, Allah, and Islam before you judge their legacy. While Prophet of Doom is meticulously researched, documented, and accurate, it's written as if you and I were old friends having a lively chat about the most important and lethal issue of our day.

One last thought before you head down this perilous path. I pray that when you have reached the journey's end, you will share my heart for the plight of Muslims. I want nothing more than to free them from Islam, and in so doing, free us from the terror their doctrine inspires.

I was to spend the next ten years (between 2003 and 2013) developing my knowledge of Islam. I decided at that time that it was my duty as a father and a grandfather to stand up and be counted. For the sake of future generations, I had to do whatever I could to make people aware of the true nature of Islam, no matter the cost.

This is because one has to understand the true nature of an enemy before one can hope to defeat him. In the words of the great Chinese general, Sun Tzu – from his book, *The Art of War*, written around 500 BC –

'If you know the enemy and know yourself, you need not fear the result of a hundred battles. If you know yourself but not the enemy, for every victory gained you will also suffer a defeat. If you know neither the enemy nor yourself, you will succumb in every battle.'

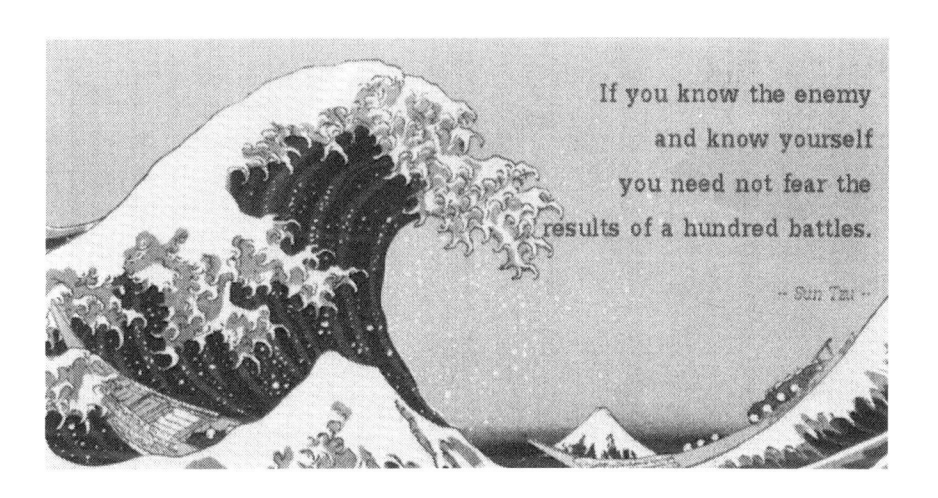

If you know the enemy and know yourself you need not fear the results of a hundred battles.

– Sun Tzu –

It's no exaggeration to say that Islam is the sworn enemy of freedom, democracy and everything that we hold dear in a civilised Western society. We have a choice. We can continue to do nothing, and to allow our political elites, church leaders and mainstream media to continue to do nothing, in which case Islam will steamroll over everything that our forefathers and ancestors have bequeathed to us, or we can fight back to defend our Judaeo-Christian values and traditions that have served us so well and which are light years ahead – in virtually every physical, moral and philosophical measurement – of anything the Islamic world has to offer.

I hope that by reading this book, and by understanding the implications of what is likely to befall our civilisation if we continue to do nothing, you may come to see not only why I have made the choice that I have, but that you may also come to see that it is a choice that every non-Muslim must consider if he is to one day face his grandchildren and answer the question – asked by so many children of previous generations under similar circumstances – 'What did you do in the war, Grandad?'

CHAPTER 10

The Pigeon Awakens

It was the morning of Saturday 29 April 2017 – the start of my second day of incarceration at HMP Thameside. I was woken by the soft yet persistent buzzing of the alarm on my digital wrist-watch. This was the one electronic item that had been returned to me from my initial registration into the prison system.

It had presumably been designated as a harmless item, and not for the first time, I wished that I had paid more attention to the James Bond and Jason Bourne films of my youth, where wrist-watches could be magically transformed into elaborate killing devices with such accessories as cheese-wires for strangling prison guards, wire saws for cutting through prison bars, and (my favourite) a wrist-watch filled with explosives designed to demolish a prison door and facilitate my escape to freedom.

But then again, you should be careful what you wish for. Knowing my luck, I would probably have just blown my arms and legs off.

It was 6:30 a.m. and for a moment I was disoriented by various unfamiliar sounds and sensations. I tried to reconcile the sounds and sensations with the environment I would normally awaken to – and then I realised where I was, and my heart plummeted into my boots.

Or at least, my anticipation was that it was where my heart would have plummeted, had I not taken the precaution of removing my footwear the previous evening before retiring to the uppermost bunk in the cell. As it was, my heart plummeted to a spot just below my ankles, whereupon it rebounded like a bungee jumper on steroids and positioned itself just above my calves, from where it proceeded to hang on to my kneecaps for dear life.

This sensation was not entirely agreeable to me, and so I stretched out my body in an attempt to return my heart to its previous location, an activity that made me realise that my previous assessment of the hardness of the prison mattress the night before was pretty much as accurate as could be. The mattress had obviously been created by a sociopathic furniture designer with the intention of bringing home to the most recalcitrant old lag the fact that his previous life of luxury was destined to be but a distant memory.

Every bone that I could identify in my body ached as though I had just gone through ten rounds with Mike Tyson, perhaps on a day when he had been serially disrespected in the ring and was consequently feeling particularly well-disposed to the notion that his opponent would deserve to be beaten to a pulp. The more I thought about it, the more I realised that this sensation applied to bones that I hadn't even been aware of during my previous sixty-four years. I made yet another mental note to adjust the Trip Advisor rating for my stay at HMP Thameside – downwards, at least for the time being.

I imagined my Trip Advisor representative – 'So, Mr. Burton, how did you enjoy your first night at the five-star HMP Thameside establishment?'

'Fine, thank you. It was very enjoyable. No problems at all.' (I am British, after all, and despite my previous grousing and grumbling, we British enjoy nothing more than displaying stoicism and understated irony in the face of adversity, a characteristic that is not always fully appreciated by those of lesser cultures.)

Sunshine streamed through the heavily-barred windows, and from my bunk I could see planes coming in to land at London City Airport, just across the River Thames and less than a mile away from where I was incarcerated.

I thought of all those carefree passengers, returning from their holidays in Tenerife and Fuerteventura, clutching their straw donkeys and their bottles of duty-free tequila, never giving a thought to what it must be like to having their liberty taken away from them.

By this time you may be wondering exactly what it was that I had done for me to find myself in this predicament. You may be saying to yourself, 'Ha – that Tim Burton is a right one. He probably deserves everything the British justice system has thrown at him.' Well, if you do happen to be thinking that at this time, then it's because I haven't yet explained fully to you the precession of events that led up to my incarceration. Keep turning the pages, dear reader, and you shall be rewarded beyond your wildest dreams.

(Actually that's not quite true, unless your wildest dreams involve your living out the rest of your life in a dark and dingy bed-sit, plagued by rats and cockroaches while your social worker lives the high life with money plundered from your bank account.)

Anyway – I digress. As the moments passed, I became aware of the soft sound of snoring emanating from the bottom bunk. John was evidently a sounder sleeper than I was, and I wasn't about to disturb him if I could possibly help it. Nevertheless, I was determined to set up some kind of a routine for the duration of my stay at HMP Thameside, and so I clambered down as quietly as I could from the top bunk and made my way to the en-suite partition, armed with my bag of toiletries.

The en-suite consisted of a shower head set into the ceiling, with metal buttons set into the wall to switch it on and off. There was what looked like to be a cast-concrete toilet set into a corner of the cell, and an equally resilient sink with metal buttons in place of taps.

I was later to find out that some prison cells did originally have standard taps with rotating handles, but that these could ingeniously be utilised as improvised handcuff-removing devices. Who would have thought it? The ingenuity of prisoners around the world (and presumably especially within HMP Thameside) knows no bounds.

I activated the shower and spent the next ten minutes luxuriating under a torrent of acceptably warm water (I dare say the appropriate Health and Safety professionals had determined what was to be considered too hot or too cold for the average prisoner, as there was no temperature adjustment device in sight) and then towelled myself off and dressed myself in my prison greens, which I was to wear for most of the next six weeks. I might not be the most sartorially dressed prisoner on the wing, but I hoped I would at least blend in with the other prisoners, much like a chameleon hoping to blend in with his background, but without the advantage of the swivelling eyes and tongue-related fly-catching abilities.

After the first two weeks on the wing, prisoners are permitted to wear their own clothes, but as my only other set of clothes comprised my dark blue suit – with which I had been hoping to impress the judge – I thought that my set of prison greens would probably be a better choice. So prison greens it was, and prison greens it remained for the duration of my stay.

John stirred on the lower bunk. 'They'll most likely be unlocking the cell at 08:00,' he said. 'Or 7:45 for meds. Have you got any medication you ought to be taking?'

As it happened, I did have some medication to take, first thing in the morning, every morning, and last thing at night, every night. This was all part and parcel of having had a history of serious heart problems over the previous three years. Part of the induction process the previous day had involved removing and impounding my medication (I had brought several days' supply with me) but I had been assured that it would be dispensed each day in line with my medical requirements, and so it proved to be the case.

I couldn't fault the procedure. The cells were unlocked at 7:45 a.m. precisely, and there was a stentorian shout from one of the prison officers – 'Meds!' Those of us who were on medication sprang out of our cells like apathetic greyhounds released from their traps, perhaps on a day when the artificial rabbit on the rail had seized up due to lack of maintenance.

Waiting outside the 'medication hatch' at HMP Thameside

This was the first opportunity I had had to take a look at some of the other residents on the wing. From what I could see, they appeared to be just like any other cross-section of society in terms of demographics – although I did notice quite a few prisoners who were obviously Muslim, each sporting the characteristic long, black Islamic-style beard without the accompanying moustache. I would have to be extremely careful in response to anything that they might ask me.

We ambled our way up to the locked and barred door that led from the wing to the Wing Dispensary. From there we were required to queue up in a more or less orderly fashion to be admitted one by one by a prison officer to the 'medication hatch' which was via a barred window to the dispensary.

The majority of the dispensary staff were female, and this, I subsequently discovered, allowed for some outrageous flirting on behalf of the prisoners – an activity which, if not actually encouraged, was far from being discouraged by the prison officers, presumably with the view in mind that a bit of harmless sexual harassment diminished the possibility of prison riots from disgruntled inmates. The #MeToo movement obviously hadn't made its way as far as HMP Thameside.

"Allo darlin',' would be the standard greeting. 'What 'ave you got for me today? 'Ow about you and me getting together when you knock off after work?'

To be fair, the ladies in the dispensary were made of stern stuff; their responses would range from the placatory, 'Now, now,' to the standard, 'Behave yourself,' to the more eloquent, 'How would you like me to kick you in the nuts?'

Naturally, I was far above such uncouth behaviour, and I contented myself with giving my name, rank and number as I handed over my precious identity card – 'Burton – Timothy M. – A Wing, Cell number AA-17.' The pharmacist consulted a computer screen, gave the command to one of the other assistants to complete the order, and after a little while, a small paper cup containing one's medication slid through the hatch, together with another small paper cup containing a couple of mouthfuls of water. One was expected to swallow the meds in front of the pharmacist. I suppose the last thing they would have wanted was for some prisoner to store up a couple of hundred paracetamol tablets and then take them all at once. Just think of the paperwork that would entail.

After the early morning dispensation of meds, each prisoner was allowed back down onto the wing to collect their breakfast (and for this, one relied upon the goodwill of one's cellmate, as by the time the dispensation of meds was concluded, the time for collecting one's breakfast was usually long passed.)

I was given a small packet of Coco Pops and a carton of milk by John.

As we returned to our cell, I said, 'Is that it, then? Coco Pops?' I have absolutely hated Coco Pops with a passion ever since I was a child. I have no idea why, unlike my pathological aversion to fish, which I put down to my mother beating me over the head with a halibut when I was three years old.

'You should be able to get something more to your liking over the next few days,' said John. 'Here's some muesli, an apple and a couple of oranges to keep you going.' He reached into his cell cupboard and retrieved several items from what looked to be like a box filled with a suspiciously large stash of pre-packed breakfast paraphernalia.

'Thanks,' I said. It might not have been breakfast at the Ritz, but it was most welcome. I resisted the temptation to enquire about the possibility of being allocated a couple of hot bacon sandwiches, perhaps on lightly toasted bread with brown sauce. No point pushing your luck at this early stage in the proceedings, I thought, and besides, bacon might well be off what was likely to be a halal-compliant menu for the next six weeks.

I poured the muesli into my plastic prison bowl, added some milk, and tucked in.

CHAPTER 11

Pigeon on the Wing

After breakfast, the cell was to remain unlocked for the next couple of hours, and I ventured out of the cell onto the communal area of the prison wing in order to discover more about the world that I was to call home for the next six weeks.

I was more than a little nervous, not knowing how I might be treated by the other prisoners, but I was to find that the prevailing atmosphere was one of benign indifference, for which I was very grateful.

I was still concerned with whether I might be recognised by the other prisoners as a notorious Islamophobe (the Independent newspaper and the Daily Mail had splashed photographs of me all over their pages during the previous month). I had no desire to be fending off unwelcome questions at this stage, at least not before I had worked out an adequate defence strategy.

This section of the wing was divided into two levels – 'AA-upper' and 'AA-lower', and there were around thirty cells on each level. A flight of stairs connected the two levels, and several prisoners seemed to be engaged in constructive employment, some cleaning the communal areas with mops and buckets, and others armed with brooms nonchalantly sweeping out the cells.

There was also a wing for laundry, where one could entrust one's prison greens to one of two enormous washing machines, although I was to find out that this was not recommended unless absolutely necessary, due to the propensity for the machines to disgorge items that had been presented for washing approximately two sizes smaller than when they went in.

There were a couple of pool tables on each level, and these were in constant use whenever the cell doors were unlocked and prisoners were given 'association time' – which amounted to around eight hours per day in total. The rest of the time, we were to be locked up in our respective cells and left to our own devices.

For me though, the main source of interest lay in the half-dozen or so chess boards, complete with chess pieces that were distributed on the various tables in the association area on the wing.

I have always loved playing the game of chess from as far back as I remember.

One of my earliest memories was of playing with an ivory chess set that one of my great-uncles had brought back, decades previously from the Far East. It was a real work of art, although as a young know-it-all, I probably didn't appreciate it then as much as I should have.

The box containing the chess pieces had been intricately carved, and the chess pieces themselves were polished with age. The board was likewise intricately carved, meticulously constructed with an eye for detail and precision that is rarely seen these days in the era of mass production.

Despite my youth, and my corresponding lack of knowledge of history, the chess set seemed to speak to me of another time and another age, far removed from my middle-class upbringing in the leafy suburbs of Surrey.

Memories of that ivory chess set inspired me to join the chess club at my secondary school, and it became my hobby of choice when many of my contemporaries at that time looked down upon such intellectual pursuits, preferring instead to participate in football, rugby and cricket.

In the manner of most schoolboys the world over, they would endlessly discuss tactics, strategy and the achievements of prominent footballers, rugby players and cricketers, at a time where such people had not yet become the celebrities that they are today.

I didn't have any sense of alienation or any negative feelings about this, as I very quickly found out that as a gangly teenager I was completely rubbish at anything that involved accurate hand-to-eye co-ordination. I was always the last person to be team-picked for a football, rugby or cricket game.

('Oh, no, we've ended up with Burton again!' was a phrase I was soon to get used to.)

I therefore resigned myself to finding other areas where I might display my undoubted expertise. I knew I had some undoubted expertise tucked away somewhere, it was just a question of finding out where it was. At least, that is what I told myself.

Strangely enough, during my last ever game of rugby at my school, when I was about fifteen years old, I found myself among a bunch of other similarly weedy players who had very similar expertise (or lack of it) in the realms of hand-to-eye co-ordination.

I don't know whether it was their sheer ineptitude that spurred me on, but I found myself scoring all eight of the tries that occurred during the game, and this inexplicably included five successful conversions which resulted in a final score of 34-0.

I remember feeling on top of the world about that, and I also remember contemplating my future as a famous rugby player 'The Captain of the Weeds' as my younger daughter pithily observed when I regaled her years later with the story – unfortunately though, from that day to this I haven't been able to kick a ball straight if my life were to depend on it.

This may have been because the day following this momentous game of rugby, I was involved in a serious road accident, caused by my recklessly cycling across a busy road junction. I had been hastily trying to make up time on my newspaper delivery round and neglected to observe the relevant road signs, thereby colliding with a yellow Mini Cooper S in the process.

I distinctly remember the colour and make of the car as I somersaulted over the roof and landed in what must have been a somewhat ungainly manner in the road behind the car. I don't suppose the driver of the Mini Cooper S remembered much about the colour of my bike. I was told later that she seemed to be pre-occupied with having a fit of the vapours, perhaps unsurprisingly under the circumstances.

I thought at the time that maybe my guardian angel was having a day off. With hindsight, I shouldn't have been so cynical. Given the nature of the accident, I was lucky not to have been killed. The incident did however leave me with several broken bones, some of which never healed correctly, and I never played rugby again after that.

That's what you get for being hubristic. They do say that Nemesis comes after Hubris.

So, chess it was. I sat down at a table next to one of the chess boards that was in use, and studied the tactics of the players, who were two young men who looked to be of Afro-Caribbean origin. After a few moments, I could see that they were both making elementary mistakes, and I felt emboldened enough to say – 'Any chance I could play the winner?'

They both turned to look at me, and regarded me with cursory interest. They reminded me of Jamaican versions of Ant and Dec. 'All right, Grandad,' said Ant. He turned to his opponent. 'On my life, if this place ain't turning into an old people's home.'

'An old people's home? A graveyard more like!' said Dec, eyeing me up and down. 'Ha! A house of the living dead!' Then they both leaned back and chuckled at each other good-humouredly at their own combined quick wit and ready repartee.

Right, I thought. *That sounds like a challenge. I'll bloody well show them what the older generation can achieve when they put their minds to it.*

I won the first game, and the next. I played several games of chess that morning, and as I started to win game after game, more and more inmates came up to watch what was going on. There is nothing like successfully playing to win in a competitive sport for restoring morale, and by the time the call came from the prison officers around 11:30 – 'Lunch!' I was starting to feel quite chipper.

However, there is also nothing like queuing for your first prison lunch to bring you back down to earth. The first thing that strikes one is the general unruliness of the inmates in the queue, which was a slightly intimidating characteristic of this and all other subsequent meals I was to experience. There was a certain amount of pushing and shoving as inmates jostled to reach the front of the queue, whereupon a prison officer would tick off names and match them against the food items.

I had already used my prison ID card and fingerprint to log into the prison computer system and order the meal in advance, so I had a reasonable expectation of what it was I was likely to receive. I was looking forward to a mouth-watering plate of spaghetti Bolognese and chips, together with strawberry-flavoured yoghurt for dessert. However, by the time I had reached the front of the queue, I found that they had run out of spaghetti Bolognese.

'How about a nice piece of fried fish?' asked the lugubrious ginger-haired inmate in charge of dispensing the food. 'It looks lovely, don't it? That'll be straight out of the River Thames this morning, mark my words. You can tell that by the tiny teeth marks left by the marauding rats.' I declined. Maybe there would come a time when I would compete with Thames water rats for prison food, but today was not that time.

'We're out of strawberry yoghurt as well,' continued Mr. Lugubrious. 'Someone's nicked that last one. You can't trust anyone in here. Thieving so-and-sos, the lot of them. It looks like we still have a couple of these manky-looking oranges left, though, so you can have one of those. Two if you like. And you can have some extra chips to make up for it. We always have loads of chips left.'

I could see that maintaining my svelte figure behind bars for the next six weeks was going to prove a challenge. Nevertheless, I graciously accepted my extra chips and manky-looking oranges, and carried my food tray over to one of the free association tables in the communal area outside my cell. I sat down to eat.

As I finished my last remaining chips, the two young Afro-Caribbean chess players I had met earlier sat down at my table. 'So, you're the Pigeon,' said Ant. 'We've heard all about you from John.'

'Ah,' I said, cautiously. 'I do hope that I'm not going to upset any pigeon-lovers in here. Although in my defence I was merely protecting my property,' and I proceeded to tell them about my pigeon-related firearm escapades. Admittedly I did embellish the story a bit, and maybe I should not have exaggerated the strength and diversity of my firearms collection, and I probably should have left out the bit where I was supposedly caught red-handed with my twelve-bore shotgun by the local police SWAT team.

'Cool story, bro,' said Dec. I'm not sure if they entirely believed me, but I needn't have worried, because apparently the back story of most inmates is expected to include a certain degree of embellishment and exaggeration, and it turned out that both Ant and Dec were kingpins of South London's cannabis underworld, who had been caught within days of each other in similar circumstances while transporting large amounts of beneficial herbs from one part of the country to another.

'You don't have any weed on you, do you? No? Okay, well, how about another game of chess?' said Ant, and we played until we were instructed by the guards to return to our cells for lock-up and roll-call.

CHAPTER 12

The Pigeon and Religion

Lock-up and rollcall are procedures at the heart of every prison system, and HMP Thameside was no different in that respect. Several times every day, the inmates were locked into their respective cells, and each cell was then inspected to make sure the requisite numbers of prisoners were contained therein. As each inspection hatch was opened, one officer would look in and call, 'One!' or, 'Two!' as a second officer wrote the details on a clipboard.

How twentieth century, I thought, living as we do in an era of electronic sensors and recording devices. Maybe I should show a little initiative and suggest to the prison administration (via the suggestion box on the landing) that bar-codes be tattooed onto prisoners' foreheads for speed and convenience.

There are those who mutter darkly that such developments are not far down the road, given that we are rapidly becoming slaves to modern technology. Already there are building access systems that rely on chips implanted under the skin of employees to restrict access to certain parts of a building and to record times of entry and exit, so one could certainly argue that it is only a matter of time before it becomes commonplace.

However, I do wonder what the Howard League for Penal Reform might have to say about that. The concept of the Mark of the Beast might be acceptable in the Book of Revelation, but HLPR would no doubt view it as a gross infringement of prisoners' rights. Still, you can't stop progress, and if such a thing were ever to come to pass, remember you read it here first.

Whilst lock-up and roll-call were underway, I took the opportunity to read through a pamphlet which had been stuffed into my bag of toiletries the previous evening. This pamphlet had been written by the management of HMP Thameside as a guide for inmates towards what was considered acceptable behaviour, and what was not. I started to read through it. This is an automatic reflex from my childhood – I'll read anything that's put in front of me. My wife finds it to be an annoying trait, but my counter-argument is that it's a handy habit to have when you are negotiating the route from Birmingham to Walton-on-the-Naze.

My cell-mate, John, was engrossed in the paperback novel that I had seen when I had entered the cell for the first time during the previous evening. 'What's that you're reading, John?' I asked. It looked like a well-thumbed and oft-read piece of writing, judging from the condition of the book. The front cover was missing, and I couldn't make out the title.

'De Profundis,' he replied, 'it's by some geezer called Oscar Wilde. It was in the cell when I got here. You can borrow it if you want. It's a bit depressing, but at least it's better than that HMP Thameside instruction manual. That makes you want to slit your wrists. It's like – do all this stuff and don't do all that stuff.'

I had read *De Profundis* in my teens. 'You find it depressing? I'm not surprised,' I said. It had been written by Oscar Wilde while he was imprisoned in Reading Gaol in 1897, and was an account of the anguish he felt at having been jailed as an unintended consequence of attempting to call out a prominent member of the British establishment. Just the thing you want to read when you're coming to terms with a substantial period of unjust incarceration for something not too dissimilar.

'Look on the bright side,' I said. 'At least the HMP Thameside instruction manual contains enough risible material to support any number of pedants specialising in grammatical inaccuracies as a basis for their stand-up comedy routine. Look at this, for example,' and I pointed at a section on the first page of the pamphlet with the following instruction –

PRISONER'S MUST KEEP THEY'RE CELLS CLEAN AND TIDY.

'What's wrong with that?' said John.

'What's wrong with it?' I said. 'What's wrong with it? It's a grammatical nightmare, that's what. Whoever penned that deserves at least twelve months' hard labour, preferably down a freezing cold Siberian salt mine with nothing to eat but starvation rations and supervised by a psychopathic prison guard armed with a sixty thousand volt cattle prod.'

John seemed amused at my apparent indignation. 'Seems a little harsh to me,' he said. He turned back to his book and left me to study the in-cell computer system instructions in the pamphlet.

I hadn't yet fully worked out how the system operated – I knew there was a method for prisoners to select items from a menu on the in-cell computer, only to see their hopes and dreams dashed at the last minute when the selected food failed to materialise, but I now saw that there was a default meal allocation was to ensure that inmates didn't die of starvation whilst trying to figure out how the system worked. I was somewhat sceptical of this. From what I could see, the default meal applications consisted of fried fish, Coco Pops, chips and manky oranges.

I suppose I shouldn't complain. Tommy Robinson, a true British patriot I admire immensely for his stance against the Islamisation of this great country, had to endure two months behind bars in 2018 with only a tin of tuna to eat every day, and lost a stone and a half in weight over that time. The Muslim inmates in that prison (HMP Onley) had discovered his presence, and as they were in charge of food allocation, there was a very real risk of him being poisoned, a situation that the Governor of Onley prison (allegedly) shamefully failed to address during his time there and which could have resulted in serious consequences.

I was to find out that the computer terminal in each cell at HMP Thameside played an integral part in the routine that determined how a prisoner spent his time, what food he could eat, and what activities he could sign up for. The computer terminal could recognise one's identity card via a card reader, combined with a fingerprint reader, and from there one could access the prison intranet with its impressive range of services. I was to find that we couldn't actually get onto the World Wide Web, either to send or receive emails, or watch video clips of cute little kittens. This made me realise that it was going to be a very tough stretch indeed, and that I had better prepare myself mentally for the inevitable withdrawal symptoms of technological cold turkey. The loss of email exchanges was one thing, but not to be able to watch video clips of cute little kittens over the next six weeks was going to be very taxing on my mental equilibrium.

There were various menu options on the computer for registering with the prison library, the gym, religious services and other activities such as art classes, language classes and IT technology courses. I was interested to see that in order to sign up for religious services, one had to declare one's religion, and that could not then be changed for the duration of one's stay. I felt that this was unduly restrictive. What if I wanted to try out the Hindu religion for a week? Or even the cult of the Flying Spaghetti Monster? Or better still, sign up during the week as a Muslim for the extra privileges of halal chicken meals and the Friday afternoons out of your cell for the communal Jumu'ah prayer, before switching back to Christianity for a Sunday morning sing-along with a happy-clappy Gospel choir?

As you may by now be able to determine, I take my religious duties and responsibilities somewhat less seriously than perhaps I ought. However, what is a religion but a set of ideas? Those ideas should be able to be subjected to intense scrutiny, especially in the case of a set of ideas that command a certain degree of ruthlessness towards non-believers (yes, Islam, I'm looking at you).

Wherever a set of ideas, masquerading as a religion, impinge on the rights of non-believers, they should very firmly be rejected. In the case of religions that follow the Golden Rule (do unto others as you would have done unto you) non-believers do not suffer overmuch; however, as the ideology of Islam does NOT follow the Golden Rule, it should be treated very differently in order to protect the rights of non-believers who would otherwise be subjugated, forcibly converted, or (as is usually the case) brutally slaughtered by a majority-Muslim population.

I hit the ENTER key on the computer keyboard and signed up as a Christian. I imagine that the keystroke must have been relayed directly to the prison chaplain, probably via the activation of a flashing red light in his office, and more than likely accompanied by the 'whoop, whoop' of a 1910 Ford Model T klaxon, because he was knocking on my cell door within ten minutes of the lunchtime lock-up and roll-call period ending.

The prison chaplain was a white-haired gentleman of around sixty years of age with a fatherly demeanour and a strong Irish brogue. 'Ah, Timothy,' he said, consulting his clipboard. 'Will we be seeing you at the Sunday Church Service tomorrow?'

Well, never let it be said that I am unwilling to try new experiences. The HMP Thameside instruction manual specified that on Sunday 30 April there was in fact a church service with a Gospel choir in attendance. *That should be interesting,* I thought. 'Yes, Father, count me in. I'll look forward to it, to be sure, to be sure.'

I can't help it. I feel compelled to mimic every Irish accent I come across.

More games of chess were to follow with Ant and Dec, together with others who by now had spread the word that there was somebody on the wing that could play reasonably well, and if not quite to the standard of Bobby Fischer or Boris Spassky, could at least be relied upon not to knock over all the pieces in a fit of pique in the event of losing a game.

I think that a display of sportsmanship should be of considerable importance in any competitive sport, not just chess. One only has to think of the tennis player John McEnroe, ('You CANNOT be serious!') or perhaps in more recent times the 2019 Cameroon Ladies Football Team who were soundly thrashed during their game against England and appeared more than somewhat miffed at some of the referee's decisions.

I say 'more than somewhat'. The Cameroon ladies, given a chance, would have beaten a squad of burly Irish footballers half to death if they had lost against the Emerald Isle.

In addition, I felt that I had to earn my reputation, in light of the saying concerning a pigeon on a chess board. (The saying is often employed against a Muslim who is losing an argument concerning Islam – like a pigeon on a chess board, he struts around, knocks over all the pieces and declares victory in spite of all the evidence to the contrary.)

The call for dinner reverberated across the landing, and there was a rush to form a disorderly queue in front of the serving hatch. I joined the end of the queue, and after what seemed like an age, received a default allocation of chilli con carne and rice, an apple and a carton of orange juice. OK, it wasn't actually what I thought I had ordered, but it was very welcome after a hard day's grafting over a hot chess board.

Then it was off to the medical dispensary to collect my evening dose of Warfarin and other medications, followed by the evening lock-up and roll-call at 6:00 p.m.

That evening I leaned back on my bunk, watching the planes take off and land at London City Airport. 'Is it like this every day?' I asked John, who had more experience of the inside of a prison than I had.

'What are you complaining about?' said John. 'You've got the Gospel choir to look forward to tomorrow. You'd better get a good night's sleep if you want to be ready for that.'

CHAPTER 13

Background to the Birmingham Taqiyya Trial

During the course of Chapter 8 in this book – Ground Zero – I endeavoured to provide the reader with an account of my journey towards understanding the true nature of Islam, and the threat that Islam poses to our Western democratic society. By 2013 I had researched the subject extensively for over ten years, and the picture that was emerging was a far cry from the notion that our political elites and our mainstream media were peddling – that Islam was somehow a 'religion of peace'.

Nothing could be further from the truth – unless of course one redefines the terms 'religion' and 'peace' to mean something completely different from the normal understanding of the words in accordance with the Judaeo-Christian values that underpin our Western civilisation.

For example, 'peace' to most of us means a state of harmony between individuals, between groups, or between countries whereby differences are tolerated and a positive effort is made to rub along together. 'Peace' in Islam is an entirely different concept, as it is the happy state of affairs that will exist when all non-Muslims have been subjugated, slaughtered or converted to Islam. That's it. There are no grey areas, no compromise or tolerance in Islam for alternative religious views.

'Religion' has been defined for millennia by the Golden Rule – 'do unto others as you would have done unto you' – alternatively, 'don't do anything to others that you would not like to have done to yourself'. Islam does not follow the Golden Rule – the world according to Islam is divided into Dar-Al-Islam (lands ruled by Islam) and Dar-Al-Harb (lands ruled by the Infidel). As far as Islam is concerned, a permanent state of war exists between the two until such time as Islam rules the entire world.

This means that Islam is not primarily a religion, and it could be argued that it is not a religion at all. It is a totalitarian political cult, spread and maintained by fear, violence, intimidation and terror, and all non-Muslims should comprehensively understand the implications and take that message on board if Western civilisation is to survive.

Don't take my word for it. Read the Islamic scriptures – the Qur'an, Hadith and Sira – for yourself. Everything you need to know is in there. You don't need to consult so-called Muslim scholars. If it is in the Qur'an, Hadith or Sira, then it is Islam. If it is not in the Qur'an, Hadith or Sira, then it is not Islam. To summarise – it's not rocket science. The Qur'an actually tells the reader that the message is clear and easy to understand – and it is.

(For those of you who want to research the subject further, I would highly recommend the writings of Robert Spencer, who has published more than a dozen books on various aspects of Islam and Jihad, and who has appeared in numerous videos and interviews. He is extremely knowledgeable – possibly the most knowledgeable non-Muslim on the subject of Islam at the time of writing – and has the distinction of never publicly having lost a theological argument against a Muslim.

I would also highly recommend the writings of Bill Warner, who runs the Centre for the Study of Political Islam (CSPI) and who has produced some easy to understand pocket guides to Islam including The Two-Hour Qur'an and The Life of Muhammad.)

During the course of 2013, several events occurred which were to change the course of my life. The first was the appalling murder of Fusilier Lee Rigby on the streets of Woolwich, in London, on 22 May. The murder shocked the nation with its sheer brutality – the soldier was run over with a car, and then stabbed and beheaded in broad daylight by two Muslims, one of whom was caught on video after the event, calmly giving an interview to a passer-by armed with a smartphone camera.

Fusilier Lee Rigby with his son, Jack

One of the Muslim murderers, Michael Adebolajo, his hands covered in blood and holding a knife and machete, explained quite clearly why he and his accomplice had done what they had. They had done it in the name of Islam, and completely in accordance with the teachings of Allah and Muhammad. Theologically speaking, he was absolutely correct. He quoted extensively from Qur'an 9:29 and explained that attacking and killing the soldier was a justified response in Islam to perceived Muslim grievances.

Only a handful of us non-Muslims, of course, recognised the allusion to Qur'an 9:29 and what it meant for our peaceful democratic society. The Prime Minister at the time, David Cameron, stood up in Parliament the following day to announce that 'Islam is a religion of peace' and that the killers were following a 'warped and twisted version of Islam'. This was quite untrue, but his goal was to play down the significance of the event and to lull the British public into a sense of false security so that we would not recognise the enormity of the Islamic threat that was bearing down on us at an ever-increasing speed like an out-of-control steamroller.

Not everyone was fooled of course, and over the next couple of months there were many well-attended peaceful demonstrations across the country. The English Defence League, for the most part comprised of patriotic citizens who were becoming increasingly alarmed at what they saw as the Islamisation of their country, and led by the charismatic Tommy Robinson, attempted to bring the truth to the British public.

They were, of course, immediately smeared by the Establishment and the mainstream media as 'racists', 'bigots', 'fascists', 'right-wing extremists', and of course the favourite catch-phrase of the left-wing media – 'Islamophobes' – which falsely implies that it is somehow 'phobic' (that is to say, implies that it must be symptomatic of a mental illness) to criticise Islam or Muslims for any reason whatsoever.

The next seismic event that influenced me was an allegation in the Sunday Telegraph in June 2013 to the effect that a prominent member of the British Establishment, Fizzy Mendacious, had been instrumental in fraudulently manipulating the statistics of his organisation, Grievance Mongers UK, in order to swindle the British taxpayer out of hundreds of thousands of pounds in grant money. Grievance Mongers UK purported to catalogue the rise in so-called 'anti-Muslim hate crimes', which could be said to be a subjective concept at best, based as it was on emotions rather than facts.

The mood of the country following Fusilier Lee Rigby's murder the previous month had led Fizzy Mendacious to falsely claim that there was a spike in 'Islamophobic' crimes. It transpired that these weren't really hate crimes at all for the most part; they were simply unkind things that people had said about Islam and Muslims on social media.

Such opinions, offensive and upsetting as they may have been to those who are notoriously perpetually offended and thin-skinned about such things, should have been protected by Article 10 of the European Convention on Human Rights, which allows for freedom of expression, the right to hold opinions, and to receive and impart information and ideas subject only to certain restrictions that are 'in accordance with law' and 'necessary in a democratic society'.

However, as it turned out, there were other people with different views on the matter.

When I read the Telegraph article, I was absolutely outraged. Here was a public figure, in receipt of hundreds of thousands of pounds of taxpayers' money, who was alleged by a respected investigative journalist from the Telegraph, Andrew Gilligan, to be fraudulently manipulating the figures of his organisation to keep the money coming in.

It wasn't just Andrew Gilligan who was saying this; the Association of Chief Police Officers (ACPO) and the Department of Communities and Local Government (DCLG) were evidently of the same opinion.

Fizzy Mendacious had been told by ACPO that his figures didn't add up, at which he reportedly threw his toys out of the pram and stormed out of an ACPO meeting, and the DCLG took the unusual step of terminating the grant, worth hundreds of thousands of pounds each year to his organisation.

I took to social media to denounce Fizzy Mendacious in the strongest possible terms. I called him a mountebank, a weasel, an unmitigated fraud, a lying Muslim scumbag and a common criminal. Most memorably, I also called him a 'Mendacious Grievance-Mongering Taqiyya-Artist'.

It was my opinion that if it had been you or I who had committed crimes on this enormous scale, the consequences would have been dire. Our feet would not have touched the ground as we would have been arrested, charged, prosecuted and whisked off to prison to contemplate a substantial jail term.

Of course, none of these dire consequences were applied to Fizzy Mendacious (OBE). He was a prominent, connected member of the Establishment, and not only that, but also an advisor to the Crown Prosecution Service; our political elites viewed him as a paragon of virtue, a so-called 'moderate' Muslim who allegedly wanted nothing more than a chance to promote 'community cohesion' and to speak out against all those so-called 'Islamophobes' who were evidently doing their best to undermine it.

However, it turned out that Fizzy Mendacious (OBE) had two weaknesses; firstly, a very high opinion of himself (it was rumoured that apparently his OBE was not an Order of the British Empire at all, but an Order of the Bloated Ego, conferred upon him by Her Majesty the Queen in a fit of absent-mindedness while she was trying to attend to an errant corgi) and secondly, he appeared to be possessed of an extremely thin skin.

He had picked up the phone to the Metropolitan Police, and had expressed his displeasure that I had seen fit to repeatedly criticise him on social media. He was not only displeased; he was offended, and when a prominent Muslim tells a police officer that he is offended, then that police officer had jolly well better do something about it. When I say that there is one law for Muslims and another for the rest of us in the 'vibrant, multicultural and diverse' society that is Britain today, it's not just my opinion, but the opinion of a great many respected thinkers in this country.

I was arrested, interviewed, charged and eventually prosecuted with Racially Aggravated Harassment – the first of two prosecutions to be discussed in this book – and duly appeared at Birmingham Magistrates' Court on Tuesday 08 April 2014 to answer the charges. What happened next is recounted over the next two chapters in the following essay – Showdown in Birmingham – and as this essay forms the only detailed written testimony of the proceedings (the clerk of the court having mysteriously mislaid her extensive jottings, written contemporaneously in full view of the court on the back of a series of scruffy envelopes) I have reproduced the essay here in full.

CHAPTER 14

Showdown in Birmingham – Part 1 of 2

I took a last mouthful of cappuccino and glanced out of the window of the restaurant over the road from the Birmingham Magistrates' Court. A small group of demonstrators had already arrived on the court steps and were busy setting up placards and handing out leaflets to curious passers-by. It was time to go.

It was Tuesday 08 April, and the time was just after 09:00. I was scheduled to appear in Court 13 of Birmingham Magistrates' Court later that morning to answer a charge of Racially Aggravated Harassment – a charge which had been brought by the Crown Prosecution Service following my interview with West Midlands Police some four months earlier. A gentleman by the name of Fizzy Mendacious had complained that I was harassing him on Twitter by referring to him as a 'Mendacious Grievance-Mongering Taqiyya-Artist' and a 'Lying Muslim Scumbag' – words which I had indeed used in relation to the gentleman in question – and he had seen a chance to exact revenge by using the forces of law and order to do his dirty work for him.

I walked across the street and introduced myself. The demonstrators with the placards and the leaflets (whom I already knew by reputation) were from Liberty GB, a political party for whom I was the Radio Officer, and there were also one or two familiar faces from other publications and political organisations that I had come to know and respect. I also recognised (from photographs in his many articles and books) Professor Hans Jansen, our expert defence witness, chatting on the courtroom steps with one or two people. The case had generated a lot of interest over the preceding four months, with the phrase 'Mendacious Grievance-Mongering Taqiyya-Artist' going around the world like wildfire – a phenomenon which had generated its own cottage industry with commemorative coffee mugs and T-shirts, each emblazoned not only with the 'Mendacious Grievance-Mongering Taqiyya-Artist' slogan but also with the distinctive features of Fizzy Mendacious himself.

It was now 09:30 – time for me to present myself at the court. I walked up the steps into the main building, an imposing edifice built in Victorian times and originally known as the Victoria Law Courts. As I walked through the door, past the security screening device, the two imposing gentlemen wielding metal detectors and the sign saying 'No Knives Allowed', I reflected on the many generations of people who had come here to answer similar charges and wondered if they had felt as I did – a feeling of awe at the magnificence of the surroundings combined with a certain trepidation at the prospect of facing serious jail time.

Birmingham Magistrates' Court

For make no mistake, the charge of Racially Aggravated Harassment is not one to be dismissed lightly. On conviction, the penalty may be up to £5,000 and six months' imprisonment. One might think that this is somewhat over-the-top for the heinous crime of calling a Mendacious Grievance-Mongering Taqiyya-Artist a – well, a Mendacious Grievance-Mongering Taqiyya-Artist – but apparently there is 'A Lot of This Going Around' according to the Crown Prosecution Service, and they wanted to put a stop to it. Never mind that the right to free speech is one of our fundamental freedoms and the cornerstone of a free democracy – if it offends one of our protected minority species then it must be prosecuted to the full extent of the law – or so the current thinking goes today, influenced as it is by the twin evils of political correctness and multiculturalism.

Court 13 is on the second floor of the building, and I made my way up the step to meet the court usher at the door. The court usher checks (amongst other things) that the people coming in and going out of the court have all mobile devices turned off, and ensures that they are seated in the right place – such as the press gallery for newspaper reporters, the public gallery for members of the public, and (of course) the dock for miscreants such as myself. The ban on all mobile devices is a bit of a nuisance – obviously the court does not want people to be recording audio or video of the proceedings, or to be taking phone calls in the middle of a case – but some of the political activists were looking to see whether they could blog or tweet live from the public gallery, and that was unfortunately not allowed. Note-taking, however, was indeed allowed, and the lady representative from New English Review settled into her chair with her pencil at the ready, as did several of the representatives from Liberty GB, and we all waited for the proceedings to start.

The judge entered the courtroom just after 10:00 a.m., and the first thing that became apparent was that my case was not the only case scheduled for Court 13 that day. There was one more case involving a dispute between two local business people. However, the other case was beset by procedural delays concerning the appropriate documentation, and was quickly adjourned to a later date. Then it was time for my case to proceed. My name and address were confirmed, the charge was read out, and it was ascertained that I wished to plead Not Guilty.

The first problem was to get the video-link working. Two enormous TV screens on the wall of the court were to facilitate the evidence to be given by Fizzy Mendacious from an undisclosed remote location, somewhere in London. Fizzy had submitted a letter to the court indicating that he was too frightened to come up to

Birmingham because the threatening nature of my tweets had made him scared for the safety of himself and his family. (I had been quite surprised when I had first heard this. I know that they say that the pen is mightier than the sword, but one would have thought that having gone out of his way to make life difficult for me by pressing charges, Fizzy would have at least had the courtesy to be present in person, in order to look me in the eye.) Nevertheless, it was his right to ask for his evidence to be given from a remote location, and even though I myself might have thought he was a complete wuss, the court had granted his request.

I glanced around the court and surveyed my surroundings. The Crown Prosecution lawyer and my defence lawyer, standing at their desks in front of the dock, were exchanging pleasantries and poring over a copy of a law manual whilst waiting for the video-link connection to be made. The Crown Prosecution lawyer seemed somewhat harassed. Some of the papers he needed were missing, and the Birmingham Magistrates' Court fax machine wasn't working, so there was quite a lengthy delay while this was being sorted out. You could tell that the judge was unimpressed by all of this. He indicated to the Crown Prosecution lawyer that he was not minded to postpone the case, and that the Crown Prosecution lawyer had best get his act together, pronto. The Crown Prosecution lawyer scurried off to get his papers in order, and the case finally started at 11:45.

Fizzy Mendacious was the first to give evidence. The officers in the undisclosed remote location asked Fizzy what religion he was – to which he replied 'Islamic – I'm a Muslim' and so he was sworn in on the Qur'an. I did think about jumping to my feet and shouting, 'Objection, Your Honour – this book gives the plaintiff divine permission to lie under oath in a British Court of Law if it furthers the cause of Islam!' but as I had been advised by my defence lawyer not to do any such thing, under threat of being charged with contempt of court, I simply gritted my teeth and remained seated.

The Crown Prosecution lawyer led Fizzy through his testimony, during which he stated that he had felt threatened, harassed, distressed, alarmed, upset, insulted and offended by my tweets. In addition his very identity and who he was as a Muslim had been viciously attacked – he had felt scared for the safety of himself and his family – who knows what 'Catstrangler' (my Twitter persona) might have done if he had turned up on his doorstep one day with a mad gleam in his eye and a blood-stained keyboard under his arm? I sighed inwardly. Oh, for heaven's sake. Talk about over-egging the pudding. Methinks the lady doth protest too much (to paraphrase Queen Gertrude in William Shakespeare's *Hamlet*).

Fizzy Mendacious was also asked about Taqiyya. He said that it was a historical concept, used by Shia Muslims a thousand years ago to defend themselves from persecution. (He didn't say that the persecution was from other Muslims.) He said that the concept of Taqiyya was mainly used today by extremist far-right groups seeking to defame Islam and Muslims. (He didn't say that Taqiyya was a generally accepted licence for Muslims to routinely lie to non-Muslims about the nature of Islam.)

But then it was the turn of my defence lawyer. He fixed Fizzy with a steely glance (as far as it is possible to fix someone with a steely glance over a video-link connection). 'I put it to you, Mr. Mendacious, that far from feeling threatened, harassed, distressed, alarmed, upset, insulted and offended by my client's tweets, you felt a sense of quiet satisfaction, didn't you? You wanted and needed those tweets to add to your online hate crime database, didn't you? In fact if you didn't get enough of such tweets, you would be hard pressed to justify your enormous public grant, wouldn't you, Mr. Mendacious? Isn't that right?'

It wasn't long before beads of sweat could be seen on Fizzy's brow – a phenomenon which was commented on by several people in the public gallery afterwards. It was generally agreed that my defence lawyer was doing a grand job of grilling Fizzy Mendacious, and I have to say that I concurred with that sentiment. My defence lawyer continued. 'Do you know what the word – mendacious – actually means? Or the word – scumbag – do you know what that actually means?'

'Of course I do, let's move on to the next question!'

'Well, Mr. Mendacious, what does it mean?'

'Next question!!'

At that point the judge intervened to explain to Fizzy that he was obliged to answer the question. It subsequently transpired that Fizzy had only a partial grasp of the subtle nuances of both words – to the extent that it made me wonder why he claimed to have been offended so much in the first place.

Fizzy Mendacious was indeed losing his cool. 'But what about all the other tweets?' he spluttered. 'Your client called Muslims "inbred welfare parasites". Your client said Muslims had "shit-for-brains". Your client is associated with extremist far-right groups. Not to mention Robert Spencer. Not to mention Pamela Geller. Your client is a menace!'

Fizzy was reminded that the court was dealing only with the three tweets that formed the subject of the charge. Then it was time to break for lunch.

CHAPTER 15

Showdown in Birmingham – Part 2 of 2

During the lunchtime period, I spoke to the court usher. He was one of those people who had been around the court system for decades and had seen it all. He probably had enough experience to have been a judge or a magistrate himself. 'You're very lucky,' he said, 'to have a district judge hearing the case. If it had been a panel of lay magistrates, they might well have had difficulty understanding all the concepts in what is turning out to be quite a complex case.' He seemed quite impressed that we had managed to secure the presence of Professor Hans Jansen in order to give evidence concerning the nature of Taqiyya and its understanding and practice by Muslims today.

After lunch, Fizzy Mendacious concluded his evidence and was then released by the judge from giving any further evidence. That was the last we saw of him. Then it was my turn to give evidence and I was sworn in on the Bible in the witness stand. It's an odd thing, but having completed the swearing-in, a sense of calm descended on me. It was as if I knew that I couldn't lose.

I had experienced the same feeling once before, when I was taking my Aikido black belt examination. Part of the examination includes a multiple attack scenario, when you are simultaneously attacked by six students on the command of a senior instructor. I remember standing in the circle of six students, who were slowly advancing towards me and waiting for the word to attack. I closed my eyes and the same sense of calmness descended on me as it did in the courtroom. The Japanese call it 'no-mind'. I knew I wasn't going to lose.

The sense is conveyed well in the attempted assassination scene with Tom Cruise in The Last Samurai.

My defence lawyer started by taking me through the use of Twitter as a social medium and my use of it with respect to my tweets. I explained that because of the nature of Islam as a totalitarian political ideology rather than a religion, I saw it as my duty to raise awareness of the threat of Islam towards non-Muslims and that Twitter was a useful tool in that regard. I talked about Taqiyya and how Fizzy Mendacious was using dissimulation when he avoided explaining how Muslims use it today to deceive non-Muslims about the true nature of Islam. I explained that in my view Islam posed a threat to our civilisation and that our political elites were ignoring a very real long-term danger in favour of short-term advantages. Then it was the turn of the Crown Prosecution lawyer.

Well, I have to say that the Crown Prosecution lawyer tried his best. He was like a dog with a bone that he wouldn't let go. 'I put it to you, Mr. Burton, that your tweets were nothing more than a racist diatribe!'

'I put it to you, sir, that they were not. Islam is not a race and Muslims are not a racial group.'

'I put it to you, Mr. Burton, that your tweets were intended purely to threaten and harass Mr. Mendacious!'

'I put it to you, sir, that they were not. My tweets were intended to scold, to criticise and to castigate Mr. Mendacious. I felt very strongly that someone running an organisation like Grievance Mongers UK should not be fraudulently misrepresenting his statistics, as alleged by Andrew Gilligan in The Telegraph, in order to receive public money.'

'I put it to you, Mr. Burton, that your tweets were racist in nature!'

'I put it to you, sir, that they were not. As I have said, Islam is not a race and Muslims are not a racial group.'

I must have repeated that phrase half a dozen times before the prosecution gave up and tried a different tack. 'You called Mr. Mendacious a lying Muslim scumbag. That is not only racist and offensive, but deeply unpleasant!'

'The definition of scumbag in the Cambridge Online Dictionary is of an unpleasant person whose behaviour and actions are unacceptable. That seems reasonable to me under the circumstances. I did not mean to imply that Mr. Mendacious was a scumbag because he was Muslim. However, I did mean to imply that there was an association between lying and being Muslim, and that is because of the doctrine of Taqiyya.'

Then the prosecution changed tack again. 'Mr. Burton, you could have written a tweet in less offensive language, telling Mr. Mendacious that you disagreed with some or all of the things on his website, inviting Mr. Mendacious to have a meeting with you and to discuss differences of opinion face to face. Why didn't you?'

I explained that Twitter constrains one's tweets to 140 characters, at which a muffled titter ran around the courtroom. I further explained that I wouldn't expect Mr. Mendacious to respond to such a message, and that my primary audience was my thousands of Twitter followers, who I wished to invite to join me in condemnation of Mr. Mendacious and his organisation.

The Crown Prosecution lawyer asked me whether I considered myself to be a journalist, and if so why my language differed so markedly from that of Andrew Gilligan in The Telegraph. I said although I might be considered a journalist in some respects, Andrew Gilligan was writing for a different audience and was probably more constrained by laws of libel than I felt myself to be. The Crown Prosecution lawyer laboured this point extensively until the judge stepped in and pointed out that it was accepted that I had used language not normally found in the Daily Telegraph, but that it might be considered fair political comment. I think that was where the Crown Prosecution lawyer realised he was starting to lose his grip on events. 'But Mr. Burton, your tweets taken as a whole were nothing more than gratuitous racial insults!'

'No, they had a specific purpose, and anyway, as I have said before, Islam is not a race, and Muslims are not a racial group.'

Shortly after that I was released from the witness stand, and Professor Hans Jansen was called. I have to say he made an excellent witness, with his extensive qualifications over many years presented to the court in detail, and he elaborated on the concept of Taqiyya, basically confirming all the points I had made and also making the point that although Fizzy Mendacious might have been well-meaning (!) he was obviously not a student of Sharia Law and was inaccurate in his explanation of Taqiyya to the court.

The prosecution and the defence were both allowed a final summary of their argument, with my defence lawyer arguing that

Article 10 of the Human Rights Act allows for fair comment in the context of free speech, and although the state does have the right to restrict free speech, those limits should be very narrowly drawn. The Crown Prosecution lawyer wasn't going to let go of the 'gratuitous racial abuse' angle and again argued the point with the judge.

The judge then began his summing-up. He noted that although some of my language had been unpleasant, and that Fizzy Mendacious might well have found it to be upsetting, that was not the test. The test was whether my comments transcended the boundaries of fair political comment and strayed into the realms of criminality through harassment. Had Mr. Burton crept up to his door one night and shouted these things through his letterbox, then it might have been perceived differently, but as it was, the use of the Twitter platform to convey the same messages was not the same thing at all, which was a point which I had elaborated upon in my essay in New English Review a couple of months earlier.

The judge also indicated that he understood that the juxtaposition of the words 'Mendacious', 'Lying' and 'Muslim' were acceptable in the context of the Islamic concept of Taqiyya, and did not therefore constitute a racial slur. This was a highly significant observation, in my opinion.

The judge indicated that Mr. Burton might wish to moderate his language in the future, but in a case involving free speech, the bar must necessarily be set very high, and that in his view, the prosecution had failed to meet that bar in trying to prove its case. He said, 'Mr. Burton is hereby found Not Guilty and formally acquitted of the charge.'

At that point a round of applause reverberated around the courtroom from the public gallery. I was a free man. The Crown Prosecution lawyer, in one futile last-ditch attempt, did then try to have a restraining order applied to me in respect of Fizzy Mendacious, but the judge was having none of it. I thought that was nice, because I did want to send a photographic memento of the day to Fizzy and Grievance Mongers UK (see below).

I would like to thank my many supporters, both in the courtroom on the day and those from around the world, who have supported me in the ongoing fight against the insidious creep of Islamic supremacism and the consequent encroachment on, and erosion of, our freedoms. This was an historic decision, whereby the judge recognised that the Islamic concept of Taqiyya was a valid reason for criticism of Islam in a political context. Although I am not a lawyer, and although I do not at this moment in time fully comprehend what constitutes a legal precedent, as opposed to what does not, I think I can safely say that this was a landmark case with enormous implications in favour of our fight, not only to expose the true nature of Islam, but also to specifically determine the relationship (concerning trust or more importantly the lack thereof) that must necessarily exist between non-Muslims and Muslims due to the Islamic doctrine of Taqiyya – which not only gives Muslims divine permission to lie to non-Muslims if it promotes the cause of Islam or prevents the denigration of Islam in the eyes of non-Muslims – but also makes lying obligatory if the goal (promoting the cause of Islam or preventing the denigration of Islam in the eyes of non-Muslims) cannot be achieved by telling the truth.

Essays from the Dark Side

Trust and Goodwill

The successful outcome of the Birmingham Taqiyya Trial in April 2014 resulted in many articles in publications around the world, written by people who realised just how much of a big deal this was when it came to determining the level of trust that should be extended to the followers of Islam who live in our midst.

This is important because our default position in the West, based on our Judaeo-Christian ethics and moral framework, is to automatically extend a basic level of trust and goodwill towards our fellow man. This works well in most instances, where trust and goodwill is recognised and reciprocated among most communities, traditions and cultures.

However, it is an unwise attitude to take towards the followers of Islam, especially towards those followers who describe themselves as 'devout Muslims' – that is, those who closely follow and adhere to the tenets of the ideology which tells them that they should never take non-Muslims as friends (Qur'an 5:51) and that they should always maintain enmity and hatred towards them in their hearts (Qur'an 60:4).

Apologists for Islam frequently try to explain away the importance of Qur'anic verses like these as 'errors in translation' or suggest that the non-Muslim reader is taking the verses out of context. But there is a well-established doctrine in Islamic tradition called 'Al-wala-wal-Bara' which translates as 'the doctrine of loyalty and disavowal' and which specifically commands Muslims to hate non-Muslims for who they are, irrespective of anything that they may or may not have done.

The very existence of the concept of 'Al-wala-wal-Bara' means (or at least it should mean in a sane world) that we as non-Muslims, always and everywhere, should treat Muslims with a certain degree of caution. It is true that not every Muslim follows the tenets of the ideology of Islam closely enough for it to be a problem in their relations with non-Muslims in the West, but some of them do, and it is far from being the tiny minority that our politicians and mainstream media would have us believe it is.

Surveys undertaken by respectable organisations such as Pew (who go to great lengths to eliminate bias and to present a fair picture of what is going on) demonstrate that at least fifty percent of Muslims living in the West are have some sympathy with Islamic teachings on this matter, and that at least twenty-five percent of Muslims are actively hostile towards non-Muslims because of these same teachings.

There will always be those who say – 'But you can't judge every Muslim because of the actions of a small number of Islamists' – and by 'Islamists' they mean Muslims who supposedly follow a 'radical' version of Islam. The judge at my subsequent trial at Southwark Crown Court clearly demonstrated – before the trial had even started – that he personally subscribed to this fallacy, as revealed by his remarks to the prosecuting lawyer.

But when the 'radical' teachings of Islam are not actually 'radical' at all, but are in truth nothing more than the mainstream teachings of Islam, what then? Especially when these teachings are being reinforced every week to every Muslim adult who visits a mosque regularly? Especially when these teachings are being reinforced every week to every Muslim child who is enrolled in after-school Qur'anic teaching in the enormous number of unofficial madrassas (Islamic schools) around the country?

Why should we automatically extend the same basic level of trust and goodwill to someone who subscribes to an ideology that tells them to hate us?

Let's put it another way; imagine being told that your entire country was going to be overrun by a plague of poisonous snakes, deliberately introduced by our betters in order to 'increase diversity'. At the same time, you are told that you must not discriminate against them, for only fifty per cent of them are likely to bite you and only twenty-five per cent of them are poisonous. What's more, any such discrimination would be 'snake-o-phobic'.

Would you accept that the very real risk of being bitten and poisoned was more than offset by a commendable demonstration of virtue-signalling your politically correct commitment to diversity?

Clue: A reasonable answer might be 'No.'

CHAPTER 16

The Revenge of Fizzy Mendacious

As may be discerned from the previous chapters concerning the Birmingham Taqiyya Trial, Fizzy Mendacious (the previously-described mendacious, grievance-mongering director of the den of rattlesnakes that was Grievance Mongers UK) was not best pleased at the outcome of the trial, resulting as it did in the acquittal of the country's most notorious racist, fascist, bigoted, right-wing extremist 'Islamophobe' (that would be me) and the subsequent dent in the international reputation of Fizzy Mendacious on the world stage.

He had had the evidence that he gave at the trial thoroughly discredited by one of the most acclaimed Islamic scholars in the academic world, and had been revealed as an unprincipled bully-boy, in turns demonstrating behaviour that was, in my humble opinion, alternately whining and petulant, interspersed with nauseating bouts of arrogance and pomposity.

His mental equilibrium was probably not improved by the subsequent (anonymous) modification of his Wikipedia page, making reference to 'The Ballad of Fizzy Mendacious' which was at that time being played regularly to the accompaniment of much side-splitting hilarity on 'The Oz Report', an Australian internet radio show run by the irrepressible and talented entrepreneur Mike Holt.

Fizzy Mendacious took to his own personal weblog to complain that he hadn't had what he considered justice in the matter. Naturally he blamed everyone else for this state of affairs, rather than reflecting on the fact that it was his own fraudulent activities – as alleged by Andrew Gilligan in the Daily Telegraph – that had given rise to the righteous indignation on my part and my subsequent caustic comments about those fraudulent activities on social media.

Interestingly enough, he was never prosecuted by the authorities for the alleged fraudulent manipulation of the figures of his organisation; and after the 2014 case, he continued to receive ever-increasing amounts of taxpayers' money from a government that was only too eager to appease him in a desperate search for so-called 'moderate' Muslims to counteract the increasing – and justifiable – suspicions that non-Muslims were having concerning the ideology of Islam.

Fizzy Mendacious complained on his weblog that the Crown Prosecution Service had, in his words, 'missed a trick' by not fielding a competent witness to counteract the narrative of Taqiyya that I had outlined for the court. Never mind the fact that my evidence was supported by Professor Hans Jansen, one of the most highly acclaimed scholars of Arabic and Islamic studies in the academic world, Fizzy evidently felt that had the CPS fielded the right candidate, then his argument that the word "Taqiyya' was a word only used today by right-wing bigots in order to defame Islam would have had greater currency.

It would appear that there is nothing like stubborn and obstinate pig-headedness in the face of irrefutable facts to win you more friends in the Establishment, for not only was Fizzy's grant of taxpayers' money subsequently reinstated the following year, it was increased to the point that Fizzy plainly felt that he should be expanding his empire, and particularly by means of hiring at least one additional case-worker.

Between April 2014 and April 2016, a period of around two years, I had been largely ignoring the activities of Fizzy Mendacious and Grievance Mongers UK. I had been active with Liberty GB, a political organisation run by Paul Weston, and I had been running the Liberty GB radio show in addition to writing articles for the Brenner Brief and the New English Review.

I had campaigned as a Member of Parliament for Birmingham Ladywood in 2015, and while I hadn't been successful in securing the seat, held as it was by a Labour-dominated cabal that was determined to keep me out of the running by utilising whatever dirty tricks that they could, I had at least had the satisfaction of knowing that they were seriously worried by the prospect of a candidate standing on a platform of anti-Islamisation.

Their tactics had included the deliberate sabotage of the Liberty GB promotional leaflet mailing campaign, and creating a hostile environment by declaring me to be (and by extension the entire Liberty GB movement to be) 'appallingly racist', a viewpoint that was expounded by the Labour incumbent, Shabana Mahmoud, live on BBC local radio.

I am sure that this was behind a physical attack on me by a group of Muslims while I was out on the streets campaigning in Ladywood. I had notified the local police each day concerning where and when I was going to be out campaigning, and on this particular day, two days before the General Election, a colleague and I were set upon by a car-load of four young Muslims who were extremely aggressive and intimidating. The end result was that after a bit of pushing and shoving, coupled with mouthfuls of verbal and racist abuse (from them, not from me), they stole my campaign materials, including my expensively acquired Liberty GB campaign board, and drove off.

Campaigning for Liberty GB outside Birmingham Central Mosque

Naturally I reported this to the police, together with the registration number of the vehicle the Muslims had been in, and fully expected a prosecution, not only for assault and theft, but also for street robbery, together with compensation for my loss. After all, I had a witness who could corroborate and back me up on everything that had occurred.

Imagine my surprise when, a couple of days later, I was notified by an apologetic young policeman that there would be no prosecution. This was despite the Muslim driver of the car having been identified and brought into the police station for questioning.

'Yeah, we did it, so what?' was his response when asked if the events had occurred as I had described them. 'And we took his campaign materials to stop any further problems.'

Quite apart from the fact that it wasn't up to him to decide what constituted a problem (when a law-abiding member of the community was acting in a lawful way while campaigning as part of the democratic process) the entire episode of street robbery, comprising as it did assault, theft and intimidation, and witnessed by my colleague, was dismissed by the Crown Prosecution Service as 'not being in the public interest' when it came to deciding whether or not to prosecute. No further action was taken.

I wrote to the CPS for clarification, as it was my opinion that if it had been myself and (say) three of my colleagues who had set upon a Muslim in the street under similar circumstances, our feet wouldn't have touched the ground as we would inevitably have been arrested, charged, prosecuted, convicted and sentenced to long jail terms.

The CPS response was again – 'prosecution would not be in the public interest'. That is to say, not in the Muslim 'public interest'. Given the propensity for Muslims to riot at the drop of a hat for the slightest grievance, I could see their point, but for me it was just one more piece in the jigsaw of confirmation that there was a two-tier level of justice in operation – one law for Muslims, and another for the rest of us.

Returning to the subject of the dirty tricks employed against me, there was also the threatening of the organisers of local hustings events prior to the election. They had employed significant levels of Mafia-like intimidation – 'Nice little church hall/community centre you have there, squire, it would be such a shame if anything were to happen to it. All sorts of nasty things happen to church halls/community centres these days, squire. Like – fires, for example. You wouldn't want a fire here, would you, squire? Then don't let that Liberty GB candidate Tim Burton anywhere near your hustings event if you know what's good for you.'

I lost count of the number of hustings organisers who phoned me up to tell me that they were dreadfully sorry that they had to disinvite me, really very sorry indeed, but the political atmosphere was just too toxic, you see, and – I did understand, didn't I?

I understood only too well. The cowardly activists on the political Left do not have any convincing arguments to counter our narrative, and so they have to resort to tactics of intimidation in order to silence us and to de-platform anyone who has the temerity to argue against them. We see the same tactics being used today at colleges, universities and elsewhere in the public arena where conservative voices are being progressively silenced. It is a very bad state of affairs that does not bode well for the continuation of democracy in our society, and it does not look like it will get better anytime soon.

In the meantime, as I have said, Fizzy Mendacious and Grievance Mongers UK were continuing to drum up dubious cases of 'Islamophobia' for a gullible government, and as a result were in receipt of ever-larger amounts of taxpayers' cash. The decision was taken (presumably by Fizzy Mendacious himself) to advertise for an additional case-worker, and this was brought to my attention in April 2016.

My first thought was that this was absolutely outrageous. In my opinion, Fizzy Mendacious and Grievance Mongers UK were doing quite enough damage to the foundations of British society already – trying to convince everyone that Muslims were somehow the victims of an oppressive, 'Islamophobic' environment that generated an unreasonable hatred of all Muslims, and that such pernicious 'Islamophobia' had to be countered by every means possible.

Never mind the fact that Muslims are, in reality, one of the least oppressed groups in British society, with the government and officialdom falling over themselves to appease them in every respect, lest they be thought of as 'racist' or 'Islamophobic' themselves.

A blind eye has been turned to one of the most horrendous scandals of the past two decades – that of Islamic grooming gangs systematically raping young, vulnerable non-Muslim female children on an industrial scale, aided and abetted by councils, the police and social services, who between them did absolutely nothing effective in the face of overwhelming evidence, but more often than not blamed the victims themselves.

Then I had a second thought.

My second thought was – *Hey, I could do that job!* They needed someone with an empathetic nature (check), who was familiar with Arabic and Urdu (check) and who could demonstrate an ability to work well as part of a team (check). The successful applicant would earn £25,000 per annum, and I could do with a bit of pin money.

Admittedly my Arabic and Urdu was limited to ordering food at Middle Eastern restaurants and cursing out the native roughnecks and roustabouts on oil rigs in North Africa, Pakistan and the Persian Gulf during my previous career as an oilfield geologist in the 1970s. But hey, I was a hard worker and I was willing to learn, and I was certain that a modern, forward-thinking organisation such as Grievance Mongers UK would give me a chance, despite the somewhat chequered history that existed between Fizzy Mendacious and me. So I sent off my CV to the Grievance Mongers organisation, together with an admittedly tongue-in-cheek covering letter which read as follows:

To whom it may concern,

I see that I have just missed the deadline of 31 March for my application to be considered for the post recently advertised on your website.

However, it's probably just as well, as those who know me consider me to be honest and trustworthy, and as such, I would most likely NOT fit in with a cowboy outfit like yours, run as it is by the Mendacious Grievance-Mongering Taqiyya-Artist-in-Chief, 'Fizzy' Mendacious.

It's a real shame, because otherwise I am qualified - nay - some might say over-qualified, to fulfill all the requirements of this position, together with the ability to dispense some much-needed honesty and integrity which appears to be sadly missing from your organisation on every level.

Fortunately, my current gainful employment will undoubtedly sustain me for the foreseeable future, so please don't worry about parachuting me into the position over the heads of your less-qualified applicants who have managed to submit their application forms by the due date.

Just as a reminder of what you are missing, I herewith attach a link to the write-up of my recent court case, as published in the New English Review.

Yours faithfully, Timothy M Burton

I had expected my CV to be ignored – or at the very most a polite letter declining my offer to serve their organisation. Imagine my surprise when I received this response:

Your communication has been passed onto the MET. Cease and desist in sending us any further communication. You have been notified.

Best Wishes, Grievance Mongers Team

It has to be borne in mind that at the time of this exchange, there were no grounds whatsoever for passing the contents of any communication between myself and Grievance Mongers UK to the Metropolitan Police. Fizzy Mendacious might have felt slightly annoyed, but no criminal offence of any sort had been committed. Having considered their reply, I considered it to be a grossly over-the-top response to a little gentle mockery from me.

Had they not responded in such a fashion, I probably would have forgotten all about it. But the response prompted me to write another tongue-in-cheek email:

To whom it may concern,

Well, that's not very Christian of you. However, my email and your reply will no doubt prove a great topic of conversation on our radio shows in the UK, Canada, Australia and the USA. So thank you very much for that!

[…]

Yours faithfully, Timothy M Burton

PS – by the way – Is there any more news on my job application?

I know that I must be the obvious front-runner with my qualifications and experience, but I should warn you that once I am hired, I will set about the place with a new broom, cleaning out the Augean stables of Taqiyya-laden manure, casting sunlight into the darkest recesses, spreading the disinfectant of truth [and] generally keeping you on your toes.

I look forward to hearing from you. Yours etc.

It wasn't long before another email came back from Grievance Mongers UK:

You have been expressly notified not to contact us. You have failed to heed this. All of the material is being sent to the police and solicitors. Any subsequent material will also be passed on for action and rest assured we will push for action against you.

Best Wishes, Grievance Mongers Team

By now I myself was feeling slightly annoyed. In my defence, and when I had occasion to later refer to it in court, I probably should have given this annoyance as a justification for responding – because I was becoming mildly exasperated, not to mention alternately incensed and outraged. Still, I thought, in for a penny, in for a pound.

In response, I sent yet another email, this time addressed to the head honcho himself, *le grand fromage*, the big cheese of Grievance Mongers UK, Fizzy Mendacious, rather than to the Grievance Mongers organisation:

For the attention of Mr. Mendacious

Good morning Fizzy old chap,

I just thought I would enquire as to how that new 'caseworker' is working out for you. Not very well by the sound of it – I detect a certain amount of desperation from within your organisation as you stoop to lower and lower depths of depravity to try and pin charges of 'racism', 'bigotry' and 'Islamophobia' onto people who have done little more than express a healthy contempt for a medieval belief system that teaches hatred and violence towards non-believers and which is completely incompatible with a free, tolerant and democratic society such as ours.

(You should have taken up my offer to come and work for you – it's difficult

to see how I would have done more harm to the public image of your organisation than you guys are doing unaided.)

[…]

Regards, Timothy M Burton

PS – I thought that you might have blocked my email address earlier this month, but it turns out that I merely made a spelling mistake when typing your email address, which meant that my email was bounced back to me. It just goes to show that even the best of us are not infallible.

Of course, the fact that you yourself haven't as yet blocked my email address demonstrates that you want - and indeed need – emails from people like me to justify your enormous and undeserved public grant. For that reason alone, if any more reasons were needed, the breath-taking hypocrisy of you and your organisation is thereby exposed for the world to see.

This was perhaps a mistake, because it allowed him to complain that he felt personally harassed by my emails. In fact, in his deposition to the court, he claimed that he felt alarmed, distressed, threatened and intimidated to the point where he was waking up in the night in terror that he might receive another communication from me in the morning. My emails were – apparently – explicitly designed to give him a bad day.

Oh, puh-leeze.

However, the next thing I knew, two of West Midland's finest were on my doorstep, and I was again arrested and charged (and subsequently prosecuted) with the harassment of a prominent Muslim member of the Establishment who had threatened to jump up and down and stamp his tiny feet if he wasn't appeased – although, of course, that wasn't how it appeared on the charge sheet.

The charge was one of Religiously Aggravated Harassment based on the fact that I had used the word 'Taqiyya' in my communications, which Fizzy Mendacious had once again insisted was a racist term solely used by non-Muslims in order to defame Islam, despite Professor Hans Jansen's assertions to the contrary at the Birmingham Taqiyya Trial in 2014.

Professor Hans Jansen – 17 November 1942 – 5 May 2015

However, I had a problem. Professor Jansen had died in 2015 and although there were a lot of potential witnesses and Islamic scholars out there who could in theory testify on my behalf, the fact that I was now seen as a notorious racist, fascist, bigoted, right-wing extremist 'Islamophobe' had sent them all scuttling for cover. I was on my own.

CHAPTER 17

The Southwark Crown Court Trial – Part 1

It was 9:30 a.m. on the morning of Monday 27 March 2017, and I was standing on the steps of Southwark Crown Court in London. My trial for Religiously Aggravated Harassment wasn't due to start until 10:30 a.m., but I like to be early for my appointments, and in any case there was a welcoming committee waiting for me.

My colleagues from Liberty GB, the political party for which I was Radio Officer, were lined up on the steps, together with a series of placards with slogans such as 'Justice for Tim Burton' and 'Truth not Taqiyya'. There were also some well-wishers who had heard about the case and who had come down to support me by sitting in the public gallery for the duration of the trial. I was very touched by this, and indeed several of them became firm friends of mine after the trial, with three of them even coming to visit me in HMP Thameside.

There were also several news photographers snapping away, although I doubted that this small demonstration of support would make it onto the front pages of the mainstream media, at least not unless something dramatic happened – such as my being struck by lightning or the earth opening to swallow me up.

Southwark Crown Court

I remember that I was in a fairly good mood that day – after all, I had won my case in 2014 against the very same mendacious, grievance-mongering Taqiyya-artist who was pursuing me now – and on very similar charges. The main difference was that I was unable to call on the expert defence witness of my choice – Professor Hans Jansen of Leiden University, an experienced scholar of Arabic and Islamic studies – because he had sadly passed away the previous year.

Ideally I would have liked to have had another expert defence witness attend in person to represent me in court, because I knew that the Crown Prosecution Service (CPS) had one of their own experts lined up, and although you might think it would be fairly simple to explain the Islamic doctrine of Taqiyya to the court, I felt sure that the CPS expert witness would support the view that the plaintiff Fizzy Mendacious had expounded – namely that Taqiyya was never used these days by Muslims, and only ever used by bigoted, racist, right-wing 'Islamophobes' in order to defame Islam.

However, my pool of available defence witnesses was almost non-existent, at least those who were able and willing to provide their services *pro bono*, and while I was sure that I would have been able to call on the likes of Raymond Ibrahim to support my defence in court, such luminaries were likely to charge a five-figure sum to attend my trial, and this was money that I simply did not have.

At the last moment, I was able to find a gentleman who was prepared to give evidence via video-link from Switzerland concerning

Taqiyya – he was a Palestinian-Christian lawyer and a scholar of Islamic theology who had a very impressive list of relevant qualifications and taught at universities all over France, Switzerland and Italy. His understanding of Taqiyya was essentially the same as mine – which was that it was in daily use as a doctrine of deceit by Muslims who wished to pull the wool over the eyes of non-Muslims in the West, with all of the implications and ramifications that I have discussed previously in this book.

We had arranged that on the second day of the trial (this was when his evidence was scheduled to be given) that he would make his way to a police station in Geneva, where a video-link would be established with Southwark Crown Court, and he would give evidence that would hopefully demolish the arguments of the CPS expert witness and allow me to leave the court as a free man.

In my mind, I could already hear the cheers of my supporters in the courtroom and see the smiles on the faces of the jurors as they acquitted me of all charges. Maybe I would get to see the incandescent rage and hear the wailing and gnashing of teeth of the plaintiff, Fizzy Mendacious, as he watched me slip through his clutches for the second time.

So I was well-prepared – or so I thought. I chatted on the steps of the court with my Liberty GB colleagues and other well-wishers until it was time to go into the court building. Some of my colleagues remained outside and the rest of us took the lift up to the third floor, where there was a waiting area just outside the allocated courtroom.

No sooner had we arrived than my barrister walked up to me and introduced herself. I had only spoken to her on the telephone previously, and it was good to be able to put a face to the name. She had a very severe expression on her face (although I thought at the time that this was probably something that barristers cultivate in order to project an aura of seriousness).

I suppose that this is a good thing – after all, the last thing you want when you are on trial for a serious charge is to see someone in a clown suit (with a red bowler hat, a big red nose, big shoes, baggy trousers with large blue and white spots, a swivelling bow tie and a honking klaxon) walking up to you with a big smile painted into their face and announcing that they are your barrister. So I was encouraged, at least to start with.

The two of us entered a side office to discuss what was about to happen. 'Now then, Mr. Burton, you do realise that this is a very serious charge, don't you? When you send an email to someone, the courts treat it very differently than if you had sent a tweet as you did in 2014.'

I couldn't see why this should be the case, as the mechanisms for blocking unwanted communications are the same in either case – just hit the block button, and *'Bob est ton oncle'* as they say in Birmingham. But I wasn't terribly worried about this as I had forwarded a dossier with my defence notes to the barrister a couple of weeks previously, and had explained all this in great detail.

'You do realise that what you wrote in your emails could be construed as offensive, don't you?' she continued. 'I mean, I am the daughter of Greek immigrants myself and even though I'm not a Muslim, I found what you wrote extremely offensive.'

I was somewhat taken aback. After all, offence is taken, not given, which is what I had been taught when I was younger, with the words 'sticks and stones may break my bones, but words shall never hurt me'. In addition, my arguments about the block button still applied, as I had explained in great detail in my essay 'When is harassment not harassment?' – a copy of which I had included in the dossier mentioned earlier.

'You did read my notes on the subject in that dossier I sent to you, didn't you?' I asked. 'There is a detailed argument in the dossier which I was rather hoping you would have had some sympathy with, at least enough to use it to wipe the floor with the prosecution and give a favourable impression to the jury.'

'Pah! – I haven't bothered reading that,' she said. 'I already have the arguments made out that we are going to use in court. I just have to warn you that the jury might not see it in the same way that you do. Anyway, it's time to go into the court.'

I was now extremely concerned. My own defence barrister hadn't even bothered to read my carefully constructed defence notes and now she was probably going to put forward a boiler-plate defence strategy that took no account of the subtle nuances of the case. But I consoled myself with the fact that she was a barrister with over twenty years' experience, or so I had been told, and she obviously knew more about defence strategy and tactics than I did.

As it happens, she wasn't my first choice for a defence barrister. My solicitor, who had represented me in the 2014 trial at Birmingham Magistrates' Court, had deemed it more appropriate for me to be represented by a barrister in London, from a set of prestigious chambers in King's Bench Walk, rather than to attend my trial himself. This was partly because it was a Crown Court trial rather than a Magistrates' Court trial – something that I had personally chosen when I first knew that I was going to be prosecuted, firstly because I wanted to be tried by twelve good men and true, a jury of my peers – and secondly because there would be a proper transcript of the trial rather than the back-of-an-envelope job that the Clerk of the Birmingham Magistrates' Court had done in 2014.

Making the choice of a Crown Court for the trial (rather than a Magistrates' Court) was admittedly a risk, because the Crown Court can levy penalties that are far more severe than a Magistrates' Court limit, which would be restricted to six months' imprisonment if I were to be found guilty. But I was absolutely convinced that just as in 2014, I would be found 'not guilty', especially after the meeting with my first barrister.

The first barrister from the King's Bench Walk chambers that I was introduced to had made a good first impression. He had looked through my dossier of notes, studied the plaintiff's statement and the police records of my initial interview when I had been arrested in 2016, and seemed very confident that I would get off.

'I can't see anything here that would justify a conviction for harassment,' he said, 'and if there is no conviction for harassment then you don't have to worry about whether or not it is racially or religiously aggravated. Even if that was an issue, you have the advantage of an expert witness giving testimony via video-link, and all we need to do is use his expert testimony to sow sufficient uncertainty in the minds of the jury to the point where your guilt cannot be established beyond reasonable doubt. In my considered opinion, you have nothing to worry about.'

That sounded wonderful, and I was all set to go into the courtroom on that basis. But a couple of weeks before the trial was due to start, he was called away to attend to a complex fraud trial that was going to take months to resolve, and it turned out that he would not be able to represent me after all.

'Not to worry,' said my solicitor, 'I've found you another barrister from the same prestigious set of chambers. They seem to think that she is just the person to defend your case. She will look after your interests just as well and you can have full confidence in her abilities, as she has over twenty years' experience.'

And so I was landed with Miss Bunny-Lover (although I only found out about her sobriquet some months later, when I had been released from prison).

We left the side office, walked across the waiting area, and made our way into the courtroom for the start of the trial. It was an inauspicious start, with her having completely dismissed my carefully prepared dossier, but I was sure that with the right arguments presented in the right way in court by an experienced defence barrister, the jury would definitely be on my side.

Unfortunately, it didn't quite work out as I had intended.

CHAPTER 18

The Southwark Crown Court Trial – Part 2

As we filed into the courtroom, I gave my details to the Court usher, and I was led to the dock at the back of the courtroom. Rather than just a fenced-off area from the rest of the courtroom, as had been the case at the Birmingham Magistrates' Court, this was an area of around six metres wide and three metres deep, surrounded by floor-to-ceiling armour-plated glass. There were at least what looked like a dozen or so chairs for me to choose from, and as I was likely to be here for four days (for that was the scheduled length of time for the trial) then some degree of comfort would be most welcome.

The dock officer escorted me into the dock, locked the door, and we sat down to await the arrival of the judge so the trial could begin. 'Let me know if you want anything, like a glass of water for example,' said the dock officer, a rotund, balding man, probably in his late fifties. He picked up a Sun newspaper from his desk in the corner of the dock, and settled down to do the crossword.

I surveyed my surroundings. To the front and left of the dock was the press gallery, with the public gallery next to it, and my supporters were already seated, some of them giving me small waves and encouraging smiles. To the front and right of the dock was the jury box, with twelve chairs neatly arranged in two rows of six. I looked closer. Those chairs seemed to be a lot more comfortable than mine. Should I ask for a replacement? I kept quiet. It probably wouldn't make a good impression on the court.

Directly ahead of me was the judges' bench, elevated several feet above the rest of the court. The Crown Court logo, with the lion and the unicorn either side of the shield and crown, was emblazoned on the far wall of the court, just behind where the judge or judges would sit.

Southwark Crown Court – Interior of Courtroom (File Photo)

In the well of the court, in between the dock and the judges' bench, were lines of benches occupied by the defence team and the prosecuting team. I recognised the prosecutor – I had met him briefly at an earlier hearing at the same time I had met with my first allocated barrister (who had by now been called away to the complex fraud trial alluded to earlier.) The prosecutor greeted me with some enthusiasm, which I found to be odd.

No doubt he was under the mistaken impression that he was likely to win this case. Little did he know that I had a foolproof defence strategy, a savvy and experienced defence barrister and a well-qualified, knowledgeable defence witness.

'Mr. Burton?' he had said as he introduced himself. 'I'm going to be prosecuting you. But don't worry, it's nothing personal. We're all just doing our jobs here.' As he said this, he gave me an oleaginous smile, the kind of smile that a demon from Hades might give you as he welcomed you to an underworld filled with burning pits of sulphur and row upon row of racks, iron maidens and other torturing devices. 'Nothing personal.'

I shuddered at the recollection. Next to him, Miss Bunny-Lover looked like Mother Theresa. I hoped that she was going to be up to the challenge of defending me against him.

A door opened at the far end of the court and the judge walked in. He wore the traditional red robes and the long wig, and he sat down at the middle of the judges' bench. He glanced at me briefly, looked with some disapproval at my supporters in the public gallery, some of whom were still smiling and waving at me, and then instructed the court usher to empanel the jury.

As this process was going on, I distinctly heard him speak to the prosecutor. They were obviously discussing some aspect of my case, because I clearly heard the judge say, in what he must have supposed was *sotto voce*:

'It's ridiculous to claim that if you are against Islam then you are not also against Muslims.'

Now I had serious cause for concern. I would have expected the judge to be impartial in this matter, and it was part of my defence that while I wholeheartedly despised the ideology of Islam with a passion, I viewed Muslims mostly as victims of that ideology, to be pitied rather than hated or despised.

This was not looking good.

But worse was to come. The court usher had completed the process of jury selection and we had our twelve jurors. They appeared to be quite diverse, that is, from a multicultural perspective. I had quite forgotten that there were now more foreigners living in London than native-born Britons. Not that that was necessarily a problem in itself, but at least one person on the jury appeared to be a Muslim, judging by his dress and demeanour.

I forget what the rest of the jury looked like. The sight of that Muslim filled me with foreboding. I knew which way he would be likely to vote, and it wouldn't be for me.

The judge addressed the jury. 'Some of you may have noticed a small demonstration outside the court today. I am instructing you to completely disregard anything that you may have heard the demonstrators say, or anything that you might have read on the placards.

'In addition, some of you may have heard about the so-called terrorist incident that took place five days ago on Westminster Bridge. I am instructing you to disregard anything relating to that incident when you undertake your deliberations.'

The 'so-called terrorist incident' was something that I was quite sure all the jurors would have heard about. Five days earlier, on 22 March 2017, a terrorist attack took place outside the Palace of Westminster in London, seat of the British Parliament. The attacker, fifty-two-year-old Khalid Masood, drove a car into pedestrians on the pavement along the south side of Westminster Bridge and Bridge Street, injuring more than fifty people, four of them fatally. He then crashed the car into the perimeter fence of the Palace grounds and ran into New Palace Yard, where he fatally stabbed an unarmed police officer. He was then shot by an armed police officer and died at the scene.

I wasn't sure how this might affect the jurors. Some of them might have been inclined to treat Muslims with more suspicion than they otherwise might have done, but equally some of them might become aware of their own potential bias and make an extra effort to treat Muslims more leniently. It could go either way.

The court was then briefly adjourned, and I was released into the waiting area outside the court. I saw my barrister and accosted her in a somewhat agitated fashion. 'Did you notice that Muslim on the jury?' I enquired. 'Can't we challenge that selection?'

She dismissed my concerns with an airy wave of her hand. 'It doesn't matter as much as you might think,' she said, 'and if we start that game then the prosecutor might challenge the selection of some of the people on the jury who might be quite sympathetic to you.'

I told her what I had heard the judge say to the prosecutor. Again, she seemed unconcerned. 'I'm sure the judge will go out of his way to be fair and unbiased,' she said, 'and in any case, we can hardly call for a replacement judge. We're stuck with him, I'm afraid.'

With that, we were called back into the court, I was locked into the dock, and the trial was underway. The rest of the morning passed with technical submissions being aired between the prosecuting barrister, the defence barrister and the judge. As lunchtime approached, the judge again turned to the jury and said, 'You may find a lot of these technical submissions difficult to follow, but don't worry, I will give you instruction at the end of the trial. All you have to do is to listen carefully and weigh the evidence before you come to your verdict.' And with that, the court adjourned for lunch.

I was released from the dock and met with some of my supporters outside the court. We repaired to a local coffee shop. Everyone was very encouraging towards me, but I was still thinking about the Muslim on the jury. How persuasive was he going to be in the jury room, with the other jurors? In any case, a devout Muslim is duty bound to side with another Muslim against the infidel, no matter what the evidence might say.

In my mind, I was already down to eleven impartial jurors from the original twelve. As I mulled this over, I saw the flashing blue lights of a fire engine in the distance, together with the urgent sound of a siren. Some poor devils must be in trouble, I thought.

The court reconvened after lunch, and once again I was locked into the dock. I sat there impatiently waiting for the jury to return and for the proceedings to restart, but nothing was happening. Ten minutes passed; then twenty, then thirty. At last the door in the side of the court leading to the jury box was opened, and the jurors filed in.

I looked at them closely. There was something not quite right about their demeanour – they appeared somewhat subdued compared to how they had been during the morning and I called my barrister over.

'What's going on?' I said. 'They don't look quite right – and one of them is missing.' I had just noticed that there were now only eleven jurors in the dock, including the Muslim gentleman.

It transpired that all the jurors had got stuck in one of the lifts on the way down to the ground floor over the lunch hour. The fire brigade had been summoned in order to release them, but one of the jurors had a panic attack and had to be taken to hospital. We really were now down to eleven jurors – or ten jurors and the Muslim gentleman, depending on how paranoid you might happen to feel. I was rapidly starting to feel very paranoid indeed, especially as the judge had just said that he would not replace the juror at this time.

The prosecuting barrister now started to outline the case for the prosecution. He told the jury that he was going to prove that I had harassed the plaintiff, Fizzy Mendacious; and not only that, but the harassment was religiously aggravated by virtue of the fact that I had used the word 'Taqiyya', which according to him, was a word with racist connotations, and grossly offensive insofar as it implied that the plaintiff employed deceit in order to pull the wool over the eyes of non-Muslims in order to further the cause of Islam.

I was reminded of the Birmingham Taqiyya Trial of 2014, where it had been alleged that Fizzy Mendacious had done *exactly* that in regard to manipulating the figures of his organisation in order to extract money from the public purse; it could certainly be said that such behaviour was designed to further the cause of Islam at the expense of the infidel, and yet here we were again over two years later, with his organisation once again raking in money from the taxpayer, and no sign of any fraud charges having been laid against him.

The prosecuting barrister finished his initial presentation to the jury, who had sat impassively throughout his somewhat lengthy talk. I couldn't discern any sign of emotion in any of them; they were probably still too traumatised by the lunchtime events to be able to take in much of what the prosecuting barrister had been saying.

By now it was just coming up to 4:00 p.m., and the judge adjourned the court until the following morning. I was once again released from the dock, and gathered with my supporters outside the court to discuss the day's events. We repaired to a local restaurant and I took advantage of the opportunity to get to know some of my colleagues and well-wishers a little better.

I'm not going to name any names here, but we all had a sufficiently good time in that restaurant to convince ourselves that this trial was going to be a walk-over, I would be hailed as a hero and that Fizzy Mendacious would be sent away with his tail between his legs. After all, despite the setbacks of the day, we still had three days left where the light of righteousness could shine through the courtroom and drive away the darkness.

I think it must have been something in the Perrier water.

CHAPTER 19

The Southwark Crown Court Trial – Part 3

My supporters and I re-convened outside the court at 9:30 the following morning – Tuesday 28 March. The previous day's events had generated some interest among the media – after all, it's not every day that an entire jury gets stuck in a lift in the Crown Court buildings – and there were some camera teams outside the court, filming some of my supporters and their placards.

I recognised one of the cameramen from a Canadian media organisation called 'The Rebel', and he asked me if I would like to do an interview to camera with him. For the next ten to fifteen minutes I outlined the background to the case for the Rebel interviewer and finished by expressing my confidence that justice would be done, as I expected that my barrister and my expert witness would wipe the floor with the opposition.

I entered the court building just before 10:00 and presented myself to the courtroom usher. Once again I was locked into the dock, behind the sheets of armoured glass, and we awaited the arrival of the judge and the jury.

The judge arrived first, and sat down behind the judges' bench before signalling to the court usher that he should invite the jurors back into the court. As they filed back into the courtroom and took their places in the jury box, I noticed a couple of things. The first was that the Muslim gentleman was still there, a brooding, malevolent presence, or so it seemed to me.

The second thing I noticed was that we seemed to be down to ten jurors.

The Muslim gentleman – who now appeared to be the foreman of the jury – passed a note to the court usher, who handed it to the judge. It transpired that one of the jurors had been taken ill overnight and dispatched to a local hospital. Initial enquiries suggested that the juror would not be coming back any time soon.

The judge considered this new information. It was within his gift to discharge the existing jury, and empanel a new jury with twelve jurors. Would he do it? It would mean a new foreman, who might not be a Muslim. However, it would mean re-starting the trial from scratch, thereby wasting one of the scheduled days of the trial.

The judge decided that we would continue with the existing ten jurors. This meant that the Muslim foreman of the jury, if he were at all persuasive, would only have to convince nine other people of my guilt, rather than the original eleven others. I estimated that my chances of acquittal had just dropped about fifteen to twenty per cent.

Not to worry, I thought, we still have a good case that a half-decent defence barrister could use to run rings round the opposition, especially with the evidence of my expert witness on the subject of Taqiyya. I resolved to remain positive, and turned my attention back to the proceedings in the courtroom.

The judge at Southwark Crown Court

The first prosecution witness was called – it was the police officer who had taken my original statement when I was first arrested in

Birmingham some months previously. He was sworn in and taken through my interview statement (which had been recorded and transcribed for the court) by the prosecuting lawyer, but listening to the evidence again, I didn't think that I had said anything particularly incriminating, apart from admitting to sending the emails in question, which as I have said, may have been mocking and satirical, but were in no way threatening or intimidating.

My defence lawyer declined to cross-examine the police officer, and he was dismissed from the witness box. The next witness to be called was Fizzy Mendacious himself.

Just as in the previous court case of 2014 at the Birmingham Taqiyya Trial, he declined to present himself in person, instead choosing to give evidence via video-link from an undisclosed location. Just as in the previous court case, I considered him to be a complete wuss for refusing to come to the court, but nevertheless it was his right not to do so, and he was sworn in via the video-link connection.

Once again I had to bite my tongue as he was sworn in on the Qur'an – an oath given by a Muslim on the Qur'an means absolutely nothing when it comes to furthering the cause of Islam, as the doctrine of Taqiyya allows a Muslim to lie with a clear conscience even under oath in a court of law.

Just as in the 2014 trial, my defence barrister declined to raise this point with the judge. I would have to rely on my expert witness to explain Taqiyya to the court, and having spoken to him previously, I was sure that he would be able to do so in a fluent and persuasive manner.

The prosecuting lawyer took Fizzy Mendacious through his evidence – and I have to say that Fizzy deserved an Oscar for the bravura performance he put on. He had been distressed and alarmed by my email communications, he had lost his appetite, he had lost sleep at night, tossing and turning in his bed as his nightmares kept him awake.

He had feared for his life and the safety of his family – it was nothing less than harassment of the worst kind. His voice rose and fell with heartfelt anguish, and when the prosecutor concluded his initial examination, I half expected the jurors to rise from their seats, give him three resounding cheers and shower the video screen with roses.

But then it was the turn of my defence barrister. She took him through his evidence whilst giving the clear impression that she didn't believe a word of it. This was quite obvious to everyone, including Fizzy himself, whose face was starting to turn red as the interrogation progressed. Just as in the 2014 trial, you could clearly see the beads of sweat forming on his brow. He was clearly becoming agitated and was starting to raise his voice.

'You don't have to shout, Mr. Mendacious,' said my barrister calmly. 'I am merely asking you why you did not block my client's emails if you felt that you were affected that badly by them. Could it be that you considered the emails to be of benefit to your organisation for the purposes of demonstrating the rampant 'Islamophobia' that you have to put up with, and the subsequent continuation of your enormous taxpayer's grant for Grievance Mongers UK?'

I thought that Fizzy was going to have an apoplectic fit. 'It's – it's not up to me to block such communications,' he spluttered, 'it's up to your client to stop sending them!'

This was such a ridiculous statement that I felt sure that my defence barrister would press home this point and demolish Fizzy's credibility there and then. But for reasons of her own, she didn't do that, instead choosing to change tack and come at him from a different direction.

'It's true, isn't it, Mr. Mendacious, that the real reason for your complaint is not that you felt harassed, alarmed, distressed, threatened and intimidated, but that you wanted revenge for having lost your case against my client in 2014? That's true, isn't it, Mr. Mendacious? Isn't it?'

Fizzy was definitely losing his cool again. 'NO! NO IT ISN'T!'

'You don't have to shout, Mr. Mendacious. The court can hear you perfectly well without you having to shout.'

The cross-examination concluded, the prosecuting barrister declined to re-examine and Fizzy Mendacious was discharged from giving further evidence. I felt that we had definitely come out of that exchange better than when we had started.

Then it was time for the CPS to introduce their star witness. This was a gentleman in his forties who was a Senior Research Fellow in Contemporary Islam. He had converted to Islam some twenty-five years previously and had an impressive range of qualifications and experience. The prosecuting barrister introduced him to the court as an expert in all things Islamic, and he gave an explanation of Taqiyya that was exactly as I had would have expected from a Muslim – that Taqiyya was rarely used by Muslims these days, and that any impression that non-Muslims might have regarding the lack of trustworthiness of Muslims when it came to Islamic matters was entirely misplaced.

The prosecution barrister took him backwards and forwards through his evidence until I could see that the jury were hanging on his every word. He was persuasive, no doubt about that, but some detailed cross-examination from my barrister based on my extensive dossier of notes that I had compiled before the trial, together with the evidence of my own expert witness, should introduce an element of uncertainty, and as my original barrister had said to me some months earlier, that was all we needed.

We adjourned for lunch. I was released from the dock, and my supporters and I repaired to what we now regarded as 'our' coffee shop – insofar as it was one of those trendy 'bijou' coffee shops, and when we were all in it, there was no room for any other patrons. We discussed the morning's events, and had a good old laugh about Fizzy's testimony in particular.

'Don't you worry, Timmy boy. Fizzy didn't do himself any favours, what with him shouting at your defence barrister and everything. And don't you worry about the Taqiyya either; your expert witness should make mincemeat of that chap from the CPS.'

We re-assembled after lunch back in the court, and once again I was locked in the dock. I was looking forward to Miss Bunny-Lover taking apart the evidence of the CPS expert witness, reducing him (or so I hoped) to a quivering wreck in the witness box.

Then my defence barrister dropped her bombshell.

First of all, she declined to cross examine the CPS expert witness in any detail, except to confirm his qualifications and experience. Then, as the cross-examination was concluded, and the judge was in the process of discharging the CPS expert witness from the witness box, she came over to the dock and whispered to me through the grill in the armoured glass: 'I don't want you to bring in your expert witness.'

I couldn't believe what I was hearing. My expert witness was at that moment sitting in a police station in Switzerland, having been sworn in and ready to give the testimony about Taqiyya over video-link that I was certain would contradict the evidence given by the CPS expert witness, and would help to introduce just the element of uncertainty that I felt was needed.

'What?' I said. 'You don't want me to bring him in? But everything has been arranged, hasn't it? Why don't you want to bring him in? His evidence could be crucial.'

My defence barrister fixed me with a steely glance. 'Mr. Burton,' she said, 'I don't want to confuse the jury. You may think that introducing contradictory evidence at this stage would be to your advantage, but the CPS expert witness has made a good impression on the jury and has explained the technical implications of Islamic doctrine. If we sow confusion in the minds of the jury at this stage it will not be to your advantage. I strongly recommend that you do not bring in your expert witness.'

I sat back in my chair, stunned. My entire defence strategy had been predicated on the testimony of my expert witness concerning Taqiyya, at least as far as the religiously aggravated part of the charge was concerned. But on the other hand, my defence barrister had twenty years of experience in handling cases of this nature, or so I had been lead to believe. I suddenly felt very out of my depth.

'I need an answer NOW,' she whispered menacingly through the grill. 'Or I won't be able to answer for what might happen. As I said, I strongly recommend that you do not call your expert witness. It's your choice, but it might all go very badly for you.'

If I had had more experience of Crown Court procedures, I might have felt able to challenge her assertions; as it was, I had no experience whatsoever, and if my barrister with her twenty years of experience recommended a particular course of action, then I felt that it would be irresponsible of me to challenge her, no matter what my personal feelings might be at the time.

'Well – alright then,' I said, 'if you're sure about this.' I was still unconvinced that was the right thing to do – and as it turned out, my misgivings were entirely justified.

There were some more technical submissions between the

prosecuting barrister, my defence barrister and the judge; the court was then adjourned until the following morning, when I was due to give evidence myself in the witness box.

My supporters and I repaired to our restaurant. Although the meal was very enjoyable, there was no doubt about it; the atmosphere was slightly subdued. Not one of my supporters thought that it was a good idea to dispense with my own expert witness.

'You'll have to rely on your charm and charisma in the witness box tomorrow, Tim,' one of them joked, 'then you'll really be in trouble.'

My supporters burst into laughter. But they were right. Tomorrow I would have to put on the performance of my life.

CHAPTER 20

The Southwark Crown Court Trial – Part 4

It was the early morning of Wednesday 29 March, and I was having a cup of coffee in my hotel room overlooking Westminster Bridge – the same bridge that Khalid Masood had wreaked such havoc on just seven days previously, killing four civilians by running them over with his car, and then stabbing an unarmed police officer to death in the grounds of Parliament itself.

The sun was just coming up over the horizon, and I wondered how much more Londoners were going to have to put up with in terms of terrorist attacks on their city. I imagined that we were just seeing the tip of the iceberg, because the inconvenient truth is that the more Muslims you have in any given Western society, the greater the incidence of low level anti-social behaviour, serious criminal violence and outright terrorism you are likely to have.

The epidemic of political correctness that has gripped our society over the last few decades has blinded otherwise sensible people to the point where they are willing to disbelieve the evidence of their own senses, and to assign all sorts of reasons to justify the behaviour of Muslims in Western societies – other than the obvious reason, which is that the ideology of Islam condones and encourages such behaviour.

Many otherwise sensible people – including the judge at my trial – are under the impression that there is a difference between 'moderate Muslims' and 'Islamists'. This is a purely artificial distinction – anyone who has studied Islam for any length of time and visited Islamic countries will tell you that Muslims themselves do not make this distinction, and that those Muslims who undertake acts of terror are not following a 'twisted version of Islam' as ex-Prime Minister

David Cameron told Parliament following the murder of Fusilier Lee Rigby on the streets of Woolwich – they are following the divine commands of Allah as handed down to the Islamic prophet Muhammad through the Angel Gabriel, and anyone who thinks otherwise is sadly mistaken.

Maybe I would have the opportunity to explain all this in front of the judge and the jury later on. What I needed was a defence barrister who understood the ideology of Islam sufficiently in order to be able to ask the right questions.

Instead of which, I was stuck with Miss Bunny-Lover. I sighed to myself.

I still had misgivings concerning the decision I had made concerning my expert defence witness. I had called him via Skype the previous evening and apologised for having put him to so much trouble, and all for nothing. He was very magnanimous about it, but he made the point that without his testimony, the jury would have completely the wrong impression of Islam and Taqiyya. I tried to present my barrister's argument as she had presented it to me, but the words rang hollow. I just couldn't convince myself that I had done the right thing by letting her talk me into this course of action.

I made my way to Southwark Crown Court and arrived at 9:30 as usual. My supporters were already there with their placards and there were still one or two camera teams in the vicinity, obviously hoping for an exclusive interview with some notorious soon-to-be-convicted criminal. I remember feeling glad that it wouldn't be me in that position.

The court reconvened at 10:00 and we all filed into the courtroom. This time, instead of being locked into the dock, I was allowed to sit in the public gallery until I was called to give evidence. The judge arrived, the ten jurors entered the jury box, and the court was in session.

The prosecutor called me to the witness box and I was sworn in on the Bible. I tried to bring to mind the same feeling of calmness that had served me so well in the 2014 trial, but I couldn't do it. I was nervous, and it was starting to show. This would never do. I gripped the rail that ran around the top of the witness box with both hands, took some deep breaths, and waited for the examination to start.

The prosecutor began by taking me through some basic statements of fact. He read out the emails that had formed the exchange of communication that had led to my being charged. Did I agree that I had written those emails? 'Yes.' Wouldn't I agree that those emails might have a negative effect on Mr. Mendacious? I pointed out that the majority of the emails weren't sent to Mr. Mendacious at all, but to his organisation, Grievance Mongers UK. Only the last email had been addressed to Fizzy himself.

'Ah yes, Mr. Burton, but you meant those emails to be seen by Mr. Mendacious, didn't you? You knew he was going to be the ultimate recipient of all those emails.'

I pointed out that there was no way I could know who might look at an email addressed to Grievance Mongers UK. Fizzy might have a staff of five, or five hundred for all I knew, with a team dedicated to handling incoming emails and separating the wheat from the chaff, so to speak. But the prosecutor was determined not to let the point go, and badgered me about it until I made the mistake of saying, 'Well, I suppose he might have been the first one to open the email, but—'

He cut me short. 'So you admit it!' he said. 'Your behaviour constituted a course of conduct amounting to harassment. The prosecution has proved its case!' And with that he slammed his folder of notes onto his desk with such force that a cloud of dust arose and hovered in the air for a moment.

He had obviously done this for effect, because although I didn't think for a moment that the prosecution had proved its case at all, the theatrical nature of his performance had definitely left an impression on the jury. They were now sitting upright in their seats, staring at the prosecutor like a family of meerkats that had just realised that an apex predator was in the room.

The Jury at Southwark Crown Court

'No further questions, Your Honour!' he said, and with that he sat down. My defence barrister stood up, and I hoped that she would cross-examine me as to my motives and demonstrate to the jury that I had done what I had, not out of personal animosity towards Mr. Mendacious on account of him being a Muslim, but because he was a crook, a liar, a cheat and a fraud with a track record of extracting money from the taxpayer under false pretences.

But Miss Bunny-Lover had other ideas.

'Would you please tell the court, Mr. Burton,' she said, 'how it was that you got your nickname of "Catstrangler?"'

This was a story that I had told many times before, and I had mentioned to my defence barrister that if she had an opportunity, then she should ask me about it in court. I didn't think that it ought to take preference over some of the more serious questions that she should be asking, but maybe it would elicit some sympathy from the jurors.

'A lot of people ask me this,' I began, 'and it's usually because they are concerned that I might be going around strangling cats. In fact, nothing could be further from the truth. I love cats – and I'm actually very fond of them to the degree that I have owned several of them, including a beautiful Burmese pedigree cat whose name was Tiger. He was my constant companion for many years when I lived on my own until one day he was struck down with feline leukaemia.' This was actually true, and I could feel the tears springing to my eyes as I recalled that day. I glanced at the jury. So far, so good. One or two of them looked sympathetic, although the Muslim foreman seemed unimpressed.

'But my nickname was given to me by my mother, who enrolled me for some after-school classes when I was about ten years of age. She had decided that I should learn a musical instrument, and as there was some sort of special offer at my school for a term's worth of violin lessons, then violin lessons it would be.

'So for the best part of a school term I practiced the violin. I was given a school violin to practice with, and I was allowed to take it home in the week to improve my technique in between lessons. At first my mother seemed pleased that I was demonstrating some sort of musical prowess – she said that musical abilities ran in her side of the family, and that her great-aunt Jessie had been an international violin player some decades previously.

'However as time went on, she became strangely more irritable and depressed. I noticed that when I practiced the violin at home she would take to going out to the shops or visiting the next-door neighbours. But she even stopped doing that after a while, because the next-door neighbours would complain about how the strains of little Timmy playing the violin would permeate through the party walls and send their highly-strung Irish setter into a frenzy, to the point where it would start bounding around on the furniture in the lounge until I stopped.

'Eventually she could stand it no longer, and came into my room in tears one day when I was in mid-practice, crying, "That's it, I can't take any more. The neighbours are threatening to lynch us both because of your violin playing, which sounds as though someone is strangling a cat." And so my fledgling violin career came to a close.

'And that's how I got my nickname "Catstrangler", Your Honour.' I addressed this remark to the judge, who by now was looking intently in my direction.

There were some smiles and a few chuckles from the jury. I sensed that I may have been starting to win them over. My defence barrister obviously thought so too, for she said, 'As it's nearly lunchtime, Your Honour, may we adjourn? I'd like to continue my cross-examination after lunch but I have a line of questioning which might take some time to develop.'

Over lunch in the coffee shop, most of my supporters were fairly enthusiastic about the morning's events. The general consensus seemed to be that the 'Catstrangler' story had been well told, and might have won me a few friends on the jury. A lot would depend on my cross-examination by the prosecuting lawyer in the afternoon, but they were certain that with the evidence that had already been presented, I shouldn't have too much trouble.

I wasn't so sure. I would have preferred my defence barrister to have made a better job of rebutting the points that the prosecuting lawyer had made. Maybe she would do that in the afternoon now that the jury were more on our side.

CHAPTER 21

The Southwark Crown Court Trial – Part 5

We assembled back in the court after lunch. I saw that we hadn't lost any more jurors, which was a mixed blessing, as if we had lost another one, the judge would have been compelled to empanel a new jury, and I might have acquired a new jury foreman as a result. However, one or two of the jurors were definitely smiling at me by now, and I thought that was a net positive benefit.

All I had to do now was to get through the cross-examination.

Miss Bunny-Lover jumped to her feet and continued with her examination. 'So, Mr. Burton, the prosecutor has described you as a racist, bigoted, far-right 'Islamophobe'. Is that how you see yourself?'

I replied that is was not, and explained in detail why not, making the points that Islam is not a race, that my views were what would have been described as 'conservative' rather than 'far-right' only a few decades ago, and that 'Islamophobia' is not even a real thing, merely a word concocted in order to stifle free speech and to discourage the justified criticism of Islam.

'But Mr. Burton, the prosecution has made you out to be hostile towards Mr. Mendacious because he is a Muslim, and not only that, but he thinks you are hostile to all Muslims. Is that true?'

I replied that it was not, and that while I may be said to be hostile to the ideology of Islam, I was definitely not hostile towards individual Muslims, whom I generally regarded as charming and courteous. Mr. Mendacious, on the other hand, I considered to be a liar, a cheat and a fraud, and my hostility to him was based on those characteristics, rather than him being a Muslim.

The examination continued along these lines, and I felt that I was at least sixty-forty in percentage terms towards getting an acquittal. After a while, my defence barrister said to the judge, 'No further questions, Your Honour,' and sat down.

The prosecutor got to his feet. 'Mr Burton,' he said, 'you have testified that you do not hate Muslims for who they are, you only hate the ideology, is that correct?'

I replied that it was. 'Then how do you explain THESE?' he said, and started to reel off a series of tweets from the notes he had in front of him.

I didn't recognise the tweets to start with – but as he continued, I realised with horror that they were tweets of mine from four years previously – which I had posted just after the murder of Fusilier Lee Rigby by Muslims on the streets of Woolwich in London.

At the time, emotions were running high – and I'm sorry to say that some of my tweets from that time were a little intemperate, and could arguably be described as derogatory to Muslims as a group. I had completely forgotten about the tweets, and as the prosecutor continued to read them out to the court, I realised that they could be used against me in a way that might not give the best impression to the jury.

'For example,' said the prosecutor – *'Are you fed up with your Muslim neighbours? Is there a mosque in your area causing problems? Then call 0800-DRONE-STRIKE now!'*

The Drone Strikes Back, I thought. The tweet had seemed incisive and witty at the time.

'What about this one?' said the prosecutor – *'I failed my history test at school today. Apparently the answer to the question of "how have Muslims evolved over time" is not "through 1,400 years of inbreeding."'*

Putting aside the fact that the link between consanguinity and first-cousin marriages between Muslims (particularly Pakistani Muslims) is well-documented, and the resultant high levels of birth defects (coupled with correspondingly low levels of intelligence) account for a sizable burden on the NHS in our country, the tweets could arguably be seen to be somewhat prejudicial to Muslims as a whole.

I was completely taken by surprise with this ambush technique of the prosecution, to the extent that I couldn't offer a coherent account of why I had written them in the first place. I found myself unable to explain that I had written them in anger; that our brave servicemen were being slaughtered on the streets of London by Muslims who were just following the commands of Allah and the Islamic prophet Muhammad as laid down in the Qur'an. Those Muslims were not 'Islamist extremists', they were good Muslims, at least in the eyes of Allah and Muhammad, which was all that mattered in Islam.

My mind had just become a complete blank when I needed it most, which was no doubt what the prosecuting barrister had intended.

'It doesn't get any better, my lord,' he said to the judge. 'This man is obviously the bigoted, racist, right-wing 'Islamophobe' that the prosecution has said he was all along.'

He turned to the jury. 'Just imagine the effect of a drone strike on a poor innocent Muslim family living in terror under the rubble of their former home in the Middle East. It doesn't bear thinking about, does it, ladies and gentlemen? And yet this man, Mr. Burton, the defendant who you see standing before you, thinks it is funny. He is a despicable human being, and you must find him Guilty, Guilty, Guilty!'

A small cloud of dust rose into the air as the prosecutor emphasised the last three words while repeatedly banging down his folder full of notes with great force onto the bench in front of him. 'No further questions, Your Honour.'

The dust slowly settled, and the judge regarded me gravely. 'We will now adjourn and re-convene at 10:00 tomorrow morning,' he said. 'I would remind you that if you fail to turn up for the rest of the hearing tomorrow then a warrant will be issued for your arrest.'

This further signalled to the jury that he, the judge, felt that I was as guilty as sin. This did not bode well for the fairness and unbiased impartiality I had been expecting from the trial judge. Maybe I could explain to Miss Bunny-Lover how those tweets came to be written, and then we could explain it to the jury in the morning.

The judge then turned to my defence barrister. 'I am instructing you that you are not to have any communication with the defendant, your client, until the court has re-convened tomorrow morning, when you will have the opportunity to further examine.'

So I wasn't even going to be allowed to explain, outside the court anyway, how those tweets came to be written. Not to worry, I was sure that Miss Bunny-Lover would re-examine me in the witness box the following morning and get to the bottom of it.

Over our evening meal in the restaurant, my supporters expressed their outrage. 'That was completely out of order,' said Frank, a spry, smartly dressed gentleman who must have been in his sixties with an authentic South London accent. 'They're not supposed to ambush you like that with evidence that hasn't been presented to the defence in advance.'

I wasn't sure of the law relating to sudden surprises of that nature. I was still smarting from the completely unexpected turn of events, and I felt that we might have a hard time recovering from it in order to undo the damage that had been inflicted.

I arrived at the court early the following morning, Thursday 30 March. I wasn't going to give the judge the pleasure of issuing an arrest warrant, and besides, I felt that I should have the opportunity to present my side of the story, even though those tweets had absolutely nothing to do with the so-called 'harassment' that I was currently charged with as a result of the so-called 'alarming, distressing and intimidating' emails sent to Fizzy Mendacious and his merry men at Grievance Mongers UK.

Some of my supporters were already on the court steps with the placards and calling out, 'Justice for Tim Burton! Truth not Taqiyya!' and they gave me three cheers as I went into the court building, which was a pleasant surprise. I presented myself to the court usher as required and the court re-convened on time at 10:00.

But when I was called to the witness box, my defence barrister didn't re-examine me at all. I had been under oath since the previous afternoon, and I hadn't been able to speak to her since then, but I felt that the least she could have done was to go over the 'ambush' evidence that the prosecution had presented to the court and to give me a chance to explain why I had written what I had at the time that I did.

Not a bit of it. 'No further questions, Your Honour,' she said, and that was that. I was released from the witness box and returned to the dock.

The judge gave his summing up to the jury – and although his words seemed impartial enough to my ears at that time, I couldn't help but feel that the antics of the prosecution on the previous afternoon would leave the jury with a lasting impression that would be hard to dispel.

The judge instructed the jury to retire – he wanted them to reach a unanimous verdict, and the rest of us were dispatched to wait outside the courtroom. We would be called back in when the verdict had been reached.

As it turned out, we didn't have to wait long. We were called back into the court and the Muslim foreman asked the judge whether a majority verdict would be acceptable. The judge replied, 'No, it has to be unanimous,' and with that we were dispatched to wait outside the courtroom again.

I was starting to feel hopeful. I could imagine the Muslim foreman of the jury trying to guilt-trip the rest of them into finding me guilty, and the other stalwart jurors standing up for me and saying, 'Don't be ridiculous, he's just a patriot who is standing up for what he believes in. Anyway, it was a good story well told concerning his nickname "Catstrangler" and his violin lessons. We can't possibly find him guilty.'

However, the jury came back with a unanimous verdict just before lunchtime. We were called back in, and I watched the Muslim foreman stand up and smirk at me as the verdict was read out – 'Guilty.' The rest of the jurors avoided eye contact with me.

The judge thanked the jury for their service, and they were dismissed through the side entrance from whence they had come. The judge then turned to me. 'Mr. Burton,' he said, 'you have been found guilty of a very serious offence. I find that your communications were grossly offensive and that you intentionally caused alarm and distress to Mr. Mendacious through your actions. You will return for sentencing at the Inner London Crown Court on Friday 28 April, and I advise you now I would not want you to go away thinking that I was not considering a custodial sentence.' And with that double negative, for which the judge himself should have received a severe custodial sentence with hard labour, the gavel came down and the trial was over.

I went to look for my barrister, but she had vanished. As well she might, I thought.

My supporters and I went to the restaurant for one final meal. My supporters did their best to cheer me up. 'Never mind, Tim, things could have been worse. You could have been remanded in custody for sentencing. Anyway, a hundred and fifty years ago you would have been transported to Australia. They'll probably let you off with a fine.'

'Thanks, guys,' I said. 'But you heard the judge – he's considering a custodial sentence, or so he says, and I don't think he was on my side from the start.'

My supporters continued to offer encouragement. 'You could always appeal the verdict,' one of them suggested. 'That defence barrister was well dodgy.'

Unfortunately, having a dodgy barrister for your defence at a Crown Court trial is no grounds for appeal, as I was to find out. But Miss Bunny-Lover would not agree that there were any grounds for an appeal whatsoever, and so for the next thirty days my attempts to have the verdict overturned fell on deaf ears. It was only when I came out of prison after six weeks in HMP Thameside that I found that there were in fact very good grounds for an appeal, if only my defence barrister Miss Bunny-Lover had undertaken the appropriate due diligence investigation that she should have done beforehand.

One of my supporters had been doing some digging and he had discovered that the so-called 'independent' expert witness called by the CPS was nothing of the sort. He had declared himself to the court as someone who would give unbiased evidence, and he had signed a statement to the effect that he knew of no connection that would call the truthfulness of his evidence into question.

Except that unbeknownst to any of us, he was the director of an organisation that he had founded some years previously, and was receiving material and moral support and patronage from a senior figure in the CPS. He hadn't disclosed this to the court, and this alone should have disqualified him from giving evidence.

How likely is it that he would have been 'independent' when his organisation was receiving substantial benefits from the very people who were asking him to testify on their behalf? The law is clear on this matter; even a suggestion that his evidence might be biased requires at the very least a disclosure to the court, and without such a disclosure in advance, his evidence would be inadmissible.

Given that the CPS had obviously felt that his evidence was crucial to securing a conviction in my case – otherwise they wouldn't have bothered with an expert witness in the first place – then under the law as it currently stands, his non-disclosure should have rendered the verdict in my case null and void.

Of course, it is one thing to know that an injustice has been done, and quite another to have it recognised and addressed by the British legal system, especially when it involves highly placed members of the Establishment. But that wasn't going to stop me trying.

However, I wasn't aware of any of these grounds for appeal during the days and weeks after the Southwark Crown Court trial – and so in due course I presented myself at the Inner London Crown Court for sentencing on 28 April 2017, which is of course where we came in at Chapter 1 of this book.

CHAPTER 22

Pigeon on a Sunday

Sunday 30 April 2017 – It's an odd thing, but the human mind is capable of adapting itself to drastically changing circumstances relatively quickly. Only a few days previously, I had been a free man, able to sample all the exotic delights of Birmingham on a whim, with no worries other than whether I would wake up with a moderate case of 'Delhi Belly' after having consumed a dodgy Chicken Tikka Masala from the local Balti House down the road from where I live.

As it was, I was now a convicted criminal, subject to Her Majesty's Prisons' rules and regulations, and severely constrained in what I could do over the next thirty-nine days in terms of just about everything, not just sampling the delights of the local takeaway, although that is still fairly high up my list of 'Great Places To Visit in Sutton Coldfield'.

However, they do say that 'stone walls do not a prison make, nor iron bars a cage' and I was determined to make the most of my predicament and not to let it get me down too much. There are those who say that this is easier said than done, but there are techniques that one can employ to mitigate the circumstances in which one may find oneself embroiled from time to time.

The first thing to do is to accept the things over which you have no control. In my case, I had been sentenced to twelve weeks in prison, which meant that I would hopefully be released in six weeks with good behaviour. So, for the next thirty-nine days I would do my very best to stay out of trouble and to navigate my way through the unknown waters that lay ahead of me.

The second thing to do is to treat your situation as a positive learning experience, and this is what I endeavoured to do over the rest of my sentence. I won't lie to you – there were times when I felt very hard done by indeed, and it would be very easy for someone with less fortitude to be crushed by the experience. The loss of control over one's life and liberty can be very difficult to deal with, and I could see that many of the other inmates exhibited signs of extreme stress during the time that I was there.

The presence of illegal drugs such as 'spice' was an ever-present problem throughout the prison, and although there were numerous posters on the prison notice boards warning against the use of this pernicious drug, there were many prisoners who had fallen under its spell. It was easy to get hold of – consignments of the drug were regularly thrown over prison walls or brought in by corrupt prison officers; and in some cases by remotely-controlled drones flown directly to the cell windows of well-connected prisoners.

You could always tell a prisoner who was under the influence of 'spice' – just think of the zombies in the TV series 'The Walking Dead' and you have a very good idea of the effect that this drug has on the average prisoner. A blank-eyed stare, shambling gait, and an inability to engage with the world are just three of the symptoms apparent.

In addition, the drug poses a challenge to all those who would help prisoners under the influence. It has been described as worse than heroin in that it cannot only render the user unconscious and at risk of death extremely quickly, but the toxic atmosphere literally surrounding such a user can be easily inhaled and may affect the person tasked with trying to help to a similarly dangerous degree.

However, assuming that one is able to steer clear of dangerous narcotics and other psychoactive substances, there is actually plenty to focus on in order to develop a positive experience.

As you may recall, I was asked earlier by the prison authorities whether I identified as Catholic, a Hindu, an Atheist, a Jain, a Buddhist or a Baptist or a Jew (to paraphrase Bob Dylan in his song Universal Soldier) and I thought it would be prudent to identify as Christian, seeing as how that was how I had been brought up. Not that I was actually a practicing Christian, in fact I saw myself then (and still see myself now) as an agnostic – one who admits to the possibility of a higher power but not necessarily within the confines of organised religion.

So on the first Sunday of my incarceration, 30 April 2017, I found myself making my way to the meeting room designated as the place of Christian worship within the prison. All those identifying as Christian were called from their cells by the prison officers, lined up at the exit of the prison block, and marched around the vast open space that doubled as a running track and a football field to a prison block on the other side, where we were patted down, identities checked – and checked again – one by one, in order to experience the solemn and profound word of the Lord.

Well, that was an eye-opener.

I had no sooner made my way into the meeting room than I became aware of a tumultuous hubbub emanating from a crowd of inmates at the front of the room. This was obviously a very popular event, and the reason why soon became apparent.

At the front of the room, on a slightly raised platform, were the members of the South East London Gospel Choir, and boy, were they dressed to impress. Modesty forbids me from describing the long legs, the exceptionally short mini-skirts and the tight blouses of the half-dozen or so well-endowed young ladies on the platform, but they seemed to be proving a big hit with those who had taken the trouble to ensure that they were right at the front and able to make the most of the sights and sounds presented to them.

The enthusiastic young ladies of the South East London Gospel Choir proceeded to belt out a range of songs that had the inmates literally dancing on their chairs and in the aisles. I couldn't fault them – they certainly knew how to appeal to their audience, to the extent that I could see the five or six prison officers who were supervising the event glancing at each other in apprehension. Was something going to kick off?

In the event, things passed off without major incident. One young Afro-Caribbean inmate fell off his chair after some particularly animated dancing and had to be carried to the First Aid room with a dodgy ankle, but other than that, the South East London Gospel Choir exuded a certain magic that I felt was almost entirely beneficial. I could certainly see how they would attract inmates to their cause.

It was around then that an earnest lady of around seventy-five or eighty years of age approached me after the South East London

Gospel Choir had completed their last number. 'Did you enjoy that?' she asked. I tentatively replied in the affirmative. 'Have you ever considered giving yourself to Christ?' she continued. Talk about trading on heightened emotions.

'Let's just say I'm open to all possibilities,' I said, 'and as an agnostic, I certainly wouldn't rule anything out at this point.'

This was her cue to unload a ton of religious literature on me, including a copy of the Bible and a tract entitled 'How to Counter the Double Curse of Booze'. Well, given that booze was quite hard to come by in prison, unless you included straining melted boot polish through six slices of Warburton's finest, I would have thought that countering the Double Curse of Booze was not of the highest priority when it came to advising prison inmates.

However, I was not about to upset someone who obviously felt very strongly about all the good works she was doing, so I simply murmured, 'Thank you,' as she departed to foist her attentions on another unsuspecting prisoner.

On the way back to the cell block I was struck by the magnificence of the Prison Garden – a cultivated area by the side of the football pitch. Someone – I dare say maybe many people over the years – had clearly put a lot of effort into developing a truly inspiring oasis of horticulture in an otherwise barren landscape. There were numerous exotic plants – although as a complete ignoramus in horticultural matters, I would have great difficulty in naming even a few of them – interspersed with vivid green bushes and trailing vines circumventing their way up a series of trellises to simulate a tropical environment. I leaned against the fence surrounding this vision of beauty for several minutes, and almost completely forgot about the reality of my oppressive surroundings.

The reality was that for the next thirty-nine days I would be subject to Her Majesty's rules and regulations, which on one level was perfectly true, but on another level I was freer to explore the limits of the capabilities of my mind. When one is subject to the mind-numbing routines of everyday life, it is quite difficult to 'think outside of the box' and to develop patterns and lines of thought which can lead one to a higher stage of enlightenment.

Having a lot of time to oneself, on the other hand, as in prison, allows one to cultivate a Zen-like environment where every thought can be analysed and expanded upon to reach conclusions that would never (or hardly ever) be attainable during normal everyday life. I was reminded of another book that I had read in my early twenties, entitled *Zen and the Art of Motorcycle Maintenance* by Robert M. Pirsig.

When I first read this book I was overwhelmed by the complexity of the thoughts, concepts and emotions described therein, but having re-read it in recent years I am struck by the profound truths that it contains. Distilled into a nutshell, the message is that there is more than one reality, and it is not always what you think it is. Only by undergoing hardship and endurance, coupled with humility and introspection, is it possible to perceive the perpetual transition between realities and to realise that many (if not most) things that one has taken for granted during their lifetime are but an illusion.

There is a Buddhist saying:- 'When the student is ready, then the teacher will appear.'

This refers to a state of preparedness on behalf of the student. The teacher may not be an actual person, but an event or a combination of circumstances that allows the student to realise a truth of which they have previously been unaware.

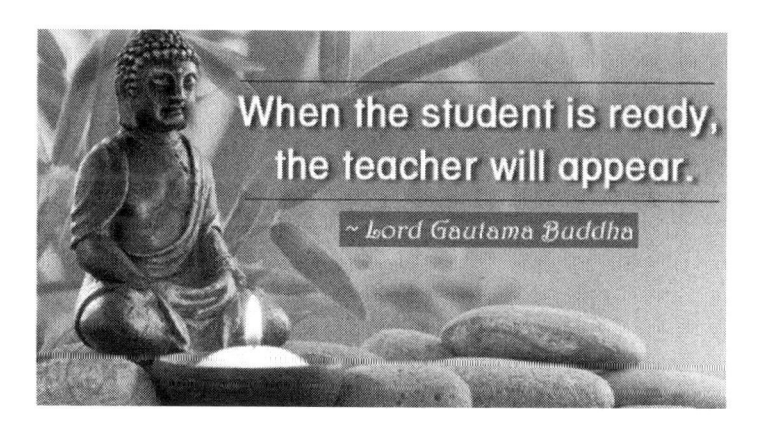

When the student is ready, the teacher will appear.
~ Lord Gautama Buddha

I arrived back at my cell in a state of euphoria. 'What's up with you then?' said John.

'What's up with me then? I'll tell you what's up with me then. I have been overwhelmed by the complexity and the beauty of the universe,' I said, suddenly afflicted with a bout of uncontrollable spluttering and coughing, 'nothing whatsoever to do with the long legs, the exceptionally short mini-skirts and tight blouses of the well-endowed young ladies of the South East London Gospel Choir.'

John cast me a glance of scepticism. 'Don't you start enjoying yourself in here,' he said, 'or the next thing you know you'll be fighting to get back in when you're out on the street, and then from there on in, it's a slippery slope to institutionalisation.'

I laughed. 'As if,' I said, and climbed up onto the top bunk to read the copy of *De Profundis* that John had loaned to me. There's nothing like the tortured writings of Oscar Wilde to dispel the physical effects of sexual arousal (or so I've heard).

CHAPTER 23

Assessment Time

Friday 12 May 2017 – It was now fourteen days since I had been taken from the Inner London Crown Court and transported to HMP Thameside – aka the 'Thameside Hilton'. During that time I had been introduced to the rules and regulations of Her Majesty's Prisons, and I had got to know a considerable number of inmates on my prison wing.

The fact that I was interested in chess certainly helped when it came to making friends – men don't just get together and talk about each other's feelings in the same way women do – an external mechanism for bonding is essential, and playing chess on a regular basis allows for bonding to take place without all the touchy-feely stuff that most men would run a mile from.

No doubt I will be inundated with letters of criticism from hundreds of men out there who are more in touch with their feminine side than I am – but please feel free to continue to write in, as I have been informed that writing paper, when shredded, makes excellent cat litter, especially for Damian (a very particular and discriminating feline belonging to an acquaintance of mine).

I'm not speaking here from personal experience, but it is rumoured that Damian's political opinions are apparently even more forthright than mine. An' that's sayin' summat, as they say in Yorkshire. Damian's political opinions are usually expressed via a stream of cat urine, and apparently he can hit a grainy newspaper photograph of Jeremy Corbyn shagging Diane Abbott nine times out of ten from a distance of three feet.

In my two weeks behind bars, I had become used to the quirks and vagaries of the prison system to the extent that I was now considered to be an 'old lag' – able to dispense solemn advice to some of the new inmates who, surprisingly enough, seemed to materialise out of nowhere (via the prison transport system) every day.

I was now able to explain the intricacies of the menu system – whereby prisoners could order their food for the week through a computer system based on fingerprint recognition – and I could show them how to select TV programs through their in-cell entertainment centre.

(I should mention that I was determined to make a concerted effort to stay away from dispensing advice on how to obtain illegal and contraband items. One could get into serious trouble for that, and leaving aside my recently acquired criminal conviction, I was keen to cultivate my image among the other prisoners as an exceptionally law-abiding criminal. Well, perhaps not too law-abiding. In the Thameside Hilton, that could land you in just as much trouble. Suffice it to say that my recipes for extracting the methanol from popular brands of boot-polish via six slices of Warburton's finest were now proving very popular.)

I use the phrase 'entertainment centre' loosely – the premise for the successful operation of the system was that you required a co-axial lead to connect to the back of the TV in your cell and for it to be set up in such a way that it was able to receive signals from the ether and display them on your TV. The first challenge was that the co-axial leads were in very short supply.

(When I say 'in short supply', I mean somewhere on the HMP inmates' spectrum between gold dust, hens' teeth and the pubic hair of expectant unicorns.)

I was advised that if I were to acquire such a co-axial lead, then I should keep it secreted about my person, otherwise it would most likely disappear and be squirreled away by one of the other inmates at the first opportunity. Apparently – whisper it quietly! – there were some acquisitive, thieving and downright dishonest persons on our wing.

Shock-horror, I hear you say! Surely not! But yes, there were indeed some inmates who would steal anything that wasn't nailed down, and that included TV co-axial leads from their fellow prisoners. As an aside, I was to find that it also included electric kettles. The ownership – or, to be more specific, non-ownership – of a common-or-garden electric kettle assumes a great deal of importance in a prison environment, as I was to find out.

The second challenge was tuning the TV in. This required the services of an inmate who was in possession of a remote control unit. In my case, I had to bet on the outcome of a chess game with the appropriate inmate in order to acquire a co-axial cable and to get him to tune my TV in to the available channels. This was relatively easy for me because I was developing my chess-playing skills each day through extensive practice.

I don't know what sacrifices the other inmates might have had to make to acquire a co-axial lead and the use of a remote control unit, but I'm sure some of them ended up in transactions that might not be considered prim and proper (or even hygienic) by one's maiden aunt. Anyway, moving on…

Having tuned in the TV, then next challenge was to select a channel to watch. In addition to the standard mainstream TV and satellite channels, there were two prison-operated DVD channels in operation twenty-four hours a day. You could say this was a mixed blessing. I use that phrase because the only DVDs available during my first two weeks were box sets of 'Prison Break'.

Talk about adding insult to injury.

Believe it or not, the last thing you want when faced with a substantial period of incarceration is a DVD box set based on the premise that if you don't break out of prison using the most violent means available to you then you are likely to die a horrible death at the hands of mobsters and psychopaths. Someone in charge of the DVD media administration at HMP Thameside obviously had a warped sense of humour.

During the first two weeks, there were numerous assessments carried out, mostly by nubile young women who seemed to have been selected for their sexual attractiveness in order to remind inmates of what they were missing. Now I may be mistaken on this last point, because when, as a man, you have been thrown against your will into an all-male environment for any length of time, then any female who is possessed of a pulse and who does not display any outward signs of debilitating illnesses such as leprosy starts to look sexually attractive.

In fact I'm not sure that even leprosy would have put me off after two weeks of enforced celibacy. Although I think I would have to draw the line at the prospect of the object of my desire not having a pulse.

I do have some principles, after all. As the famous comedian Groucho Marx once remarked – 'Those are my principles. If you don't like them – well, I have others.'

I remember my first assessment well. A prison officer poked his head around my cell door one morning and announced that my presence was required outside. Could I possibly make myself respectable and meet my assessor at a table in the communal area outside my cell, if I would be so kind?

As I recall, his actual words were – 'Burton, you've got a visitor. Get outside now, and don't keep the lady waiting.' Now, that was an instruction that was hard to refuse.

I duly obliged and sat down in the communal area with a buxom brunette who looked as though she was on day release from the Cheltenham Academy for Exceedingly Demure Young Ladies. She had an cultured and refined accent, a face which was the very epitome of health and beauty, and a figure that wouldn't have looked out of place on a Playboy centrefold – or at the very least, sprawled lasciviously in a skimpy bikini across the bonnet of my Ferrari – perhaps before I had loaned it out to Jeremy Clarkson for an episode of Top Gear.

I'm joking, of course. I would never loan out my Ferrari to Jeremy Clarkson. Not after he punched that Irish chef for not cooking his steak correctly. I am most definitely not a fan of culinary-related violence.

'So how are they treating you?' she purred. 'Can I ask you a few questions? Are you suffering from any ailments? Allergies? Are you addicted to drink, drugs or any form of narcotics? How is your food? Have you any complaints that are not being addressed?'

She ticked off various boxes on a sheet of paper on her clipboard as I gave her my answers. The question about having allergies, I was to find, formed an indispensable part of any questionnaire in the prison system.

Strangely enough, due to my medical history over the previous three or four years, I had found that it formed an indispensable part of any questionnaire within the National Health Service as well. I could well imagine a future conversation going like this:

Doctor: 'Well, Mr. Burton, if you could just stop bleeding for a moment while we retrieve your severed limbs from the floor of the ambulance, I need to ask you if you have any allergies. Hay fever is particularly prevalent at this time of year, and we wouldn't want you to suffer unnecessarily.'

Maybe I'm just being oversensitive.

My reply would be along the lines of: 'Now that you mention it, Doctor, it turns out that I'm allergic to complete strangers continually asking me whether I am allergic to anything.'

Anyway, the questions from of the Exceedingly Demure Young Lady from the Cheltenham Academy finally came to an end. I was quite sorry to see her go, really. She left me with the promise that she would be back for a further Educational Assessment in the prison library within the next few days. Woo-hoo! I couldn't wait.

Maybe I could inveigle her into smuggling a cake into the prison with a file in it? Or persuade her to take my place in the cell while I dressed up as a washerwoman and made my escape past the unsuspecting prison staff. Unfortunately the aforementioned prison staff seems to be alert to such ruses these days. Whoever would have thought that reading *The Wind in the Willows* was so essential for custodial effectiveness?

Sure enough, after a few days the Exceedingly Demure Young Lady was back, with another series of questions designed to establish my level of educational attainment. Now, having graduated from Wallington County Grammar School in a leafy Surrey suburb some forty-seven years previously – with a diploma for flicking ink-soaked paper pellets from a wooden ruler with a high degree of accuracy over a range of ten metres – I considered myself to be fairly high up on the educational spectrum, at least compared to some of the less fortunate members of the prison population.

HMP Thameside Prison Library

'You'll still have to go for an English Language, Mathematics and Computer Skills assessment next Saturday,' she said, 'and it's important that you do well. HMP Thameside prides itself on making sure that all inmates leave with the requisite skills to enable them to become productive members of society.'

Personally I would have thought that some courses in advanced computer hacking, crypto-currency fraud and loan-sharking techniques would have been more useful to me at my time of life, but I forbore from saying so just in case the powers-that-be had an opportunity to review my comments and to decide that my release in four or five weeks' time would be inappropriate.

It's a funny thing, but being in an environment with people who might well be eligible for Professorships in Advanced Criminality makes one unconscionably competitive, and I resolved to do as well as I could to achieve a respectable result in the forthcoming educational assessment.

The following Saturday I was directed to a classroom with another fifteen to twenty old lags to undergo an English Language, Mathematics and Computer Skills assessment. I took my place in front of a computer terminal. I noticed a sign above the screen that read 'Anyone caught stealing a mouse will be punished with the loss of all inmate privileges'. Blimey, I thought, that's a bit much. What was it about computer mice that would attract such a draconian punishment? I could envisage a possible scenario:

'OK, Fingers, now remember we are going to steal 100,000 boxes of high-end computer mice from this warehouse. Ignore the substantial quantities of cocaine, heroin, high-powered military armaments and the squillions of forged 500-euro notes that are lying about unguarded. We might end up doing serious time in the nick if we get caught with that lot.'

'You're joking, aren't you boss? If they catch us with those computer mice they'll throw away the key. Just let us keep the Class A drugs, the rocket-propelled grenades and the forged currency – and we can unload them onto Barry the Baptist at the Sutton Coldfield Sunday Market Stall without any risk and no questions asked.'

(Barry the Baptist was a familiar figure in the Sutton Coldfield underworld. Like his namesake in the film 'Lock, Stock and Two Smoking Barrels', his specialist subject was half-drowning recalcitrant debtors by holding their heads underwater until they paid up. They don't mess around when it comes to unpaid debts in Sutton Coldfield, I can tell you.)

In any event, my fears were unfounded. The English Language, Mathematics and Computer Skills assessment proved to be a doddle. I suppose being an IT consultant for the previous thirty years might have helped matters, as would having English as my native language and the ability to total up an invoice in my head and calculate the result while subtracting a discount and adding VAT. Maybe I shouldn't have been so smug about it. There were a lot of people on the wing who didn't have the first idea about such matters.

'You've passed,' the assessment supervisor informed me. 'Not only that, but I don't think we've ever seen anyone in here scoring Level 3 (the highest level) in English Language, Mathematics and Computer Skills. You're obviously destined for great things.'

I detected a certain amount of cynicism in his voice. Hardly surprising, I suppose, given that I was ostensibly in HMP Thameside as a serial pigeon killer. Opportunities for career advancement in that field were limited, to say the least.

'Great things' might just mean making it to the end of my sentence without being brutally murdered by any number of inmates who might secretly be lifelong members of the internationally feared assassination department of the notorious RSPB.

I needn't have worried. The Royal Society for the Protection of Birds doesn't take any prisoners.

CHAPTER 24

A New Wing for the Pigeon

Monday 22 May 2017 – A couple of days after my assessment in English Language, Mathematics and Computer Skills, I was approached by a prison officer as I was preparing for another exciting, fun-filled day on the wing. I have heard it said that being in prison is like being in a combat zone with the army – long periods of boredom punctuated by short bursts of terror.

It's not a perfect analogy of course – for example, I hadn't as yet been issued with my own sniper rifle, nor indeed had I yet been enrolled on a high explosives handling course, but I dare say that the Howard League for Penal Reform would be addressing these very issues as I write.

Maintaining prisoners' morale is a high priority for the HLPR, and I am sure that a series of courses based on the correct handling of small arms, heavy machine guns and high explosives would have an overall positive effect on the mental well-being of most prisoners.

To be fair, the officers at HMP Thameside appeared to be working diligently to reduce the possibilities of boredom setting in, at least during 'times of association' when prisoners were allowed out of their cells. My cell-mate John was in the prison gym and pumping iron, and I was halfway through a game of chess with another inmate in the communal area.

The prison officer said to me, 'Get your stuff together. You're moving.'

I thought for a moment. 'Is this a good thing or a bad thing?' I asked. I had got used to the prison routine and there didn't seem to be any immediate threats to my well-being, but perhaps someone had complained that I was winning too many games of chess.

Was I likely to be thrown into solitary confinement with only bread to eat and water to drink until the end of my sentence? Or had someone at the RSPB – the Royal Society for the Protection of Birds – been pulling strings to have me transferred to a 'Cat A' prison with the other pigeon murderers?

The nearest Category A prison was HMP Belmarsh, just up the road from where I was in HMP Thameside. It wasn't all bad news, if that were to be the case. Maybe I could get the 'Mad Mullah' – Anjem Choudary – to sign my autograph book. He was currently cooling his heels in Belmarsh, serving a five-and-a-half-year sentence for glorifying terrorism. A signature from him in my autograph book would definitely earn me some brownie points at the next meeting of the Sutton Coldfield Wheel-Tappers and Shunters Social Club.

'We're moving you to Cat C,' said the officer, 'be ready in ten minutes.' On hearing this, I was somewhat relieved. Category C was one step down in terms of serious crime and psychopathic behaviour from Category B, and while it was not exactly a five-star upgrade to my current circumstances, the chances were that it wouldn't be any worse.

'Do you know why I'm being moved?' I asked.

He handed me a couple of prison-issue polythene bags. 'No idea. Orders from above.'

I was later to find out that Paul Weston, the chairman of Liberty GB, the organisation of which I had been Radio Officer, had written in no uncertain terms to the Governor of HMP Thameside, reminding him of his duty of care towards vulnerable prisoners such as myself.

By vulnerable, I don't mean physically or mentally weak – many years of studying the Japanese martial art of Aikido had toughened me up to the point where I could probably handle any sort of one-on-one confrontation – but the risk of large numbers of Muslims ganging up on me if the true nature of my conviction were discovered had obviously given the Governor pause for thought.

It would not look good for public relations if I were to be harassed – not to mention brutally slaughtered, systematically dismembered and turned into kebab meat for the benefit of the local Muslim prison population.

I scooped my belongings together into the large prison-issue polythene bags and was escorted out of the Category B prison block by two prison officers through an interminable series of imposing metal doors which were mysteriously unlocked as I approached and then locked again behind me.

Prison officers must spend years choreographing this seamless operation, although I never tested it to the point where they might be persuaded to unlock the main door leading to the outside of the prison. I thought that there would be little point pushing my luck at this stage in the process.

However, I determined that at the next opportunity I would recommend the officers as candidates for the forthcoming series of Strictly Come Door-Unlocking, an innovative TV entertainment series that I had invented during idle hours of reverie, and which I intended to host once I was released.

In my mind's eye, it would have all the attributes of a hit TV show, a cross between Strictly Come Dancing and Prison Break, but with more sequins and less of the brutal on-screen slaughter. I think that the officers of HMP Thameside would win it hands down.

I was led across the prison grounds, past the football field and the prison garden to another prison block, virtually identical in appearance to the one I had just left. I half expected to see a welcoming party with balloons, party poppers and signs on sticks saying 'You made it! Welcome to Category C!' but I was sadly disappointed. They might have at least baked me a cake.

The prison officers who had escorted me to the new block handed me over to another two prison officers. I hadn't been handcuffed or shackled, but obviously they weren't going to take any chances. A large sheaf of paperwork changed hands. One of the new officers scrutinised the paperwork carefully.

'Let's see. Oh, yes, Burton. You'll be in a cell on your own.' I still wasn't sure whether this was a good thing or a bad thing. Did this mean solitary confinement? Apparently not. 'Doors locked at 6:00 p.m. Open again at 7:45 a.m. for medication. Other than that you can use the communal area apart from lock-up and roll-call between

12:00 and 14:00. You're not going to cause us any trouble, are you?'

Trouble? Moi? 'I sincerely promise to be on my best behaviour, Officer.'

The officer regarded me with a certain degree of wariness. 'Is that right? Follow me, then.'

I was led to a cell on H-wing in the Category C block and the door was locked behind me. I surveyed my new surroundings for a moment or two. Not so very different from the Category B cell I had just vacated, I thought. On the desk in the corner was a battered-looking computer terminal, comprising of a screen, keyboard and mouse, which I had by now established was for use as an ordering system for meals and for general prison enquiries such as arranging library visits and medical requests.

The terminal also doubled as a TV, and it was perched precariously on the desk in the corner of the cell, next to four or five dog-eared hard-back books from the prison library. There was a single bunk (with the obligatory thin avocado green mattress and a pile of used bedding, presumably left behind by the previous inmate) and an open cupboard with shelves for personal belongings.

For ablutions, there was an en-suite shower area, toilet and hand basin. There was only one chair, which prompted me to note that it was going to make it difficult if I wanted to host any dinner parties in my cell. For that matter, there was a distinct lack of candelabra, napkins and wine glasses.

But more importantly, there was no kettle in the cell. This was going to be a problem. If I wanted to offer any of my guests a mug of tea or coffee I would have to make do with lukewarm water from the hot tap. Still, worse things happen at sea, I thought, and I started to unpack my belongings.

I reached into one of my polythene prison bags and extracted my precious co-axial cable. I plugged it in to the TV system and it immediately burst into life. It had apparently been pre-tuned for the mainstream TV channels! Things were looking up.

I switched to the DVD box-set channel. There was Series 1-4 of 'Line of Duty' (a gritty and realistic police detective drama series.) Hey, not bad at all! Better than 'Prison Break' by a long chalk. I could get used to this! And indeed, for the duration of my sentence, whenever I had nothing else to occupy me, I would watch the entire box set of 'Line of Duty' many times over, to the point where I could recite verbatim what words the characters were going to say before they actually said them.

I don't want you to think that this was all I had to do with my time. Over the next few weeks, I spent as much time as was allowed in the prison library and I tried to play as many games of chess as I could each day. In addition, I tried to set aside at least two hours a day for meditation – my Aikido training had acclimatised me to an hour every morning and every evening, and the hours of enforced solitude in my cell contributed immensely to the transition to a meditative state at those times.

Aikido meditation is a technique that is for everyone, not just for martial art enthusiasts. It is definitely worth cultivating as it brings long-term benefits to the average human frame. It simply involves positioning your body into a comfortable (and preferably kneeling or seated) relaxed stance, and then focusing on taking a series of deep, regular breaths until your mind drifts away from your immediate surroundings.

Once you have your breath under control – maybe four breath cycles in and out every minute, one every fifteen seconds or so, after about five or ten minutes your mind enters a different phase – and you start to leave behind material concerns and to be more open to contemplating a veritable wealth of abstract concepts, such as life, death and the meaning of the universe.

An hour or so of Aikido meditation really does bring with it a more positive outlook on life, no matter what your immediate circumstances may be, and I found it to be of immense help to me over the subsequent days and weeks, which at this moment appeared to be stretching interminably ahead.

As my Aikido teacher used to say – if a technique is not working for you, then your physical side may not be, at the moment, completely in tune with your spiritual side. His advice was always to persevere, for success will come eventually.

As I alluded to in a previous chapter, there is a Buddhist saying – 'When the student is ready, then the teacher will appear.'

> "When the student is ready,
> ...the teacher will appear"
>
> ~Buddha

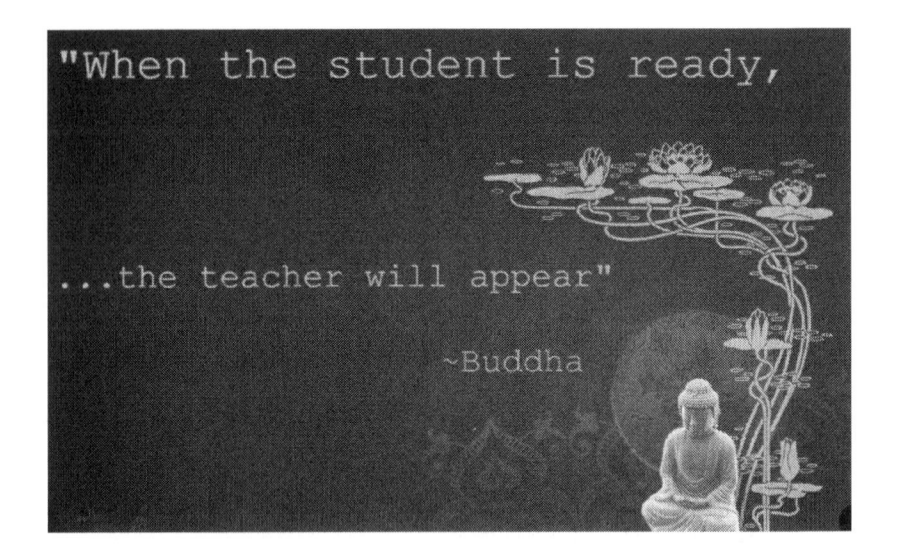

(I remember pulling this very statement – written on a piece of paper in the style of a Chinese fortune cookie – out of a Christmas cracker and reading it out in front of the family over a turkey dinner, when admittedly there was a high degree of inebriation and a certain lack of philosophical awareness around the table. The response was along the lines of – 'That can't be right! The teacher should be in the classroom waiting for the students to arrive!')

Sometimes you can lead a horse to water, but you can't make them drink.

***

The communal area was very similar to the Category B environment I had left behind, although over time I did notice that the Category C prisoners seemed more relaxed than those in Category B. There was very little aggressive confrontation between prisoners and guards, or between the prisoners themselves as far as I could see.

However, I reminded myself to be aware of the possible dangers from the Muslim population of around ten to fifteen per cent (as far as I could ascertain) in the Category C environment of HMP Thameside. It only needed one leak of the real reason behind my criminal conviction to the general prison population and I could be in real trouble.

I finished unpacking, left my cell and sat down at one of the communal tables with a chess-board in front of me. I had found that simply doing this was enough to pique the interest of at least a few of the chess aficionados on the wing. Sure enough, scenting new blood, a steady trickle of prisoners introduced themselves and challenged me to a series of chess games.

My chess-playing skills were still at a comparatively high level and over the next few days I managed to chalk up a respectable number of victories. Not too respectable though, it never does for the 'new boy' to appear too clever, something I had learned early on in my life while growing up and attending a typically middle-class English grammar school.

I remember one such 'new boy', Watkins Minor, who had been transferred to our school during the course of Year Six. He was a rotund, bespectacled boy with a mop of blond hair, and he appeared determined to demonstrate his superiority to the rest of us by coming top in all the school activities he participated in.

No doubt he felt that by demonstrating such superiority, reminiscent of Percy Bysshe Shelley's Ozymandias – 'Look on my works, ye mighty, and despair!' It would stand him in good stead during his remaining school years and earn him our undying admiration.

However, in the manner of most healthy pre-teenage boys with a sense of social justice in what was a typically middle-class English grammar school of the 1960s, we systematically disabused him of that notion with the standard school punishment of tarring and feathering, and then tying him up and locking him with a bicycle chain to the apple tree in the garden outside the school staff room.

Admittedly he was somewhat subdued for a few days after that, but I still maintain to this day that we probably did him a favour by teaching him such a valuable lesson so early in life.

All in all, 'Category C' life in HMP Thameside had much to recommend it. I wouldn't say that I would be sorry to leave at the end of my sentence, but I resolved to upgrade the facilities to at least a three-star rating on the travel site Trip Advisor.

As my imaginary Trip Advisor representative would say: 'So, Mr. Burton, how would you rate the facilities of Category C at HMP Thameside?'

Me: 'To be honest, I did notice some dust on the top of my wardrobe. It was only faintly detectable on the outside of my white glove, but it was definitely there. And the sheets on the bed should have been changed prior to my arrival. Other than that I would definitely give it three stars.'

Damn. I forgot to mention the lack of a kettle. But it was too late. The Trip Advisor representative (figuratively speaking) had left the cell, the door had been locked behind him, and there was the gradually diminishing sound of footsteps in the corridor outside, faintly reverberating until all that I could hear was the sound of silence.

CHAPTER 25

The Kettle

Thursday 25 May 2017 – I was settling into my new life on the wing of Category C block in HMP Thameside. It was Thursday morning, and I had assumed my accustomed position in the communal area, hunched over a chess board whilst drinking a lukewarm mug of tea – courtesy of the hot tap in my cell (in the absence of a dedicated desktop plug-in water-heating device.)

The absence of such a device (a.k.a. an electric kettle) was a nuisance, and I had been debating with myself for a couple of days about whether or not to lodge a complaint with my imaginary Trip Advisor representative.

No doubt he would have told me that electric kettles occupied a similar position on the HMP Thameside scale of desirable accoutrements as co-axial TV leads, Tasmanian alligator feathers and the excrement of rocking horses. I surmised that it was just one of those things I would have to put up with.

In the meantime I was simultaneously contemplating my next move against an opponent with all the charisma and chess-board skills of a village idiot on his day off. He had left his king exposed in a fool's-mate position, a basic error that was about to cost him dearly.

All of a sudden, a Muslim hove into view from the other end of the communal area. I noticed that he seemed to be heading in my direction.

This particular Muslim looked as though he was trying extremely hard to win the 'HMP Thameside Devout Muslim of the Year' award, and I felt that his appearance warranted further examination.

He was in possession of a large bushy black beard reaching halfway down his chest, which made him look like a Pakistani version of Father Christmas, but without the red suit and the accompanying jovial ho-ho-ho disposition.

He was wearing a multi-coloured prayer cap which looked as though it had been made in a kaleidoscope factory by an overzealous operative who had just been told that silver glitter was all the rage this year, and who had been instructed to spare no expense in the manufacturing process.

The final touch was a long khaki-coloured djellaba reaching down to his ankles – an ensemble which contrasted fetchingly with his olive-green fur-lined parka jacket and matching olive-green socks and fur-lined slippers.

Most tellingly, he also had the notorious terrorist instruction manual – in the form of a green and gold hard-backed Qur'an – tucked under his arm.

Yes, I thought, that was definitely a one hundred per cent stove-enamelled, copper-bottomed, dyed-in-the-wool Muslim without the shadow of a doubt.

He bore down on me with all the unnerving accuracy of an incoming Exocet missile zooming in on an unsuspecting squirrel. I braced myself for the worst. Just because someone sports a natty matching parka, socks and slippers combination, it doesn't mean that they aren't out to get you, and in prison it is a good idea to be on the alert and to prepare accordingly.

Never let it be said that life in prison makes you paranoid about such things.

'Hey Grandad,' he said – which I had found was the standard greeting for anyone over the age of sixty in the prison. 'My name is Rohani. Can you help me with my English language homework? I hear you're good at this. We need to complete all the tasks before my personal liaison officer visits next week, insh'allah.'

Word of my proficiency in the assessment process while I had been in the Category B section of the prison was something that had obviously spread quickly. However, something about his opening statement intrigued me.

Personal liaison officer? I thought. How come I didn't have a 'personal liaison officer'? I was rapidly coming to the conclusion that there was one rule for some people and another rule for others in the prison system. It was almost as if there was a privileged group of inmates whose demands and needs took priority over the rest of the prison population.

Now it would seem that 'personal liaison officers' could be added to this ever-growing list. No wonder conversions to Islam in prison were on the rise. If it had not been for the beguiling attractions of the young ladies of the South East London Gospel Choir (who were currently playing a starring role in the overnight maintenance of my nocturnal fantasies) then I could easily see how a conversion to the satanic world of Islam might be worth a try.

I'm only kidding. I am not so easily persuaded. It would take far more than the prospect of my own personal liaison officer for me to convert to a genocidal totalitarian ideology with global ambitions of supremacy.

Even the prospect of seventy-two virgins in Paradise wouldn't be enough. I am sure that most Muslims don't realise that seventy-two virgins imply the additional prospect of seventy-two potential mothers-in-law, ready to nag you for all eternity if you don't keep the house tidy, make sure that the lawn is mowed regularly and the hedges are kept neatly trimmed.

However, the delights of Islam obviously do appeal to many prison inmates. For example, it is not unknown for self-declared Muslims to enjoy a raft of extra privileges in British prisons, such as halal meals, extra time out of one's cell for communal prayer on a Friday, and even (in some of the more progressive prisons) toilets orientated to face away from Mecca on the grounds that if Muslims knowingly defecate while facing Mecca then it would be the first step on a slippery slope to eternal damnation.

The metaphor 'slippery slope' is probably not the most tactful one to use in such a context, but I am sure that you know what I mean.

While such privileges are no doubt meant to assuage religious sensitivities, it only encourages the Muslim community to consider themselves as superior to the rest of us mere mortals. Unfortunately this ridiculous notion is reinforced by the teachings in Islamic texts –

such as Qur'an 3:110 – where Muslims are informed that they are 'the best of people'.

That would be laughable if it weren't so tragic. Since when did the ideology of Islam produce people superior to any others on this planet, when even a casual glance at the statistics available reveals that in every country where the ideology of Muhammad holds sway, the inhabitants of that country are right at the bottom of virtually every measurable yardstick of success?

If the teachings of Qur'an 3:110 were not bad enough, another verse – Qur'an 98:6 –informs Muslims that non-believers are 'the worst of creatures'. Apologists for Islam frequently argue that this doesn't apply to each and every non-believer, only to those who reject Islam, 'even though they know it to be the one true religion' – which of course is nothing more than sophistry.

Sophistry, the use of clever but false arguments, with the specific intention of deceiving the unwary, are meat and drink to Muslims when it comes to defending Islam in front of non-believers. I know this from my own personal experiences leading up to the Birmingham Taqiyya Trial in April 2014 (which I describe in detail in Chapter 13).

All things considered, I was grateful that I had made the decision to keep the real reason for my detention to myself. A conviction for Religiously Aggravated Harassment might be somewhat complicated to explain to a devout Muslim, and I didn't want to generate any unnecessary ill-feeling whilst confined inside the enclosed space of HMP Thameside.

I glanced down at the chess board. The fool's-mate gambit would have to wait. I murmured my apologies to my opponent, and moved over to another table to sit opposite Rohani.

'So, you're the Pigeon, eh?' said Rohani. 'I have heard about you from my friends. You blow pigeons apart with a .44 Magnum, eh? Or was it a .50 Barrett? Like Dirty Harry, insh'allah. Maybe I should call you Dirty Harry.'

I wasn't about to enlighten him concerning the limitations of my armoury. This was because my trusty .22 air rifle was nowhere near approaching the capabilities of a .44 Magnum or indeed a .50 Barrett (with its 2,800 FPS muzzle velocity and effective range of over 2,000 yards, it is obviously the ideal weapon for discouraging our feathered friends from nesting under the roof panels, and I had resolved to save up for one after I had been released). 'Oh yes,' I said nonchalantly, 'no pigeon is safe from me and my .44 Magnum. Do you feel lucky, punk?'

I pointed my fingers at him and with my best Clint Eastwood impression, mimed the action of a hammer being pulled back on a .44 Magnum. It was obviously a good impression as far as impressions go.

Rohani regarded me impassively for a moment and then smiled broadly.

'Ha-ha! You and your famous British sense of humour! You and me are now good friends, yes? Now you can help me with this homework. I have to atone for my sins, insh'allah.'

Rohani's homework was indeed an act of atonement. It comprised a series of questions relating to his offences of car-jacking a few months earlier. It was obviously designed to appeal to the conscience of a wrong-doer.

There was of course – implicit in this process – the premise within the prison homework questionnaire that the conscience of a Muslim was identical to the conscience of a non-believer. This is not necessarily true and is a frankly dangerous supposition which is, in my humble opinion, at the root of many if not all the differences, fallacies and misapprehensions between Muslims and non-believers. They simply do not think the same way as we do, which is – without a doubt – due to the teachings of the Qur'an and the Islamic Prophet Muhammad.

This was not something I was about to point out to Rohani at this time. In my experience, Muslims for the most part do not take kindly to points of view that may disagree with the Qur'an or indeed disagree with the views or the behaviour of the Islamic Prophet Muhammad, no matter how heinous such views and behaviour may be to those of us brought up with the honourable and decent traditions of our Judaeo-Christian heritage.

I looked over Rohani's homework and started to read out some questions.

Question 1 – 'Describe how your victims must have felt when you attacked them in the street and stole their vehicle.'

Rohani: 'Yeah, I suppose they might have been a bit upset. But then that's infidels for you. Serves them right for having a posh motor though, innit.'

Me: 'No, Rohani, Muslim or not, they were more than likely extremely traumatised. It isn't nice having your prized possessions taken away from you by a knife-wielding psychopath.'

Rohani: 'Oh. Yes. Right. I suppose.'

Question 2 – 'Describe how your family must have felt when you were arrested for your crimes.'

Rohani: 'Yeah, well, they probably thought I was a chip off the old block. My dad was a senior commander in the Taliban, you know. He could shoot the eye out of a chicken at fifty paces. My mum was always telling him off about that. She needed those chickens for the eggs to sell at the market.'

Me: 'No, Rohani, as Muslims living in the West, they would have been extremely ashamed that you had failed to live up to the high standards expected of a well-integrated law-abiding citizen in a civilised democracy.'

Rohani: 'Oh. Yes. Right. I suppose.'

Question 3 – 'Describe what you would do if you were faced with the same situation in the future.'

Rohani: 'Yeah, well I would try harder not to get caught, wouldn't I?'

Me: 'No, Rohani, you would have seen the error of your ways and resolved to be a good citizen in the future by not stealing from other innocent law-abiding citizens, Muslims or not, and by making amends to your victims.'

Rohani: 'Oh. Yes. Right. I suppose – I suppose we had better be writing this down. My personal liaison officer will want to see this. Please write it down for me. You want a Kit-Kat?' He held out a chocolate bar in front of me. He obviously felt that I was easily bribed.

I sighed inwardly. This was going to be hard work. I could see that he was expecting me to be his personal scribe. To be fair, Rohani's handwriting and grasp of written English left something to be desired.

Not that my own handwriting was anything to write home about.

'What did you do with these vehicles that you car-jacked?' I asked. 'You obviously wouldn't be able to keep them for any length of time.'

'You'd be surprised,' said Rohani. 'My first cousin makes a good living churning out forged documents and cloned number plates – and my uncle has a chop shop in Bradford where you can get pretty much any car part that you might want.

'Not only that,' he said, warming to his theme, 'top-end Range Rovers and Jaguars fetch a fortune in the Middle East, where they are not so fussy about the paperwork. They are ever so easy to steal and disguise. I just change the plates and drive them to a container ship in Hull, where—'

'Don't tell me,' I said, 'you have a relative who is a container ship captain. And another one who is a Customs Officer, perhaps?'

Rohani smiled at me, a big gap-toothed smile full of innocence. 'I suppose some people might say that I shouldn't have got involved, but it's all part of the family business. In Islam, family is everything.'

He continued, 'And it was great fun! So much fun! The expressions on the infidels' faces when I held a knife to their throats and threatened to behead them! And of course I only ever stole cars from infidels, which is the most important thing, insh'allah.'

He uttered the last words with some trepidation, and glanced behind him, as if half-expecting to see the archangel Gabriel himself standing there, a frown etched into his brow and his wings gently rustling in disapproval as he thumbed through a sheaf of paperwork relating to a dodgy Range Rover.

Or worse still, a Range Rover that had mistakenly been taken from an innocent Muslim – which would have been in dire contradiction, naturally, of the numerous edicts concerning Range Rovers and other top-end vehicles that had been handed down by Allah over the centuries and subsequently incorporated into the Qur'an.

I was reminded of a well-known verse that had never made it into the Qur'an, having allegedly been written down on a palm leaf and eaten by a goat in the seventh century:

'O ye who believe! Never steal a camel from another Muslim, because he is your brother. But verily, the camel of the infidel is yours to do with what you will.

And one day that camel will have air conditioning, adjustable suspension and reclining seats, and you will be at ease while the infidel gnashes his teeth and walks upon the desert sands.'

Oh well, that's OK then, I thought. That's the most important thing. No Muslims had been harmed during the execution of these crimes. I could definitely see Rohani being a productive member of society when he was finally released. All things considered, I felt it was my civic duty to help him.

Not only that, but I felt that it was right to show some compassion. I could see that Rohani had been to Hull and back.

In any case, you never know when you might end up needing a particularly hard-to-come-by distributor cap for a Ferrari. Or more likely, a set of tasty alloy wheels and tyres and some furry dice to hang from the rear-view mirror of a souped-up Ford Fiesta. Last but not least, helping Rohani with answering the questions in his English Language homework wasn't entirely without its compensations.

A day or so later, there was a knock on my cell door. It was association time and the cell doors had been unlocked a few moments previously. A familiar face appeared.

'You want a kettle?' said Rohani, looking around my cell and expertly assessing my electrical appliances – or lack thereof. 'I can get you a kettle.'

To be fair, he was as good as his word, bringing me an electric kettle later on that day, and for the rest of my time in HMP Thameside I was able at least to brew up a decent cup of tea whenever I felt that I needed a little bit of cheering up.

I know what you're thinking – 'Why, that Tim Burton doesn't know he's born. When I was a nipper, my Uncle Albert had to do a ten-stretch in Winson Green for nicking smoked salmon off the fish counter at Tesco's, and he never had all the creature comforts that they lavish on prisoners these days. Electric kettles? Luxury. Uncle Albert was lucky if he was able to get a sup of tea out of a damp dish-cloth during all the time he was inside. Pampered, that's what that Tim Burton is.'

Well, if you are thinking that, you're probably right. But if you ever find yourself in a prison cell without a kettle, please feel free to write and let me know how much you enjoyed the experience.

CHAPTER 26

Visitors

Tuesday 30 May 2017 – For some weeks now I had been looking forward to the prospect of meeting someone from the outside, in the form of a process known in the prison as 'Visiting Time'.

For those of you familiar with soap operas such as Coronation Street, EastEnders and Emmerdale, where characters are being banged up every other week, and subsequently visited with a never-ending procession of their loved ones at little or no notice, it might seem like an obvious and integral part of the humane and considerate prison environment in the UK.

However, in reality the process is fraught with bear pits and elephant traps, no doubt designed to bring home to all those involved that incarceration is not meant to be a walk in the park, and communications with loved ones on the outside of the prison should be only conducted with extreme difficulty.

It wasn't all the fault of other people, as I was to find out. In order to initiate communication with people on the outside, it was necessary to employ a certain level of handwriting skills, in order just to send the most elementary of letters to prospective visitors on prison notepaper.

Although I had access to a computer terminal in my cell, there was no word processing software, no email software and no way of electronically communicating my thoughts to the outside world, so I would have to call on those very same handwriting skills, painstakingly perfected in the British educational system after years of being rapped over the knuckles with a wooden ruler by the formidable Mrs. Anderson, head of English at my local primary school, St Norberts in Carshalton Beeches, Surrey.

What could possibly go wrong, I hear you say? I will tell you what could go wrong. I used to win prizes for my handwriting skills at school, but half a century later I would find that those handwriting skills had deserted me.

Half a century of conducting my communications via a typewriter and a computer keyboard had left me with all the calligraphic skills of a dyslexic chimpanzee.

A chimpanzee, furthermore, who having been tasked with writing the complete works of Shakespeare, along with an infinite number of other chimpanzees, had unfortunately found it all to be too much to cope with, and seeing no other way out, had overdosed on a combination of crack cocaine and methylated spirits.

I had received letters from several good friend and colleagues who had expressed a desire to come and visit me, and all I could do was to scrawl a missive on prison notepaper that looked as though a demented spider had decided to dip its feet in an old-style ink-pot, dance the Light Fantastic across my notepad and gracefully expire in a blob of noxious fluid in the bottom right-hand corner, signing itself off with, 'All the best, because I know you'll miss me when you're next on the Web.'

I found this extremely disconcerting. As I said, I had won prizes at my school some fifty-odd years previously – at the time, I had invested in a plethora of Parker pens, numerous bottles of Indian ink and other writing implements – and with broad brush strokes, judiciously placed full stops, expertly located commas and quotation marks, I had swept the board with my calligraphic expertise.

Where had it all gone? I had no idea. The phrase 'use it or lose it' came to mind, and I resolved to recover my handwriting skills in prison by writing 'the quick brown fox jumps over the lazy dog' on innumerable sheets of notepaper every single day until I could at least write a coherent letter to someone on the outside.

In the meantime I had been fighting a running battle with the prison authorities to have them accept some nominated names, addresses and telephone numbers for potential communication. This was a problem because I was not allowed to communicate directly with anyone from Liberty GB, and it was only with great difficulty that I was able to nominate some good friends of mine, who I will from now on refer to as Margita, Emma and Charles (although not necessarily in that order).

These three fine people had attended my trial at Southwark Crown Court, and they had very kindly distributed the details of my trials and tribulations far and wide through the counter-jihad support network. Now, they had expressed a desire to come and visit me, and I had to pull out all the stops to make that happen.

I had to nominate the appropriate telephone numbers and have them approved – a process which took over a month – and once the approval came through, I had to set aside some of my weekly allowance to contact them via telephone and set up a meeting.

Every time you make a phone call from prison, it costs you a substantial sum which is deducted from your minuscule £15 weekly allowance, and setting up a meeting is a process fraught with difficulties which could have been derived from Dante's seventh circle of Hell.

My potential visitors then had to submit a request to the prison for a visit, the prison administrators would let me know, and then I had to inform the prison administrators that I would agree to such a meeting taking place.

It sounds simple, but as I said, it takes a long time to arrange. Of course, time is something that most prisoners have a lot of in HMP Thameside.

That the one proper visit I had took place at all was something of a miracle. (I don't count the visit from two SO-15 counter-terror officers that took place a couple of days earlier.)

On that occasion, I had been invited for an interview on a Sunday afternoon. I remember thinking that they must have been desperately short of some overtime payments to give up their Sunday afternoon to visit me in prison.

The two SO-15 counter-terrorism officers introduced themselves to me with a cheery, 'Don't worry; you're not in any trouble. We're just here to conduct a random survey on how you are being treated at HMP Thameside.'

The hackles on my neck rose. No police officer conducts a 'random survey'. Random surveys are the prerogative of organisations such as the statistical gatherers of information such as Pew and Mass Observation. The police only target people of specific interest.

'So how are you getting on?' said the first SO-15 counter-terrorism officer.

'I can't complain,' I said, 'but I can't help but wonder how you selected me for your visit to one of Her Majesty's Prisons. I'm sure you have better things to do.'

The officers looked at each other. 'Actually we wanted to ask you about what you were planning to do once you had been released,' said the second SO-15 counter-terrorism officer. 'You know, whether you had seen the error of your ways and were remorseful, or perhaps had decided to repent.'

Remorse and repentance might have been high up on their agenda, but it was not even on my radar. 'You must be joking,' I said, 'I am going to be making speeches, writing articles and transmitting my thoughts concerning Islam and its deleterious effects around the globe on radio, TV, social media and YouTube channels until the Grim Reaper knocks on my door and invites me to participate in some scythe-sharpening exercises.'

This was obviously not what they had wanted to hear. 'But why would you persist in publicly expressing anti-Islamic views after having been locked up?' said the first SO-15 counter-terrorism officer. 'And by the way, please call me Ray.' He gestured to his colleague. 'This is Dave, by the way.'

Ray and Dave were in for a surprise.

For the next forty-five minutes I proceeded to explain (quoting chapter and verse from the Qur'an) to Ray and Dave as to why the entire counter-terrorism narrative was flawed, and why they would never achieve any success while they clung to the view that Islam was at its core a 'peaceful religion.' (The reality of course being that it was a genocidal totalitarian ideology with ambitions of global supremacy at the expense of all non-believers.)

I also explained (again quoting chapter and verse from the Qur'an) that their media-inspired world-view where so-called 'Islamist terrorists' were essentially twisting and misinterpreting the so-called 'peaceful religion' to justify their violent attacks on non-believers –

was likewise essentially flawed.

I told them in no uncertain terms that I felt that it was my duty to make every single non-believer aware of the dangers of allowing the ideology of Islam to occupy the public space in any capacity whatsoever – even if that awareness meant that some politically incorrect decisions would have to be taken by those in power to maintain and reinforce national security.

I spoke of the need to halt Muslim immigration and to stop the building of new mosques, the need to monitor existing mosques, and the need to remove Muslims from positions of power in local and national government, the police, military, judiciary and educational infrastructure, primarily because of the divinely-commanded duty of every Muslim to promote Islam at the expense of the non-believer at every opportunity.

At the end of the forty-five-minute interview there was a stunned silence from the SO-15 counter-terrorism officers. 'You seem to know an awful lot more about Islam than all the other people – including Muslims – that we have talked to in recent months,' said Dave. 'Maybe we could talk to you again once you are on the outside in a couple of weeks?'

'Sure,' I said, 'no problem.' But they never followed it up. They did telephone me a few weeks later to claim that they had been called away on a more pressing engagement – would I mind very much if they postponed or cancelled their visit?

I could sympathise with the myriad priorities that the officers of SO-15 would have to deal with. Perhaps Anjem Choudary, the 'Mad Mullah', locked away up the road in Belmarsh, urgently needed somebody to clip his toenails.

***

The promised day for my contact with the outside world eventually arrived, and on the Tuesday before I was released, the visit from Charles, Margita and Emma took place.

It was an unforgettable experience.

It was up there with my earliest childhood recollections – of a day in the park with my parents in the summer sunshine, the day I managed to ride my bicycle without falling off, and the day I won first prize for my calligraphy at school.

(Then of course there was the day I made the acquaintance of a large number of very aggressive black and yellow winged insects whilst I was eating jam sandwiches *al fresco* and subsequently ended up at the local hospital A&E with multiple wasp stings.)

Well, maybe I wouldn't include that last one. However, they were memorable times.

The cell door was unlocked. 'Oi, Burton, you've got visitors.'

Two prison officers collected me from my cell. (Over the previous few weeks, everything involved in moving me from one place to another had been done in the presence of at least two prison officers. I was obviously a hardened criminal who – left to his own devices and with a series of mighty leaps and bounds – would stop at nothing to escape the clutches of the prison system.)

I was led to the preparation area and instructed to don a vivid fluorescent purple and yellow vest over the prison greens that I had been wearing for the previous four or five weeks.

I have to say that these colours clashed more than I would have liked. I could think of more than one camp performance artist from the world of theatre who would have said something along the lines of – 'Oh dear – that purple and yellow does NOT go with that green, darling.'

I don't wish to be overly melodramatic, but I could definitely see how that colour combination would produce nausea in someone of a delicate disposition.

From the preparation area, I was led to the visiting area and signed in using the secure fingerprint recognition system. I seriously considered the process that I would have to employ in the future if I were to make my escape (which would probably involve sawing off a prison officer's finger and using it to fool the fingerprint recognition process).

HMP Thameside Visiting Area

I'm only kidding. It's surprisingly difficult in prison to obtain a saw that would be suitable. I would probably have to resort biting the officer's finger off with my teeth.

You can see that I have thought this through.

(I was still using my own finger. I hadn't as yet found a prison officer prepared to donate a finger in exchange for a packet of cornflakes and a month's supply of toothpaste, which was all I had in the way of bargaining chips.)

Once I had been signed in via the secure fingerprint recognition system, I was then allocated a table number and was led to the seating area where my three visitors were waiting.

It seemed to me as if I had never met three more beautiful human beings in my entire life. When you have been incarcerated behind bars for almost six weeks, then you really appreciate the company of people who share your worldview, and Emma, Charles and Margita were together and separately the epitome of human kindness.

And I'm not just saying that because they bought coffee for me – proper vending-machine coffee too (supposedly meant for visitors only) and not the ersatz coffee supplied as standard for consumption by prisoners.

When I say this, I don't wish to cause unnecessary offence to the no doubt highly respected purveyors of coffee granules to the prison population of the UK. Also I suppose, at the end of the day I should have been grateful.

After all, I could have been restricted to a bread and water diet with the odd tin of tuna thrown in, along the lines of the treatment afforded to Tommy Robinson while he was incarcerated at HMP Onley.

But if the purveyors of coffee granules could have chosen something that tasted a bit more like coffee and a bit less like second-hand grit from the bottom of a budgie cage, then I'm sure it would have been met with much appreciation.

I sipped at my vending-machine coffee. Nectar from the Gods would not have tasted any better. We talked about all the things leading up to my trial, the trial itself and my subsequent imprisonment. I tried to make light of it but I started to get quite emotional, which is something that doesn't often happen to me.

I don't remember everything that I said, but in the heat of the moment I do remember hugging and kissing each of my visitors on the cheek several times more than I should have under the circumstances.

This produced a variety of interesting responses.

Emma was a strikingly beautiful young lady. She spoke perfect English with a slight trace of a German accent. She had beautiful blue-grey eyes that looked straight into your soul, and a flawless facial complexion that could have come straight from a Chanel cosmetic advertisement. As she was being subjected to my unwarranted attentions, she blushed fetchingly. I loved it.

Charles was a retired insurance underwriter and a professional musician. He was a quiet and thoughtful man, as straight as a die and around the same age as myself, which probably explained why he spluttered profusely at my thoroughly inappropriate exhibition of tactile enthusiasm.

Margita (who was married to Charles) seemed to take it all in her stride. As a college teacher (and as another strikingly beautiful woman with a soft and sexy Eastern European accent) she was no doubt used to having to fend off the attentions of randy old reprobates like me.

I only had a week to go before my release date, but I remember that I was ecstatic that these three wonderful people had taken time out of their busy day to visit me.

You know who you are, and you will always be in my thoughts.

The visit ended, and having said our goodbyes to each other, I was escorted out of the visiting area, across the courtyard back to the Category C block, and from there to my cell. The door clicked shut behind me with an air of finality, and I was alone once again.

CHAPTER 27

Release of the Pigeon

The soft, insistent beep from my digital wristwatch roused me from my slumbers. It was 6:30 a.m. on Friday 08 June 2017 – the day I had been informed that with good luck and a following wind, I ought to be released from the confines of HMP Thameside after having served six weeks of a twelve-week sentence.

'You never know, though,' one of the old lags had said to me a couple of days previously. 'They might let your release date come and go just for the hell of it. Why, only a couple of months ago there was a prisoner here who was due for release – that was a Friday too, as I remember – and they never let him out, or the next day, or the next one after that.

'When they finally came for him on the following Monday he was curled up in a foetal position in the corner of his cell, gibbering unintelligibly. It drove him clean round the bend, apparently. Still, I'm sure you're made of stronger stuff than that.' And at this point he looked me up and down with an expression on his face that suggested that he wasn't sure about it at all.

'Thanks very much for the encouragement,' I said. 'As it happens, I will be quite sorry to leave the Thameside Hilton. I've been made to feel very welcome.'

This was true insofar as nobody had yet attacked me with a razor blade, or had tried to poison me or to beat me up in my cell. With two days left to go on my sentence I was starting to get quite optimistic that I would be released without having to sign for a separate consignment of body parts that might be handed to me in a blood-stained plastic bag at the end of my stay.

I didn't know exactly what was likely to happen – some of the prisoners had said that the most common scenario was to release prisoners early in the morning; others had said that it was just as likely that I would be released last thing at night, just before lights out.

I have to say I didn't fancy that. Given that turn of events, I would have to negotiate my way around the streets of Plumstead in the dark, with all my worldly possessions in my rucksack and the prospect of footpads around every corner just waiting to pick off newly released prisoners, like cats waiting to pounce on unsuspecting baby pigeons as they ventured out of their nest for the first time.

Then again, with my reputation as a serial pigeon killer... They do say karma's a bitch.

As it transpired, I needn't have worried. I went through the usual routine – showered, shaved, dressed, meditated for an hour, and then released to pick up my medication at 7:45 a.m.

The young lady at the medication hatch consulted her computer. 'Looks like you'll be leaving us today, Timothy. You'll have to be a good boy from now on.'

I took the proffered medication and swallowed it with a sip of water from a small cardboard cup. 'I'll miss our friendly chats,' she said, and smiled as she turned away.

It is little things like that – a dash of human kindness in a world of sorrow – that keep you going.

I returned to my cell, sat on the bed and listened out for approaching footsteps. Sure enough, shortly after 8:30 a.m., a prison officer poked his head around the door of my cell and threw in two large, clear polythene bags.

'Get your stuff together, Burton. You're leaving in ten minutes.'

I grabbed everything that wasn't nailed down in my cell – apart from the mattress and bedding, which I decided in a sudden burst of altruism to leave for the next occupant – and started to shove it into the two clear polythene bags. There seemed to be a lot of stuff. I was going to have to leave some of it behind.

I was still trying to work out what to take and what to leave when the prison officer returned. 'Come on, Burton, it's not that difficult. Leave that kettle, you won't need that. And leave your TV co-axial cable. You won't need that. And those are prison library books, you won't need those either. Not unless you want to get arrested all over again for nicking prison property.'

I followed the officer out of the cell with my two polythene bags slung over my shoulder, and we made our way out of the building, one unlocked door at a time, into the warm June early morning sunshine.

The officer unlocked the gate to the Reception area, and handed me over to two other officers who were waiting for me.

'Follow me this way, Burton. We'll get you processed and then you can be on your way.'

I was led to a changing area and given another large polythene bag which looked familiar. It was the bag that I had last seen in the labyrinth underneath the Inner London Crown Court some six weeks previously, and it had my rucksack and all my own clothes in it. I changed out of my prison greens into my dark blue suit.

'Do you want to keep any of your prison clothes?' asked one of the officers.

I thought for a moment. Some people say that I have the acquisitive nature of a greedy jackdaw who has just won the opportunity to take part in a two-minute supermarket dash around Tesco, but I felt that being reminded of the prison every time I put on the green tracksuit or the white trainers for a night out on the town might be a step too far even for me.

'No, thanks, I'll leave them behind for someone else,' I said. 'I'm just glad my suit jacket and trousers still fit me after six weeks of haute cuisine at your establishment.'

In fact my suit jacket and trousers fitted me very well. A month and a half of high living at the Thameside Hilton had left me with the lean and svelte body of a whippet. I had lost over a stone in weight and if anyone from Slimming World, or Weight Watchers had come up to me at that very moment and asked me if there was anywhere I could recommend for them to hold their slimming classes, I would have replied that I knew just the place for them.

I stood in front of the same Senior Custody Officer that I had met on my way into the prison. The last time I laid eyes on him, his demeanour had been that of a bulldog who had been chewing on a wasp. This time he was all smiles and sunshine.

'Just sign here, Mr. Burton. This is to say you have received everything back that you arrived with, apart from your mobile phone. We'll give that back to you just as you step out of the prison gate. The batteries will probably be a bit flat by now, so you might want to find somewhere to charge them up. And no, you can't charge them in here. Here's the balance of your prison account in cash, including some expenses for today's meals, making a total of £83.06.

'And last but not least, here's your travel warrant to Birmingham. You'll need to report to the probation office no later than 15:00 this afternoon, or you'll be in breach of your probation conditions and could be returned to jail.'

'You can't be serious!' I said. I had calculated that it would probably take six hours to get back to Birmingham from Thameside, given that I would have to find my way to Plumstead station, catch a train from Plumstead into London's Cannon Street, make my way across London to Euston station, travel up to Birmingham via the Virgin Express and then find my way to the probation office from Birmingham New Street Station.

They were serious.

I looked at my watch. It was now 9:30 a.m. This was going to be a challenge.

Another prison officer escorted me to the gate leading to the outside world, and handed my mobile phone back to me as the gate slowly slid open. 'Don't come back,' he said, albeit in a friendly manner. 'Although we've enjoyed your company, it doesn't pay to push your luck.'

I was a free man once again.

The lady in the ticket office at Plumstead station scrutinised my travel warrant carefully. No doubt she was used to scallywags like me trying to hitch a free ride on Britain's rail network with forged travel documents. To be fair, the print quality of the travel warrant was low enough that a moderately good forger could probably use one to blag his way around the country for a long time without getting caught.

'So, you're going to Birmingham, then?' she asked warily, as if anyone wishing to travel to Birmingham was in dire need of some psychotherapy.

'Yes,' I replied. I could see her point. The Birmingham of today was not the same Birmingham that I had known some forty-seven years previously when I had arrived as a fresh-faced undergraduate to take up a course at Aston University studying geology. To be sure, the city had undergone a structural transformation, with new buildings and landscapes springing up everywhere, but there was now also a depressingly large number of Muslims.

When I say this, I don't want you to think that I have hostility towards Muslims as individuals. Certainly, I had made jokes at their expense which had later come back to bite me in court, but my attitude towards them could best be described as cautious rather than hostile, an attitude that is entirely justified considering the track record of Islam and its deleterious effects on non-Muslims over the past 1,400 years.

In my experience, when talking to Muslims as individuals, for the most part they exude an aura of civility and courtesy. However, as a demographic, they have brought with them to the West such vibrant cultural traditions as the brutal honour killings of their female relatives, the industrial-scale sexual grooming of non-Muslim children and the slaughtering of livestock in the street to mark the end of Ramadan.

This is not to mention a casual unfriendliness by many Muslims towards non-Muslims, as per the dictates of the Islamic ideology (which can be seen in Qur'an 5:51 and 60:4).

In addition, there is often an excessive degree of untidiness in and around the public areas in which the Muslims predominate, and an accompanying cavalier approach to public hygiene occasionally results in the outbreak of diseases which hitherto had been largely eradicated in the West, such as tuberculosis.

The observations concerning public hygiene and the excessive degree of untidiness are not simply based on 'unthinking prejudice', 'Islamophobia' or any other form of lazy stereotyping that some on the 'woke' end of the political spectrum might attribute to those of us who disagree with their left-wing philosophy.

To illustrate this, some years ago, a young council manager in charge of analysing various council reports in the City of Birmingham discovered that there was an unusually high concentration of garbage – up to five times what might normally be expected – accumulating on a regular basis in certain public areas of the city.

Reports were coming in from garbage truck personnel, street cleaners and other operatives responsible for keeping the city streets clean, to the effect that these areas were significantly untidy and a risk to public health. What could possibly be the cause?

After much thought, and having no doubt cross-referenced the phenomenon with other data relating to the city demographics, the manager came to the conclusion that the inhabitants of these areas, who were mostly immigrants rather than native Britons, merely needed a light educational course on the importance of keeping public areas tidy. He no doubt thought that a surge of public-spiritedness would be the result.

After all, he must have thought, the campaign to 'Keep Britain Tidy' had had an enormous positive effect on the country in the 1950s and 1960s, and while not every area might have been instantly transformed into a sparkling example of landscape management worthy of a 'Prettiest Village of the Year' award, it made most people realise how much more pleasant it was to live in a relatively clean and tidy area.

Imagine his surprise when, after having organised leaflets to be delivered to every household in the affected areas, the council was inundated with complaints from a certain section of the predominantly immigrant population.

In particular, leaders from various Muslim communities descended on the Town Hall to voice their indignation that Muslims could be tarred with the same brush as other immigrants or non-believers when it came to matters of public hygiene and cleanliness.

After all, went the argument, everyone knows that the Muslims are exemplary when it comes to cleanliness, washing five times a day before prayers and supplied with detailed instructions from the Islamic scriptures on how to keep themselves clean even in the most intimate of circumstances.

(I'm not kidding here. There are Islamic scripture-based articles on 'Muslim guidance on anal hygiene' available on the Internet which you can peruse if you are so inclined.)

Unsurprisingly perhaps, the point was missed in spectacular fashion. Just because one maintains a certain level of personal cleanliness, it does not necessarily translate to a high level of public-spiritedness, and one only has to look at any public area in any city in any Islamic country to see how true that is.

I don't know what became of that manager, but I don't think he won 'Council Worker of the Month' award. Some say that his head was put on a spike outside the Town Hall as a warning to others concerning the importance of appeasing Muslim sensitivities, but I am fairly sure that this is merely another unfounded and unsubstantiated rumour.

After a while, it is hardly surprising that a combination of these factors – unfriendliness, untidiness, a lack of public-spiritedness and other vibrant cultural traditions, some of which I alluded to earlier – makes the areas in which Muslims live unpalatable to most Westerners, which gives rise to the phenomenon that is often referred to as 'white flight' but which our political elites, the left-wing establishment and media inevitably put down to 'Islamophobia' and 'racism'.

The lady in the ticket office at Plumstead station slid the tickets across the counter to me. 'There's a train in seven minutes. You'll have to get your skates on to get across London. I bet they've pulled the old probation office challenge on you. They do that all the time.'

I laughed airily, as if the prospect of an imminent recall to prison was of little or no consequence to an old lag like me. But inside I was starting to become a little concerned. I had been hoping for more than just a few hours' freedom before I was recalled to prison on such a technicality.

However, just under five hours later, a few minutes before the allotted time of 3:00 p.m., I was ascending the steps just outside the Birmingham Probation Office. The train connections had been smooth and uneventful, and I had even had time to enjoy a mug of Virgin Rail's Earl Grey tea whilst charging up my mobile phone via a thoughtfully placed electrical socket next to my chair. After six weeks' incarceration, I felt that a little luxury was long overdue.

I had even had time to answer the accumulated six weeks' worth of text messages, many of which were from relatives and well-wishers, along the lines of, 'How did you get on at court today?', 'I called you but you didn't answer, please let me know how you got on at court today', and, 'I'm worried now, why haven't you called me to let me know how you got on at court today?'

These messages were not terribly surprising, as despite explicit instructions to my solicitor, he had failed to let my nearest and dearest know what had happened to me six weeks previously, and then, having realised his omission a couple of days later, told them that I was in Wandsworth, a completely different prison altogether.

I don't like to speak ill of my solicitor – at the end of the day, he was the solicitor who enabled my 2014 case (the Birmingham Taqiyya Trial) to reach its successful conclusion. But I suppose it's entirely possible that he had other things on his mind when it came to the 2017 trial – to the extent that he failed to keep up with my stream of enquiries during the run-up to the trial and on one occasion scheduled a Pre-Trial Preparation hearing with my barrister in London on the wrong day altogether. (Having kept the judge waiting at Southwark Crown Court for four hours while the mistake was rectified, I am surprised that he wasn't dragged out of his office to be hung, drawn and quartered as an example to others.)

But then again, I suppose we're all human. Although I still haven't forgiven him for landing me with Miss Bunny-Lover.

***

I made my way to the Birmingham Probation Office reception area and gave my details to the young lady behind the desk. She consulted her computer screen and then gave me a look of deep disapproval. 'Timothy Burton?' she said, in a piercing voice that would have had Genghis Khan trembling in his boots. 'You should have been here three hours ago.'

***

Genghis Khan arrives earlier than expected at the Birmingham Probation Office.

CHAPTER 28

A Year of Probation

For a moment, I had thought that my few hours of freedom 'on the outside' were going to be my last. Fortunately, however, the discrepancy of three hours alluded to by the young lady on the reception desk at the Birmingham Probation Office turned out to be an 'administrative mistake' (yeah, right, more likely a practical joke by the Thameside staff), which was just as well as I had no desire to be recalled to prison on the same day I had been released. I was escorted to a small office and offered a cup of coffee from the vending machine in the corridor outside.

'Wait there,' said the young lady from the reception desk. Her attitude seemed to have softened a bit. 'Your designated probation officer should be with you shortly.'

A few moments later, my designated probation officer walked in. His name was Mark and I warmed to him straightaway. We had a brief discussion about my circumstances and then spent the next twenty minutes discussing politics and philosophy.

He explained that for the next twelve months I would be under the supervision of the probation service. This was something that had only come into force relatively recently. Prior to that, the term of probation that I would have expected would only have been six weeks.

The door to the office opened and Mark's assistant came in with some notes about my case. She looked to be in her early twenties and was wearing long black robes and a hijab. 'This is Fatima,' said Mark, 'and she's training to be a fully qualified probation officer. Is it all right if she asks you a few questions?'

'Sure,' I said. This was going to be interesting.

The first thing I found was that Fatima had a very strange attitude towards the giving and taking of offence. 'It says here that the judge considered your remarks to Fizzy Mendacious to be grossly offensive. Don't you feel remorseful about that?'

'The first thing you have to realise is that the problem with Fizzy Mendacious,' I said, 'in common with a great many Muslims – present company excluded, I'm sure – is that he is extremely thin-skinned. The words I used were certainly mocking and satirical, but they were not threatening or intimidating, and only a complete wuss would have found them to be cause for alarm or distress.'

'But Mr. Mendacious found them to be very offensive!' She was clearly aghast at the idea that someone might offend a Muslim with impunity and not feel remorseful about it afterwards.

'Judging by his past behaviour, Mr. Mendacious finds a lot of things offensive,' I said, 'and the world would be a better place if certain people didn't go around looking for things to be offended by.

'In fact, there's a Buddhist quotation along those lines,' I said. 'Where would I find enough leather to cover the entire surface of the earth? But with leather soles beneath my feet, it's as if the whole world has been covered.' I delivered this quotation in a solemn, Zen-like voice.

Fatima stared at me for a moment. She was clearly lost for words. 'Excuse me,' she said, and she stood up abruptly and left the room.

'I don't think she's coming back,' I said.

'Not to worry,' said my probation officer cheerfully, 'just keep out of trouble and we'll send someone round to your house every couple of weeks to check up on you.'

I had every intention of keeping out of trouble.

Sure enough, a couple of weeks later, I had a visit from Sarah, a pleasant lady in her fifties who had been tasked to check up on all the rascals, scallywags and ne'er-do-wells in the Sutton Coldfield area. There were a lot of them, well, a lot of us, apparently. She had a workload of about 100 'clients' which meant about ten visits per day over a ten-day fortnight, so I resolved not to take up too much of her time. She seemed interested to know that I was going to challenge my conviction and sentence with the information that had come to light due to the perseverance of my supporters while I was in HMP Thameside.

Over the following twelve months she appeared on my doorstep, regular as clockwork, and ticked off the various boxes on her clipboard notes. Apparently I was the ideal 'client' with no terribly bad habits – at least none that would be likely to earn me another stay behind bars – and she always seemed pleased to see me and Mrs. B.

She credited Mrs. B. with keeping me out of trouble, and there was probably some truth in that. Mrs. B. had rescued me from myself on many occasions over the past few years, and without her my life would have been immeasurably poorer. Not that I'm ever going to tell her that of course, because it will go to her head.

One of the other things that happened a few weeks after I had been released was a visit from two police officers. Like Ray and Dave, they were from SO-15 (Counter-Terrorism) and they obviously wanted to make sure that I wasn't planning anything of a malign or vengeful nature.

I explained that I fully intended to keep spreading the word about the baleful ideology of Islam, and I explained in great detail, just as I had with Ray and Dave in Thameside, why we should make every non-Muslim aware of the threat that Islam poses to every free society and democracy in the West.

When I had finished, there was silence for a moment. 'Have you considered talking to an imam?' said one of the SO-15 officers. 'Maybe he would give you an alternative view of Islam that you haven't considered.'

'I'm sure he would,' I said, 'but there wouldn't be any point because of the doctrine of Taqiyya. I tell you what though – give him this list of "38 questions to ask a Muslim" by Hugh Fitzgerald from the New English Review, and see if he wants to discuss it face-to-face in a video interview.' I passed them the list of questions from my research folder.

The '38 questions to ask a Muslim' are designed to elicit a response that cannot but help to paint Islam in an unflattering light. They are fairly simple to present and mostly are of the most anodyne and simple-minded sort, but it is important that they are delivered in the most deeply sincere way. The idea is to draw out your Muslim interlocutor into a position where he has to defend a particularly unpalatable aspect of Islamic theology.

Of course, there is always the possibility that once your interlocutor realises that you actually know something about Islam, and that Taqiyya is out of the question, he might accuse you of being an 'Islamophobe' not interested in 'real dialogue', and attempt to inveigle any onlookers that there may happen to be to take his side against you, the troublemaker. You have to be ready with sweetness-and-light, affecting an innocent, 'Goodness gracious, my friend, I just want to know, that's all,' attitude, which definitely helps, in my experience, to keep the bystanders on your side and increasingly sceptical of the deceitful mountebank.

You should come prepared with a few dozen questions, to which you possess the answers, with the relevant supporting passages from the Qur'an or Hadith or Sira easily retrievable from your smartphone or note-cards. Even though your Muslim interlocutor sees that you are well-prepared, he can't cut you off right away; he's got to let you ask at least a few questions. He may try to find excuses to end the entire Q-and-A session, or at least to stop taking your questions. But that will make him look bad, which is precisely what you want.

All of a sudden, the Muslim who made such a big deal about his openness will show himself unwilling to answer perfectly reasonable questions. Your goal is to rattle him, to get him to try to cut you off in front of others, who will then realise that this business of 'Ask Me Anything' stops the minute anyone raises an unappetising aspect of Islam. You've spoiled his game, no matter what he does.

Anyway, that was the last I saw of the SO-15 officers – they never followed up with the idea of a video interview, which was a shame, because I'm sure it would have made great viewing. Hugh Fitzgerald has a list of 38 answers to go with the 38 questions, and they are all designed to make a typical Taqiyya-artist feel very uncomfortable.

In the meantime, my attempts to get the British legal system to recognise that I had grounds for appeal were proving to be an uphill struggle. I had written to Southwark Crown Court with all the relevant information, demanding that the CPS witness be charged with contempt of court for his failure to disclose his connections with the CPS to the court. I didn't hear anything for four months, despite writing and phoning repeatedly, and then I had an email back suggesting that it was not within the jurisdiction of the Crown Court, and that I should pursue it with the Queen's Bench Division of the High Court. I wrote to the Queen's Bench Division of the High Court, and received no reply whatsoever.

I even wrote to the Royal Courts of Justice – I have an old school friend who is a Master at the Royal Courts of Justice – but still no luck.

This didn't entirely surprise me, as I had found out that the CPS expert witness had given evidence in a number of high-profile terrorism cases under similar circumstances, which meant that if my conviction were to be overturned, then those cases would need to be re-visited as well, which would have been terribly embarrassing for the Government of the day. The order had most likely been given to make sure that my complaint went to the bottom of the pile and that it should never see the light of day.

I even tried initiating a private prosecution, which was shut down in fairly short order by a judge at the Birmingham Magistrates' Court. He was of the opinion that the CPS expert witness had not acted maliciously when he failed to disclose his connections, and threw my case out. This was actually wrong in law, because the 'intent' was not the issue; it was the act of non-disclosure that was punishable, no matter the reason.

At the time of writing I am gathering the resources to challenge the British legal system further. As I have discovered, trying to negotiate and challenge the legal system is an expensive business, and I know of various people who have spent hundreds of thousands of pounds on such endeavours to no avail.

However, I have the added incentive of incorporating into my complaint a challenge to the status of Islam in the UK – not many people know this, but the status of Islam as a religion has never been tested in the courts. We assume it is a religion because that is what Muslims themselves have told us, but religions have to follow the Golden Rule (do unto others as you would have done unto you) and Islam does not follow that rule.

As things stand at the moment, there is probably no judge in the land who would put his head above the parapet and declare Islam to be 'not a religion' – but times change, and once the concepts of political correctness and multiculturalism have been consigned to the dustbin of history, then we may see a return to common sense and the banning of Islam from the public arena in the West.

For people are free to believe whatever they want – that the moon is made of green cheese, that the earth is flat – as long as the manifestation of their belief system does not impinge on other people. Unfortunately Islam encourages its followers to impose their beliefs on others, and as we have seen over 1,400 years of Islamic history, that never ends well for us non-Muslims.

Civilisations all over the Middle East, from North Africa to India and beyond, have been ground into dust by the advance of this totalitarian ideology over the past 1,400 years. The process has not always been the same – sometimes there have been outright conquests of countries by Islam through war – but what we have seen in recent decades in Western countries is a process of gradual colonisation, where Muslims have initially presented themselves as peaceful, and then changed tactics as they grow their numbers.

This process has been well documented by Dr. Peter Hammond in a book entitled *Slavery, Terrorism and Islam* – and to summarise, as long as the Muslim population remains around 1% of any given country they are likely to be regarded as a peace-loving minority and not as a threat to anyone. In fact, they may be featured in articles and films, stereotyped for their colourful uniqueness, as up to relatively recently in the United States, Australia and Canada.

However, at 2% and 3% they begin to proselytise from other ethnic minorities and disaffected groups with major recruiting from the jails and among street gangs, as in Denmark, Norway and Spain:

From 5% on they exercise an inordinate influence in proportion to their percentage of the population, which is approximately where we are in the UK at the time of writing.

They will push for the introduction of halal (clean by Islamic standards) food, thereby securing food preparation jobs for Muslims. They will increase pressure on supermarket chains to feature it on their shelves – along with threats for failure to comply, as in Switzerland, the United Kingdom and the Philippines.

At this point, they will work to get the ruling government to allow them to rule themselves under Sharia, the Islamic Law. The ultimate goal of Islam is not to convert the world but to establish Sharia law over the entire world.

When Muslims reach 10% of the population, they will increase lawlessness as a means of complaint about their conditions, for example, car-burnings in many large cities in France. Any non-Muslim action that offends Islam will result in uprisings and threats, as in the case of the infamous 'Mohammed cartoons' a few years ago.

After Muslims reach 20% of the population, one may expect hair-trigger rioting, jihad militia formations, sporadic killings and church and synagogue burning, as in Nigeria and Ethiopia.

At 40% you will find widespread massacres, chronic terror attacks and ongoing militia warfare, as in Bosnia, Chad and Lebanon.

From 60% you may expect unfettered persecution of non-believers and other religions, sporadic ethnic cleansing (genocide), use of Sharia Law as a weapon and the enforcement of Jizya, the tax placed on infidels, as in Iraq and the Sudan.

After 80% you can expect state-run ethnic cleansing and genocide, as in Bangladesh, Egypt, Gaza, Indonesia, Iran, Jordan, Morocco, Pakistan, Syria, and Turkey.

100% will usher in the peace of 'Dar-es-Salaam' – the Islamic House of Peace – (there's supposed to be peace because everybody is a Muslim) as in Afghanistan, Saudi Arabia, Somalia and Yemen.

Of course, that's not actually the case. To satisfy their blood lust, Muslims then start killing each other for a variety of reasons.

This is why the Islamisation of the West in general, and the UK in particular, must be resisted. The iniquitous process of Islamisation must not only stop, it must be reversed, otherwise our Judaeo-Christian civilisation, arguably the most advanced civilisation that the world has ever seen, will suffer the same fate as the Persians, the Byzantines, and the other civilisations of old that I alluded to earlier, and disappear forever.

What follows next (as an appendix) is a series of essays written over the past seven years or so, discussing various aspects of the topics that I have touched upon in this book. I hope that you will find them to be of interest and that you will be inspired to find out more about the subject of Political Islam and the ideology that underpins it.

Know your enemy – and remember the words of Sun Tzu – *'If you know the enemy and know yourself, you need not fear the result of a hundred battles. If you know yourself but not the enemy, for every victory gained you will also suffer a defeat. If you know neither the enemy nor yourself, you will succumb in every battle.'*

Dear reader, we must stand together now, you and I – for if we do not stand together against the greatest threat that our civilisation has ever known – then who will protect our children and grandchildren, and safeguard their legacy for future generations?

APPENDIX

Essays from the Dark Side

Contents:

Essay – What should we do about the Muslims living among us? (Part 1 of 2)

Essay – What should we do about the Muslims living among us? (Part 2 of 2)

Essay – Why Islam should not be considered as a Religion under UK law

Essay – The Problematic Definition of Islamophobia (Part 1)

Essay – The Problematic Definition of Islamophobia (Part 2)

Essay – The Problematic Definition of Islamophobia (Part 3)

What should we do about the Muslims living among us?

Part 1 of 2

In our civilised Western democracies, based as they are on Judaeo-Christian principles, we have many Muslims who are undoubtedly as innocent of terrorism, political subversion, and Islamic supremacism as we are ourselves. But we have a problem, don't we? These innocent fellow countrymen of ours – as well as the terrorists, subversives, and supremacists – all call themselves 'Muslims'.

Many non-Muslims explain the situation to themselves that 'there are extremists in every religion' and let it go at that. But those of us who have studied Islamic doctrine and Islamic history have discovered that 'letting it go at that' would be a big mistake. And of course, those who simply look at the news can see that there must be something about Islam that produces more 'extremists' than other religions.

In fact, the so-called 'extremists' are no more 'extreme' than many devout followers of other religions. The difference is that the teachings devout Muslims follow are more definitively hostile toward non-believers than the teachings of any other mainstream religion.

So we are in a quandary, and so are the innocents who call themselves Muslims (but who ignore or are unaware of Islam's intolerant teachings). We don't want to make the mistake of over-generalising and becoming hostile to someone just because he says he's a Muslim. But equally we don't want to support or encourage or befriend a Muslim who is following the teachings of the Qur'an. This is because the Qur'an says that it is okay to pretend to be a non-

Muslim's friend, but to never actually be their friend, and it also says 'kill the unbelievers wherever you find them'. These are not the beliefs or motivations we want in a friend, or in someone we invite home to dinner, or even in someone we speak freely with.

We know how to deal with orthodox Muslims who are actively pushing for concessions from the West, but what about in our personal lives? Should we live in suspicion of all Muslims? Should we automatically hate someone we know is a Muslim? Would you want to live that way? No, probably not. Should you ignore what you know about Islamic doctrine and treat everyone the same? That doesn't seem sensible either.

We're in a real quandary, and so are heterodox Muslims who have rejected the worst of Muhammad's teachings.

Our difficulty can be resolved with a simple change in our personal policy. We can consistently treat the Muslims among us a particular way and it will solve our problem and hopefully bring this issue into the light of day where we can reasonably deal with it like adults.

Before I describe the personal policy I advocate, I need to clarify something. An 'innocent Muslim' – or what has often been called a 'moderate Muslim' – would necessarily have to reject jihad except in the sense of a 'personal inner struggle'. That would be a Muslim who rejects (or is unaware of) 97 per cent of the references to jihad in the Hadith. For a Muslim to be truly innocent, she or he must reject (or be unaware of) much of the 'sacred' example of Muhammad, which means rejecting (or being unaware of) the 91 passages in the Qur'an that tell Muslims to follow Muhammad's example.

An innocent Muslim must also reject (or be unaware of) the intolerance, hatred, and violence toward non-Muslims in the Qur'an. And an innocent Muslim would reject (or be unaware of) the subordinated position of women in Islamic doctrine.

For any non-Muslim who has studied Islamic doctrine, the above description is a reasonable starting point for a Muslim we can welcome in our midst.

What brought this up was reflecting over the last eighteen years, as I describe in Chapter 8 – Ground Zero. And in that time, I and many others in the counter-jihad movement have heard from hundreds of Muslims, all of them arguing that we don't know what we're talking about because 'true Islam' is peaceful and tolerant.

In all that time, we have never heard from a Muslim – not once – anything that acknowledged the existence of the immense number of passages in the Qur'an that non-Muslims find disagreeable – passages that anyone with an IQ over seventy could understand are disagreeable to non-Muslims. And not once have any of these Muslims acknowledged the existence of the egregious example of Muhammad – an example anyone with the slightest amount of human empathy would understand might be offensive or even frightening to non-Muslims.

What we've heard again and again was – that it's all taken out of context, and that the terrorists have it all wrong and nobody else except the terrorists believe in or follow such teachings, or the teachings don't exist.

Over the years we've come across an infinitesimally small number of genuinely jihad-rejecting Muslims. And of course, if someone genuinely rejects the hatred, political ambition and calls to violence in Islamic doctrine, they don't complain to us about what we write here on counterjihadwarrior.com. They don't have a problem with criticism of Islamic doctrine (they are strong critics of the doctrine themselves).

But after rejecting so much of Islam (given our definition of an 'innocent Muslim' above), even Muslims have a hard time understanding why such a person would call himself a 'Muslim,' but who are we to say how any person should define himself?

HERE IS THE SOLUTION

Our primary problem is that we don't know how to treat the Muslims in our midst, and the 'innocent Muslims' don't know how to identify themselves as 'jihad-rejecting Muslims'. Here is the solution: We should stop coddling the innocent Muslims and start being very matter-of-fact about our situation. We need to stop talking around this issue. We need to stop avoiding the source of the problem. We need to deal with Muslims forthrightly with this attitude: 'you either firmly reject jihad or we must assume you embrace it. It is counterproductive for everyone for us to bend over backwards trying to prove how tolerant we are.'

If Muslims want to be welcomed into this society, they need to start standing up and making their voices heard. They must openly acknowledge and unambiguously and categorically reject the hatred, misogyny, and violence in their core doctrines, or we must assume they don't.

Many of us are reading their source books. We know the doctrine. We would be foolish not to assume a Muslim believes in Islamic doctrine. So it is up to Muslims to tell us they do not believe in that doctrine, and to say specifically which parts of the doctrine they do not endorse.

What we require is that Muslims openly reassure us as to where their loyalties lie. Has anyone ever heard any Muslim do this at any time over the last eighteen years? And yet Muslims are in a far worse situation than they need be. They claim to experience a great deal of suspicion and hostility in our society – and polls do indeed show that levels of suspicion and hostility are increasing. But what do Muslims do? Usually they blame us for the suspicion and hostility, and imply that the problem is 'Islamophobia' or our lack of 'tolerance'.

So here's the situation: We've become aware of Islamic doctrine and we don't like it, so we naturally wonder where the Muslims among us stand. But instead of saying, 'We acknowledge the intolerance and violence of our core doctrines, and we reject them totally,' Muslims tend to open up with hostility, and so deepen our suspicions. The hostility and finger-pointing and the avoidance of honesty are exactly what we would expect from someone who believes in the supremacist, intolerant teachings of Islam.

And weak, vague assurances are not good enough. Statements such as 'we reject the killing of innocents' don't work anymore because too many of us know already that nowhere in the Qur'an does it imply non-Muslims are innocent. It implies just the opposite.

Muslims need to be clear and explicit, and we need to demand that of them without apology. From a non-Muslim's perspective, our open demand for honesty is a rational response to the facts, and nothing to be embarrassed about.

We need to make it clear what someone must do to be welcome in this society if they call themselves a Muslim. And we need to be clear that our 'tough-love' attitude toward them is a sane response to what we know of their ideology.

Imagine you were putting an avowed communist in charge of running the country, or involved at a senior level in law enforcement, or in counter-terrorism, or in the police or the military, or in local government, or in teaching our children, or even in writing school textbooks. You wouldn't do it without very firm assurances from him that he completely rejects the basic tenets and the economic model of communism. You have to demand that assurance because you are familiar with the basic tenets of the communist ideology.

You have to assume when someone says he's a communist that he believes in the communist ideology. It's an assumption we can take for granted. Otherwise, what does it mean to say you're a communist?

That's what it means: That you believe in the communist ideology.

It is exactly the same with Islam: You say you're a Muslim. That means you believe in the Islamic ideology. That, in itself, is not a problem. Everyone should be free to believe whatever they want. However, we are familiar with Islam's teachings. So no, we don't want you running the country, or involved at a senior level in law enforcement, or in counter-terrorism, or in the police or the military, or in local government, or in teaching our children, or even in writing school textbooks, unless you can assure us about what parts of that ideology you reject. This should be plain common sense, but of course, it only makes sense to someone who is familiar with the Islamic ideology.

If you assume it is impossible for a religion to advocate intolerance, supremacism, misogyny and violence to non-believers, this policy and this attitude would not make sense. If you assume the teachings of any religion could be used to justify anything, it would not make sense to you either. But if you are a non-Muslim and you've read the Qur'an, you know what I'm talking about.

Others are coming to the same conclusion, and I've seen many more direct challenges to Muslims who say they are moderate. They are being asked pointed questions like, 'Do you repudiate what Hamas is doing in Gaza?' and, 'I am a Buddhist; do you consider me to be a kafir?' These are steps in the right direction.

But more interviewers need to become educated enough about Islam that they can ask stronger, more specific questions. And this challenge needs to become incessant from all of us, everywhere. Muslims must be made to face the discomfort. They must realise they have to come right out and say, 'Yes, there is a political agenda in Islam, and I completely reject it,' or they will not be welcomed or trusted (let alone invited to any misguided 'interfaith dialogues for peace and understanding').

For someone who is unfamiliar with Islamic doctrine, all this would sound terrible and unfair, but surely we would do the same for any person who openly declared their endorsement of a seditious or treasonous or intolerant or violent ideology and who wanted to live among us as equals.

What should we do about

the Muslims living among us?

Part 2 of 2

In Part 1 of this essay I outlined the nature of the problem we face concerning the Islamisation of our civilised societies. There is a solution, but it requires both political will on our side, and a minimum level of goodwill on the other side. It should not be beyond the wit of man to make this work, but as with any enterprise, it is prudent to explore any and all potential obstacles so that they may more readily be overcome. Part Two deals with this exploration.

WHY THE 'TOUGH LOVE' ATTITUDE IS NECESSARY

There are three main reasons behind the reluctance of Muslims to say what parts of Islamic doctrine they reject:

1. It says in the Islamic doctrine they can't reject any part of the Islamic doctrine.

2. They fear for their lives. According to Islamic doctrine, the penalty for apostasy is death. They might also merely fear to be ostracised by their community. Heterodoxy, even if not accompanied by the death penalty, can be socially penalised severely in Muslim communities.

3. They don't reject it. They are going along with the Western society program until Muslims have greater political strength, at which time, they will start applying the political, supremacist teachings of

Islam. This approach must not be discounted, given the history of Islam and Jihad, and the patterns of modern Islamisation. (See Dr. Peter Hammond's discussion of this phenomenon in Chapter 28 of this book, where he describes very clearly the stages of Islamisation as the Muslim population increases.)

It would take a very brave person, even if he was truly one who rejected jihad, to volunteer an admission of apostasy. We must, in a sense, force their hand and then help protect those who reject jihad from the very real risk of reprisals.

This issue must be forced into the open or we will continue to suffer in a confused and paralysed limbo while orthodox Muslims paint all of us into a corner (the non-Muslims and jihad-rejecting Muslims alike) by continuing their Islamisation of the West.

SUSPICION AND HOSTILITY

In numerous videos and TV programmes exploring the attitudes of British Muslims, most of whom present themselves as regular British citizens, the Muslims often seem baffled as to why non-Muslims might look at them suspiciously, but they also often seem equally self-righteous about how silly and misguided that is, and not one of the British Muslims in the videos or TV programmes so much as mentions the supremacism and intolerance at the core of their doctrines. Worse still, they act as if no such doctrines existed. They act as if such a notion was preposterous.

One Muslim woman in one of the videos even pointed out that believers of other religions don't get this kind of scrutiny or prejudice. Statements like this need to be robustly challenged. An appropriate response would be – 'That's right. It's been a long time since anyone worried about the Methodists or Lutherans rioting, beheading people, flying planes into buildings, infiltrating governments, threatening violence to silence their critics, changing the contents of public school textbooks, or blowing up trains and buses. You shouldn't be surprised if your ideology comes under scrutiny. Ideology actually counts for something.'

We don't have a situation where religions are all the same but one is being picked on unfairly. We have a situation where most religions share many principles about universal love and kindness, but Islam does not. According to Islamic doctrine, Muslims are the best of people – and non-Muslims are the worst of people who deserve to suffer in this life and burn in the afterlife.

One Muslim man in one of the videos implies that if only people could get to know him and his family, their suspicions would disappear. Again, statements like this need to be robustly challenged. An appropriate response would be – 'Whether or not your family members are personable is not what concerns us. We wonder whether you believe in jihad in any form. We wonder whether you pay your zakat and thus potentially fund suicide bombers. We wonder whether you participate in Muslim organisations under the umbrella of the Muslim Brotherhood and we wonder whether you've aligned yourself with the Brotherhood's goal to sabotage and undermine our government. We wonder if you believe in reverse integration and if you're striving in the way of Allah to Islamise our country as the Qur'an commands you to do. We wonder whether you follow the Qur'anic teachings to never make friends with non-Muslims – to go ahead and fake it, but never actually befriend them or like them.'

If he is actively working toward Islam's prime directive, no amount of 'getting to know him and his family' will matter. What might matter is if he acknowledged those teachings and told us he rejected them. That would at least be a start. But in the video, you hear nothing that even approaches that level of honesty.

If these British Muslims are really so baffled, they should read their own doctrines. And if they have read them, their 'bafflement' is a deceit because anyone reading the Qur'an or Muhammad's words and deeds would not be baffled in the slightest. It would be obvious what non-Muslims don't like about it.

THE NEXT GENERATION

Why does it matter? These Muslims are not a threat to national security, are they? Why not let them continue in their innocence?

Because they are having children, and in a recent study in Britain, researchers found that second-generation Muslims are more 'radical' than their immigrant parents. That is, they hold more orthodox views. In other words, they believe in Islam's prime directive. They are more committed to jihad than their first-generation parents.

Why would this be? Because all these 'perfectly nice Muslims' in the videos are raising their children without ever telling them that supremacist and intolerant teachings are strewn throughout the Qur'an and Sunnah, and without saying, 'But we completely reject those teachings.' No, they say nothing of the sort. They do just the opposite. They tell them being a Muslim is wonderful, that the Qur'an is the word of the Almighty, and that Muslims are being unfairly persecuted by non-Muslims around the world.

So our young Muslim grows up alienated from his surrounding culture and ignorant of Islamic doctrine and yet considering it an elemental foundation of his identity that he is a Muslim. This makes him fairly easy to recruit by devout Muslims who simply tell the kid to read the Qur'an and discover his obligations as a Muslim. The teenager is only too eager to see his parents as hypocrites, and becomes a devout Muslim, committed to jihad like it says in the Qur'an he is supposed to be. The result: Second-generation Muslims are more radical than their immigrant parents.

We are constantly being reassured with bland statements from our political elites, the mainstream media, church leaders, university professors and many so-called 'Muslim moderates', along the lines of 'frank reappraisals of the Qur'an are under way, some of which include a tougher look at its calls for militancy.' They present these statements as though they should put all our worries to rest.

Some Muslims are taking a tougher look? That is not a big relief. Islamic doctrines are clear, straightforward, and easy to find. They don't need to be 'looked at' – they have been looked at, studied, memorised, clarified, and analysed for 1,400 years. And they were pretty clear and straightforward to begin with. They don't need to be looked at. They need to be vociferously repudiated, explicitly and forcefully.

Violent and intolerant teachings in Islamic doctrine are not superfluous addenda that can be easily discarded; they are embedded deep in the core of Islam throughout its doctrine and throughout its history. And orthodox Muslims are acting on these passages all over the world, killing people, destroying property, wrecking lives, and worming their way into positions of power. They're doing it right now, today.

Someone will die today because of these doctrines. By any definition, the situation is urgent. A 'tougher look' doesn't cut it. Not even close. Do our political elites, the mainstream media, church leaders, university professors and the many 'Muslim moderates' really think we can all relax now because some Muslim intellectuals at a few universities are taking a 'tougher look'? You must be joking.

IMMIGRATION

Another common complaint is that Muslim immigrants are not treated equally or fairly in our Western societies. It is especially important to address this point given the tidal wave of Muslim immigration that has taken place in Europe ever since 2015, when the German chancellor Angela Merkel opened the floodgates to so-called 'refugees'.

Quite apart from the fact that around 85% of these 'refugees' are young Muslim men of fighting age, rather than families with children, the tsunami of immigration has brought with it enormously increased levels of criminality, delinquency and fanaticism. We are supposed to feel sorry for them. But if they feel that they are being unfairly treated, then they should prove people wrong, just like every immigrant group before has had to do.

Almost everywhere, when immigrants arrive on foreign shores, they face prejudice. However, if they work hard and prove themselves loyal members of that society, they are eventually accepted and embraced.

That's how it works. You want to be on our team? Then prove yourself worthy. We don't owe you anything. We've already let you move here – the rest is up to you. If anything, you owe us.

To every immigrant, we should say this: we know the ideology you supposedly believe in. You say you're a Muslim. We naturally assume you believe in Islam. We assume you are an adherent of Islamic doctrine, which would mean you believe in the supremacism and intolerance inherent in your ideology. Either stop calling yourself a Muslim or explicitly say, 'I reject jihad, I reject Muhammad's political, supremacist model, and I embrace Western values of freedom, women's rights, religious equality, etc.' It takes all of ten seconds to say that, so what's the problem? If you can't honestly say those things, then our suspicions are correct, so stop whining and get used to permanent rejection because you do not belong in this society.

DISCRIMINATION

We are frequently told that we should not discriminate on the basis of religion, and most Western countries have laws against unfair discrimination of this type. However, the public declaration of ideology through one's actions and behaviour (including the way one dresses in public) will always influence the behavioural response of others.

When you know something about an ideology, you treat the person differently, and so you should. You don't feed a Jain a steak dinner when they come to your house (Jains believe you should not kill any living creature). You don't invite a Buddhist with you on a deer hunt (Buddhists refrain from harming living beings).

If you know about someone's ideology, you usually will (and definitely should) treat them differently.

And in the same way, if someone's ideology calls for unrelenting jihad against non-Muslims until the whole world submits to Islamic law, generally speaking, you don't invite them to come live in your country and bring their wives. And if they are already in your country, you usually will (and definitely should) be wary of them until they prove their devotion and loyalty to your country and the principles your society is founded on.

This should be common sense. If it doesn't make sense to you, your first step should be to read the Qur'an, together with commentary from Robert Spencer and Bill Warner.

For those who categorically reject jihad in their speech and action, we should treat them like anyone else. No better, no worse.

I know many will think, 'I don't care what they say. They could be lying.' And of course that's true. But this is the place to start. The next step is to see if their actions match their words. This is true with anyone. If someone says they are on your team, you don't automatically trust them with your children. You get to know them. If their behaviour doesn't match what they say, you stop trusting them, just as you should.

But the point is, none of us should be at all shy about speaking frankly about the principles in Islamic doctrine. Speak openly about it, and ask Muslims directly where they stand.

This policy will be hard on everyone in the short run but ultimately it will solve a huge problem we now face, which is that heterodox Muslims are reluctant to speak up about what they really believe, and that leaves us not knowing how to treat them. Who is committed to jihad and who isn't? We don't know who to trust or how to treat them. We are collectively filled with an awkward uncertainty about Islam.

Meanwhile, true believers in jihad are busy facilitating the Islamisation of the West while we hesitate, paralysed by our uncertainty. This has got to stop immediately.

We call on all non-Muslims in the free world to join us in this stand – to put the onus on each individual Muslim (not just 'Muslim organisations'). We must make this clear to every person who calls himself a Muslim: If you do not openly reject the doctrine of jihad when given an opportunity to do so, we must assume you abide by it and believe in it since it is a central part of your religious doctrine.

The result will be an openness and clarity that will allow us to move forward, stopping the orthodox Muslims from proceeding with their Islamisation project, freeing the heterodox Muslims from their prison of silence, and freeing ourselves from having to live with uncertainty, suspiciousness, or hatred in our day-to-day lives.

Why Islam should not be considered as a religion under UK law

This article is of particular relevance to a March 2018 case of Religiously Aggravated Harassment in Folkestone Magistrates' Court concerning Paul Golding, the leader of Britain First – and is also relevant to the March 2017 case in Southwark Crown Court where the author of this article was similarly charged.

It may well also be relevant to numerous other cases of Religiously Aggravated Harassment that have been prosecuted since the Racial and Religious Hatred Act came into force in 2006.

If only the legal system would take the following arguments into account, and find in our favour (as it undoubtedly should) then in addition to quashing the above-mentioned convictions of Religiously Aggravated Harassment, we would solve a great many of our problems with Islam overnight. Considering that Islam is shaping up to be the world's most intractable problem of the 21st century, this would be a most worthwhile goal, and one arguably deserving of a great deal of attention.

The author of this article attempted to have the subject debated in court in 2017, but was informed that there was no way that any judge in the UK would entertain such an idea in the current political climate, which is a sad indictment of the craven and cowardly attitude of those in power who should – in an ideal world – uphold the law without fear or favour, compared to the current policies of appeasement in relation to the increasingly arrogant and aggressive followers of the most barbaric, backward, misogynistic and totalitarian ideology the world has ever seen.

The basic argument is as follows: Islam should not be

considered a religion in UK law because it does not meet certain criteria laid down by the European Court of Human Rights (ECtHR) which is currently the highest authority in our legal system.

In a case going back to 1982 it was stated that: in order to qualify for protection under Article 9 of the European Convention on Human Rights (ECHR) (Freedom of thought, conscience and religion), religious and philosophical beliefs must be "worthy of respect in a democratic society, be not incompatible with human dignity and not conflict with the fundamental rights of others."

If it is lawful to protect religious beliefs that meet these criteria, it must be unlawful to protect (via legal recognition) religious beliefs that do not meet these criteria, because such beliefs must either be not worthy of respect in a democratic society (Islam is unquestionably anti-democratic) and/or incompatible with human dignity (the dignity of women, for instance, who are mere chattels in Islam) and/or conflict with the fundamental rights of others (such as gays, including gay Muslims, who, under Sharia law, must be killed).

Following on from this, the logic would be that, in law, you cannot harass a person based on their religion if, in law, that person has no religion (what they believe is not recognised, in law, as a religion and therefore does not qualify for the legal protections that apply, in law, to religions recognised as such).

In other words, 'religious harassment of a Muslim' is, in UK law, a contradiction in terms; it is a legal impossibility.

While Islam has been treated as a religion in numerous cases over the years, this issue has never been argued before a court; courts have just assumed that Islam is a religion in law. In other words, there is no binding precedent on this issue.

This may sound surprising, but you can perhaps understand why courts would avoid this issue like the plague, even if it occurred to them that they might consider it in the first place. But courts do not hesitate to apply these criteria to other philosophical or religious beliefs – so why should Islam be exempt?

Consider the sheer idiocy of the proposition that a set of beliefs which are incompatible with the human rights of others (say, sacrificing babies on the first Tuesday of every month), which would not be protected under Article 9 ECHR as philosophical beliefs, would be protected simply because they are 'religious beliefs'.

Would you protect Nazi beliefs if Nazis believed that Hitler was God? Of course you would not. **Yet there is a direct parallel with Islam.** Does it call for anti-Semitism? Yes. Does it have an inbuilt sense of supremacism? Yes. What about a quest for worldwide domination by any means available, including fear, violence, intimidation and terror? Yes again. It can easily be seen that Islam has much more in common with Nazism than it does with, say, Judaism or Christianity.

In another case from 2005, it was stated that "Article 9 embraces freedom of thought, conscience and religion. The atheist, the agnostic, and the sceptic are as much entitled to freedom to hold and manifest their beliefs as the theist. These beliefs are placed on an equal footing for the purpose of this guaranteed freedom." Thus, if its manifestation is to attract protection under Article 9 then a non-religious belief, as much as a religious belief, **must satisfy the modest threshold requirements** implicit in this Article.

With regard to the 'modest threshold requirements', these are stated in Article 9 as follows: "Everyone, therefore, is entitled to hold whatever beliefs he wishes. But when questions of 'manifestation' arise, as they usually do in this type of case, a belief must satisfy some modest, objective minimum requirements. These threshold requirements are implicit in Article 9 of the European Convention and comparable guarantees in other human rights instruments.

"The belief must be consistent with basic standards of human dignity or integrity. Manifestation of a religious belief, for instance, which involved subjecting others to torture or inhuman punishment, would not qualify for protection.

"The belief must relate to matters more than merely trivial. It must possess an adequate degree of seriousness and importance. As has been said, it must be a belief on a fundamental problem. With religious belief this requisite is readily satisfied.

"The belief must also be coherent in the sense of being intelligible and capable of being understood. But again, too much should not be demanded in this regard. Typically, religion involves belief in the supernatural. It is not always susceptible to lucid exposition or, still less, rational justification. The language used is often the language of allegory, symbol and metaphor.

"Depending on the subject matter, individuals cannot always be expected to express themselves with cogency or precision. Nor are an individual's beliefs fixed and static. The beliefs of every individual are prone to change over his or her lifetime. Overall, these threshold requirements should not be set at a level which would deprive minority beliefs of the protection they are intended to have under the Convention."

The bottom line is: A person can believe whatever he likes but his beliefs must meet the threshold requirements to be recognised and afforded protection in law.

It is true that Islam is given as an example of a religion in the explanatory notes to s.44 Equality Act 2006, but explanatory notes are not definitive of the meaning of an Act. Also, the explanatory notes state:

'Section 44 defines what is meant by "religion or belief" for the purposes of this Act. Section 44(a) defines "religion" as "any religion", a broad definition in line with the freedom of religion guaranteed by Article 9 of the ECHR.'

This makes it clear that, for the purposes of the Equality Act 2006, a religion can only be recognised and treated as a religion if it meets the criteria for Article 9 ECHR (because Article 9 ECHR does not recognise or protect beliefs or religions that do not meet the criteria specified in Campbell and Cosans v United Kingdom [1982] ECHR 1).

In any event, even if a statute did provide that Islam is a religion, the statute would itself be unlawful under Article 9 ECHR, given that the ECHR (and the case law of the ECtHR, which interprets the ECHR) overrides domestic law, whether it is statute or other.

Let's see how many people out there would support a Judicial Review (the legal mechanism whereby a senior judge would be obliged to consider the proposition that Islam should no longer be considered a religion in law.

It is admittedly an expensive process, **however, if a mere 3,000 people (out of our non-Muslim population of around 60 million) were to donate just £20 each then we could take the first step on the road to free our country from the tyranny of Islam.**

Please register your interest by leaving a message of support at the email address: tim@counterjihadwarrior.com – or if you can, please donate via the Tim Burton Legal Defence Fund on the home page at: http://www.counterjihadwarrior.com.

We owe it to our children and grandchildren to do everything we can to help provide them with a better world, free from the threat of Islam, Sharia law, and all the other manifestations of this barbaric, misogynistic 7th-century totalitarian ideology. Please help us to meet this goal if you possibly can.

The Problematic Definition of Islamophobia

Part 1 of 3

May 2019 – Once again, there are concerted efforts being made by 'the great and the good' to criminalise so-called 'Islamophobia' by enshrining the concept in law as a manifestation of 'racism'. This follows similar previous attempts by such luminaries as Baroness Sayeeda Warsi and Fizzy Mendacious OBE to reduce or eliminate our ability as non-Muslims to criticise the ideology of Islam.

The All-Party Parliamentary Group (APPG) on British Muslims proposes to define Islamophobia as: 'rooted in racism and is a type of racism that targets expressions of Muslimness or perceived Muslimness.'

Quite apart from the fact that 'Muslimness' is just another made-up word, as is the word 'Islamophobia' itself, this definition is so broad that it will allow any expression of concern about a Muslim, or the ideology, or the history of that ideology, to be seen as some sort of unlawful discrimination.

The reason that this is important is that if the ability to criticise Islam is taken away from us, then we will be led, like lambs to the slaughter, towards a totalitarian, dysfunctional society based on the ramblings of a 7th-century Middle Eastern warlord. Look no further than any Islamic-dominated country in the world, such as Pakistan, to see what an appalling prospect that would be.

The latest attempt has (for the time being) been rejected by the government, but it is only a matter of time before the proposal is re-hashed and comes before the government in a different form. The Labour and Liberal Democrat political parties, the Mayor of London – currently Sadiq Khan – and a number of local authorities in the UK have already adopted the APPG definition.

There is a growing tendency in official discourse to use terms that are ill-defined or even undefined. This practice is especially worrisome when the topics being discussed are contentious, causing heated debates on both sides of an issue. Under these circumstances, it is crucial that precise, unambiguous definitions be provided, and that all parties discussing the issues agree on those definitions.

The term 'Islamophobia' has been used repeatedly in publications, papers, and interventions submitted by or to OSCE (the Organisation for Security and Co-operation in Europe).

As a relevant example of its widespread usage, consider 'Guidelines for Educators on Countering Intolerance and Discrimination against Muslims: Addressing Islamophobia through Education', which was published jointly by OSCE/ODIHR, the Council of Europe, and UNESCO in 2011. The document contains 49 instances of the word 'Islamophobia', yet the closest it comes to a definition of the term is this brief description found on page 17:

'Islamophobia, a term which is widely used by NGOs and frequently appears in the media, tends to denote fear, hatred or prejudice against Islam and Muslims.' The above passage does not qualify in any way as a definition of 'Islamophobia', and yet the word forms the basis for an entire guidebook officially published by OSCE. It is completely unacceptable that an undefined term be employed in such a manner, especially when the topic referenced is currently so controversial.

At the Supplementary Human Dimension meeting in Vienna on July 12, 2013, in response to the repeated use of the term 'Islamophobia' during various OSCE proceedings, Mission Europa Netzwerk Karl Martell requested a definition of the word.

In response, the Turkish government representative Mr. Umut Topcuoglu quoted a definition of 'Islamophobia' that had been used previously. The definition itself was written by Ömür Orhun, the former Personal Representative of the Chairman-in-Office of the OSCE on Combating Intolerance and Discrimination against Muslims, and currently the Adviser and Special Envoy of the Secretary General of the Organisation for Islamic Cooperation (OIC). The inclusion of this definition without disclaimer in the official record of an OSCE event (OSCE 'Supplementary Human Dimension' meeting in Vienna, 11-12 July 2013) has made it 'de facto' an official OSCE definition:

Islamophobia is a **contemporary** *form of* **racism** *and* **xenophobia** *motivated by* **unfounded fear, mistrust, and hatred** *of Muslims and Islam. Islamophobia is also manifested through* **intolerance, discrimination, unequal treatment, prejudice, stereotyping, hostility,** *and* **adverse public discourse.** *Differentiating* **from classical racism and xenophobia***, Islamophobia is mainly based on* **stigmatisation** *of a religion and its followers, and as such, Islamophobia is an affront to the* **human rights and dignity** *of Muslims.*

The wording of this definition bears a close resemblance to that of an earlier definition of 'Islamophobia', which (perhaps unsurprisingly) was also written by Ambassador Orhun and published by the Organisation of Islamic Cooperation in 2011:

'Islamophobia is a contemporary form of racism and xenophobia motivated by unfounded fear, mistrust and hatred of Muslims and Islam. Islamophobia is also manifested through intolerance, discrimination and adverse public discourse against Muslims and Islam. Differentiating from classical racism and xenophobia, Islamophobia is mainly based on radicalisation of Islam and its followers.'

It is therefore no exaggeration to say that the definition of 'Islamophobia' officially recognised by the OSCE is essentially the same as the definition promulgated by the Organisation of Islamic Cooperation.

This is a clear conflict of interest. It is analogous to allowing a government regulatory agency to assign an industrial firm the task of writing the official regulations that define how that same firm is treated by the government. Such governmental practices are considered unethical and corrupt in all Western countries, including the participating states of the OSCE. The same standards recognised by governments should also apply to the OSCE: Organisations with a vested interest in defining a particular term to their own advantage must not be permitted to write the official definition of said term.

In addition to the above, care must be taken in further defining the terms used in the proposed definition of 'Islamophobia.' Terms such as 'racism', 'xenophobia', 'fear', 'unfounded mistrust and hatred', 'intolerance', discrimination', and 'adverse public discourse' are themselves loaded with recently acquired new meanings, which alone is reason enough to render the definition questionable for any scholarly use. Words that are commonly used to demonise, intimidate, and marginalise certain viewpoints are always unacceptable in presentations that affect public policy. Unless the controversial 'loaded' terms are themselves clearly defined, they should be excluded.

Although the term 'Islamophobia' was coined over a century ago, the use of the term gained traction in Britain during the Salman Rushdie 'Satanic Verses' affair in the late 1980s. This was an attempt by fundamentalist Muslims to silence critics such as Rushdie and his supporters for free speech by arguing that only the wider 'Islamophobia' of British society and state allowed this to pass unpunished. The implication was clear: criticism of Islam is tantamount to 'Islamophobia' and is therefore out of bounds. This is not a position that freedom-loving people living in a Western democracy can accept – and nor should they.

When the Runnymede Trust issued its infamous landmark report in 1997, the term 'Islamophobia' meant a shorthand way of referring to 'an unfounded dread or hatred of Islam – and, by extension, to an unfounded fear or dislike of all or most Muslims'.

However both the Runnymede report and its model have failed to stand the test of time and a detailed analysis highlights a number of serious flaws. The most obvious disadvantage of the term is that it is understood to be a 'phobia'. As phobias are irrational, such an accusation makes people defensive and defiant, in turn making reflective dialogue all but impossible.

A phobia, by definition, is irrational. Not only does the use of the word stigmatise those so designated – which was as far as the author cared to take his objection   it requires that those who apply it demonstrate the irrationality of the purported fear. In order to make the case, one would have to prove that the designated 'phobic' had in fact nothing to fear from Islam. In most cases this would be difficult to do, and any attempt to examine the data needed for such a proof would subject the mass behaviour of Muslims to scrutiny, which would cause controversy – and would in itself be considered evidence of 'Islamophobia'.

Thus the definition of the word 'Islamophobia' is problematic, and any proof of the existence of the condition it describes is difficult or impossible to obtain. Nevertheless, the word has gained widespread currency, appearing more and more frequently over the past ten years or so. In December 2004, then-Secretary-General of the United Nations Kofi Annan, speaking at a seminar entitled 'Confronting Islamophobia' in New York, referred to Islamophobia as an 'increasingly widespread bigotry'. The Organisation of the Islamic Conference (now the Organisation for Islamic Cooperation, OIC) established an 'Islamophobia Observatory' in 2007, and it has been issuing reports annually ever since. In April 2012 the OIC inaugurated a TV channel to counter 'Islamophobia'.

In May 2013, Dr. Hatem Bazian, the director of the Islamophobia Research and Documentation Project at UC Berkeley Center for Race and Gender, wrote:

'Thus, the crime of the terrorist is immediate, while that of the 'Islamophobes' is long-lasting, for it creates and impresses on our collective public mind the logic of hate and racism that is then packaged to further justify the logic of 'clash of ignorance' that is foundational [sic] to their [Sudden Ignorance] Syndrome.'

This statement implies a moral equivalence between 'Islamophobes' and terrorists who kill innocent bystanders with powerful bombs. To make such a comparison using such a hazily defined word is to skate onto the thinnest of ethical ice.

The increasing use of an ill-defined word in heated polemics becomes significant when the term is meant to punish, intimidate, and silence those who criticise Islam and Sharia. If the word cannot be avoided, it is absolutely essential that it be precisely defined, and that the definition must be acceptable to Muslims, critics of Islam, and disinterested parties alike.

The Problematic Definition of Islamophobia

Part 2 of 3

As we have said in Part 1 of this essay, the official OSCE definition of 'Islamophobia' is as follows:

*Islamophobia is a **contemporary** form of **racism** and **xenophobia** motivated by **unfounded fear, mistrust, and hatred** of Muslims and Islam. Islamophobia is also manifested through **intolerance, discrimination, unequal treatment, prejudice, stereotyping, hostility,** and **adverse public discourse.** Differentiating **from classical racism and xenophobia**, Islamophobia is mainly based on **stigmatisation** of a religion and its followers, and as such, Islamophobia is an affront to the **human rights and dignity** of Muslims.*

Several of the terms highlighted above are 'loaded', in the sense that they are either of recent coinage or have recently acquired new meanings, and are commonly used to demonise, intimidate, and marginalise people who hold certain political opinions. These words are controversial, and thus should not be used in any official definition without themselves being defined. The other words and phrases highlighted are problematic in various ways, even when the words themselves are well-defined and uncontroversial in their common usage.

Any terms whose contextual meaning might be unclear are defined. The definitions used below are all taken from the online version of the Merriam-Webster Dictionary.

***

Contemporary (adjective) is a perplexing qualifier for the conditions identified as the components of Islamophobia. The relevant definition of contemporary in Merriam-Webster is: 'marked by characteristics of the present period: modern, current.'

Is 'contemporary' racism different from that displayed by, say, the garrison manning the walls of Vienna during the Ottoman siege of Vienna in 1683? If so, what is the difference?

If there is no inherent distinction between the racism practiced centuries ago and that which exists today, then the use of the term 'contemporary' is functionally meaningless, and should be abandoned.

Racism is a loaded word of relatively recent coinage (1933), and is as much a tool of political manipulation as 'Islamophobia'. The definitions of the term that are relevant to this discussion are as follows:

i) a belief that race is the primary determinant of human traits and capacities and that racial differences produce an inherent superiority of a particular race, and

ii) racial prejudice or discrimination.

Let us imagine that a white European or North American expressed an opinion implying a prejudice against the following men, or a belief in their inferiority:

Mustafa Cerić, a Bosnian imam who called for Sharia in Bosnia; Abdul Wahid Pedersen, a Danish convert to Islam who in 2009 refused to condemn the practice of stoning, which he maintained is ordained by Allah; Ibrahim Hooper, Communications Director, Council on American-Islamic Relations (CAIR, an unindicted co-conspirator in the 2008 Holy Land Foundation terror financing trial).

All three of these men are white Caucasians. As a result, any 'prejudice or discrimination' against them cannot be termed 'racism'. Therefore it does not constitute 'Islamophobia'.

The obvious conclusion is that any feeling or opinion about Islam or Muslims cannot depend on 'racism'.

Xenophobia is another modern word (1903), and is also loaded. Like 'Islamophobia' and 'racism', it was arguably invented as a means to intimidate opponents of a dominant political ideology. Merriam-

Webster assigns it the following definition:

'Fear and hatred of strangers or foreigners or of anything that is strange or foreign'

Given this definition, how might 'xenophobia' be applicable to 'Islamophobia'?

Consider the Egyptian city of Minya, which recently experienced extensive violence at the hands of supporters of the Muslim Brotherhood. During August 2013, over the space of a few days, Islamic fundamentalists attacked and burned churches, orphanages, and homes belonging to Christians. The attackers chose their targets on the basis of religion; that is, buildings were set on fire because they were owned or occupied by Christians.

If those Christians are now afraid of Muslims or hate them, their feelings are not directed towards 'strangers, foreigners or anything that is strange or foreign'. Those who attacked them were their neighbours, and were in some cases personally known to them. Local Muslims were very familiar to Coptic Christians in Minya; they lived in the same community and spoke the same dialect.

The fear and hatred of Muslims by Christians in Minya therefore cannot be described as 'xenophobia'.

Stereotyping is another loaded word that is commonly used to stigmatise anyone who criticises, or even simply observes and comments on, the behaviour of members of a designated 'protected' group.

The dictionary tells us that 'stereotyping' is the making of a stereotype:

'Something conforming to a fixed or general pattern; especially: a standardised mental picture that is held in common by members of a group and that represents an oversimplified opinion, prejudiced attitude, or uncritical judgement.' Determining exactly what constitutes an 'oversimplified opinion' requires a very subjective judgement. How much can an opinion be simplified before it is 'oversimplified'? How much generalisation about a distinct group is allowed before it becomes a 'prejudiced attitude'?

The following sentence is an example of simplification, but would probably be considered an acceptable description of Islamic practice: 'Most faithful Muslims face Mecca and pray five times a day, bowing and putting their foreheads against the floor while kneeling.' This is an accurate representation of the behaviour of average Muslims when they gather for corporate worship, and may be readily observed in public.

This sentence, on the other hand, might not fare as well: 'Muslim protesters often shout "Massacre those who insult Islam" and similar slogans while carrying signs that read "Death to all those who insult the Prophet" or other threats against non-Muslims.' It is descriptively accurate – many such examples have been observed at demonstrations and have been recorded and published by the news media – but the observation does not reflect well on Muslims or Islam. Thus it would commonly be seen as 'stereotyping', and cited as evidence of 'Islamophobia'.

To summarise: a realistic précis of the behaviour of Muslims may be considered acceptable and innocuous, or unacceptable 'stereotyping', depending on the content of what is observed.

Hostility – According to the Merriam-Webster dictionary, hostility means: 'conflict, opposition, or resistance in thought or principle'.

As examples of conflict and opposition in religious matters, consider the following news reports, all of which describe incidents that occurred in Indonesia in the spring and summer of 2013.

First, from March 25, 2013 – On the eve of Palm Sunday, Islamist groups made serious threats against Catholics in Jakarta, telling the priest and the faithful to cancel their scheduled weekend celebrations. Their hatred was triggered by the fact that the place of worship is located inside a school, which, in their opinion, 'should not be used' for religious services.

From July 1, 2013 – Islamic extremists are threatening to block celebrations for the 50th anniversary of the priestly ordination of Fr. Gregorius Utomo, scheduled for tomorrow, July 2. Relatives, friends and the faithful have organised a series of events and a solemn Eucharistic celebration, scheduled in the private chapel of prayer known as Wisma Tyas Dalem (House of the Sacred Heart). ... In recent days, on the eve of the celebrations, the fundamentalists of the Islamic Defenders Front (FPI) have, however, warned Fr. Utomo and faithful to stop all religious activities in program: they accuse the priest of using the house 'in an illegal manner.'

From July 19, 2013 – The Islamist pressures against Christian communities in Aceh 'have become intolerable. Within a year, with non-existent legal pretexts, 17 house churches have been closed: these also include Catholic chapels. The Islamisation of the province continues, just as promised by the governor Abdullah.' It is the sense of the Annual Report published by IndonesianChristian.org, a Protestant organisation which monitors the situation of the Christian community in Indonesia.

From September 9, 2013 – The Sharia 'Police' and security officials in the district of West Aceh, the Indonesian province where Islamic law is in force, arrested Pastor Hendri Budi Kusumo and four other people, members of the Indonesian Mission Evangelist Church. The incident occurred last week, but only emerged in the past hours. According to reports the religious police – in charge of enforcing Islamic rules and customs – accused the five of 'proselytism', because they were trying to 'convert Muslims to Christianity in the area of Aceh.'

Indonesia is a majority-Muslim country whose constitution guarantees religious freedom. The above examples show a persistent hostility displayed by Indonesian Muslims towards the country's large Christian minority. Such behaviour in most cases is unlawful. One searches in vain for similar news stories involving Christian hostility towards Muslims in Indonesia.

Once again, this does not preclude the possibility of hostile attitudes displayed by non-Muslims against Muslims in Indonesia or anywhere else. However, the persistent focus on a single type of sectarian hostility at the expense of others is further evidence that the proceedings of the OSCE often treat Islam differently from other religions.

Adverse Public Discourse – Like other phrases used in Mr. Topcuoglu's definition of 'Islamophobia', the meaning of 'adverse public discourse' depends on subjective perceptions, and is therefore susceptible to misuse for political purposes.

The dictionary definition of adverse: Causing harm, or harmful (as in drug abuse).

We will examine two examples of public discourse and consider which might be described as 'harmful'.

Geert Wilders is the leader of the most popular political party in the Netherlands. He is often characterised as an 'Islamophobe', and his speeches and writings are widely considered adverse to Islam. Mr. Wilders made the following statements in March 2013:

'In the Netherlands, there are almost 500 honor crimes each year, with on average one honor killing each month; Honor crimes are committed almost exclusively in an Islamic context; In Amsterdam alone, between 200 to 300 Islamic women have been imprisoned in their homes by male relatives; Some 30,000 women in the country have suffered female genital mutilation. Every year, about 50 girls [sic] are mutilated in this way in the Netherlands; In September 2010, of all women in women's shelters, 26% were of Turkish origin, 24% of Moroccan origin, 27% of Iraqi origin, and 23% of various mostly non-Western) countries.'

Although what Mr. Wilders said may be considered hurtful to Muslims, it is factually-based, and the points he raises may be confirmed by examining official government statistics and accessing archives of media news stories.

It is useful to compare the above remarks with those of Sheikh Yusuf Al-Qaradawi. Sheikh Qaradawi is the spiritual leader of the Muslim Brotherhood, the organisation to which former Egyptian President Mohamed Morsi belongs. The sheikh said the following on Al-Jazeera TV in January 2009:

'Throughout history, Allah has imposed upon the [Jews] people who would punish them for their corruption. The last punishment was carried out by Hitler. By means of all the things he did to them – even though they exaggerated this issue – he managed to put them in their place. This was divine punishment for them. Allah willing, the next time will be at the hand of the believers.'

Unlike Mr. Wilders' assertions, Sheikh Qaradawi's statements are not based on verifiable factual information or statistics. Furthermore, they are demonstrably harmful, and may even constitute incitement to genocide.

Yet while Mr. Wilders is routinely condemned for his 'adverse public discourse', Yusuf Al Qaradawi's utterances are not denounced by any other major non-Muslim political leader, not to mention any Islamic leaders.

This malleability of the meaning of 'adverse public discourse' illustrates the political manipulation of terms in order to arrive at pre-ordained conclusions. In this case, the predetermined consensus is that Geert Wilders is an 'Islamophobe' and Sheikh Yusuf Al-Qaradawi is a 'prominent Muslim spiritual leader'. Assigning 'adverse public discourse' to the one and not to the other serves to reinforce the intended result.

The Problematic Definition of Islamophobia

Part 3 of 3

As we have already said in Part 1 and Part 2 of this essay, the official OSCE definition of 'Islamophobia' is as follows:

*Islamophobia is a **contemporary** form of **racism** and **xenophobia** motivated by **unfounded fear, mistrust, and hatred** of Muslims and Islam. Islamophobia is also manifested through **intolerance, discrimination, unequal treatment, prejudice, stereotyping, hostility,** and **adverse public discourse.** Differentiating **from classical racism and xenophobia**, Islamophobia is mainly based on **stigmatisation** of a religion and its followers, and as such, Islamophobia is an affront to the **human rights and dignity** of Muslims.*

Several of the terms highlighted above are 'loaded', in the sense that they are either of recent coinage or have recently acquired new meanings, and are commonly used to demonise, intimidate, and marginalise people who hold certain political opinions. These words are controversial, and thus should not be used in any official definition without themselves being defined. The other words and phrases highlighted are problematic in various ways, even when the words themselves are well-defined and uncontroversial in their common usage.

Any terms whose contextual meaning might be unclear are defined. The definitions used below are all taken from the online version of the Merriam-Webster Dictionary.

***

Classical Racism and Xenophobia – 'Racism' and 'xenophobia' have already been covered above. The addition of 'classical' as a modifier of these terms is perplexing.

What are 'classical racism' and 'classical xenophobia'? Mr. Topcuoglu seems to 'differentiate' these terms from other varieties of 'racism' or 'xenophobia'. What might those varieties be?

Returning to the dictionary, we learn that classical means: i) standard, classic or ii) authoritative, traditional.

How can racism be 'standard', 'classic', or 'authoritative'? Do racists recognise a common 'authority'? This makes no sense.

There the only plausible interpretation must be 'traditional'. But from what 'tradition' of racism does 'Islamophobia' differ? Are we to pinpoint modern differences of opinion with Adolf Hitler? Or with Georges-Louis Leclerc, or with Le Comte de Buffon?

What criteria are we obliged to choose?

There has been a concerted effort over the past ten or fifteen years to codify 'Islamophobia' as a form of 'racism' in the official terminology employed by the United Nations. One presumes that Mr. Topcuoglu is continuing this process with his definition.

If 'Islamophobia' is to become a new form of 'racism' – as distinct from the 'classical' variety or any other species of the term – then the precise correlation must be specified. As we observed in the above section on 'racism', there is no logical way in which Islam may be considered equivalent to a race.

Stigmatisation of a Religion and its Followers – 'Stigmatisation' means 'the process of stigmatising'. To stigmatise is defined as 'to describe or identify in opprobrious terms'.

The definition of 'religion' is 'the service and worship of God or the supernatural'.

We are frequently reminded by Muslims that Islam encompasses far more than religion; it is not simply a matter of serving and worshipping God. Among other things it is an entire legal system, whose strictures and requirements are mandatory for all Muslims. In 'Islamic Finance: An Introduction' by Saulat Pervez on the 'Why Islam?' website, we read:

'Muslims often try to explain that Islam is more than a religion. They contend that Islam is actually a 'way of life,' with the Quran and the life traditions of the Prophet Muhammad providing a blueprint for daily life. From marriage and family life to lawful food and drink, from modesty in dress and excellence in social manners to ethics in trade and finance, Islam encompasses all aspects of our existence.'

So what is the legal code that Muslims follow to determine which behaviours are 'lawful'? The most authoritative source is 'Umdat al-salik wa 'uddat al-nasik', or The Reliance of the Traveller and Tools of the Worshipper. It is commonly referred to as Reliance of the Traveller when cited in English.

The English translation is an authoritative source on Sunni Islamic law, because it is certified as such by Al-Azhar University in Cairo. There is no higher authority on Sunni Islamic doctrine than Al-Azhar; it is the closest equivalent to the Vatican that may be found in Islam.

At the beginning of Book A, 'Sacred Knowledge' (p. 2), we read: (Abd al-Wahhab Khallaf) There is no disagreement among the scholars of the Muslims that the source of legal rulings for all the acts of those who are morally responsible is Allah Most Glorious.

In Book B (b7.1), al-Misri details the four necessary integral elements of consensus. If those are met, the ruling agreed upon is authoritative (b7.2):

When the four necessary integrals of consensus exist, the ruling agreed upon is an authoritative part of sacred law that is obligatory to obey and not lawful to disobey. Nor can 'mujtahids' (Islamic scholars) of a succeeding era make the thing an object of new 'ijtihad' (a process whereby a previously agreed ruling may be re-examined and possibly altered). Because the agreed-upon ruling, verified by scholarly consensus, is an absolute legal ruling, it does not admit of ever being contravened or annulled.

In other words, Islamic law is fixed and eternal, and mortals may not change it. It is also authoritative; that is; it is binding upon all observant Muslims.

Since Islamic law is an integral part of Islam, to oppose Islam is to oppose Sharia (Islamic law). Furthermore, the primary issue for many so-called 'Islamophobes' is Islamic law, because the tenets of Sharia, as laid out in Reliance of the Traveller and other manuals of Islamic jurisprudence, are contrary to the Universal Declaration of Human Rights as well as the European Declaration of Human Rights and the

Constitution of the United States.

For that reason, opposition to Islamic law is no more 'phobic' than opposing the Napoleonic Code or the Code of Hammurabi. Based on the commandments of their religion, Muslims might find themselves in opposition to Mosaic Law, the English Common Law, or the U.S. Constitution. Yet no one would question their right to express such opposition, nor accuse them of being 'Christian-o-phobes' for their principled stance.

If the definition of 'Islamophobia' hinges on fear or hatred of a religion, then it manifestly fails in most instances where it is applied. Such designations are erroneous, since the vast majority of those who oppose Islam specifically oppose Islamic law (Sharia), as laid down in the Qur'an and the Hadith, and codified in the fiqh (the body of Islamic jurisprudence).

Furthermore, such opposition to Sharia cannot be characterised as 'stigmatisation', provided that it quotes Islamic law accurately, recognises established precedents, and cites real examples.

The problematical 'loaded' and 'controversial' terms have been extensively discussed in the earlier part of this essay. It is obvious that the definition of Islamophobia as presented here fails to meet even minimal standards of logic, coherence, and objectivity. As such it should be rejected for any further usage, especially in OSCE proceedings.

As mentioned above, six of the terms used in the definition ('racism', 'xenophobia', 'intolerance', 'discrimination', 'prejudice', and 'stereotyping') are 'loaded', in the sense that they are either of recent coinage or have recently acquired new meanings, The definition fails utterly through its inclusion of three phrases ('unequal treatment', 'stigmatisation of a religion and its followers', and 'unfounded fear, mistrust, and hatred').

Specifically: **'Unequal treatment'**. Islam itself (via Sharia) treats non-Muslims differently from Muslims. Under the given definition, Muslims would themselves be guilty of 'Islamophobia'. This is a logical absurdity, and the definition falls because of it.

Stigmatisation of a religion and its followers – The overwhelming majority of the critics of Islam do not, for the most part 'describe or identify the Islamic ideology in opprobrious terms'. Their critiques are focused almost entirely on the tenets of Islamic law (and the practical implementation of those tenets), which are not at all religious. Criticism of the religious elements of Islam is rare, mild, and often non-existent. This term therefore deflects the discussion into a 'straw man' argument, and the definition falls because of it.

Unfounded fear, mistrust, and hatred – This is the heart, the core of the definition of 'Islamophobia'. Any fear, mistrust, or hatred of Islam must be shown to be unfounded if it is to constitute Islamophobia. As previously demonstrated, millions of non-Muslims all over the world have well-founded empirical reasons to fear Islam, and thus cannot possibly be described as 'Islamophobes'. Furthermore, any investigation into the basis for the fear of Islam – which requires research into and discussion of the collective behaviour of self-identified Muslims in real world situations – is almost always itself condemned as 'Islamophobia'. Therefore the definition of 'Islamophobia' makes the word into a self-referential term. This is a violation of logic, and the definition falls because of it.

Other logical failures detailed in the previous section include those for 'racism', 'xenophobia', and 'stereotyping'. Additional logical problems are presented by 'contemporary' (incoherent usage in context), and 'classical racism and xenophobia' (demands clarification of the meaning of 'classical' in this context).

Five other terms ('intolerance', 'discrimination', 'prejudice', 'hostility', and 'adverse public discourse') were analysed and shown to be applicable to Islam itself. This is not a logical argument against their appearance in the definition – it would be a 'tu quoque' fallacy to make such an assertion – but it adds weight to the failure of the definition on logical grounds. **Reciprocity of behaviour, commonly referred to as the 'Golden Rule', is a core cultural value in Western societies.** Islam's manifest failure to exhibit normative reciprocity argues persuasively against the inclusion of these five terms in any definition of 'Islamophobia'.

A good recommendation would be to appoint a committee whose duty will be to establish a definition of Islamophobia that is acceptable by consensus. The makeup of the committee should include Muslims, Jews, Christians, and atheists. The non-Muslims on the committee should include in equal numbers supporters of Islam, critics of Islam, and people with no opinion on Islam.

The All-Party Parliamentary Group (APPG) referred to in the earlier part of this essay proposes to define Islamophobia as: 'rooted in racism and is a type of racism that targets expressions of Muslimness or perceived Muslimness.' Arguably this definition is even worse than the more detailed definition adopted by OSCE, because of the made-up word 'Muslimness'.

What is 'Muslimness', after all? Perhaps it is the propensity for adult males to wear their prayer hats and 'shalwar kameez' while walking around in public sporting long black beards? Perhaps it is the inclination for adult females to resemble letterboxes in public (as the former Mayor of London, Boris Johnson once memorably said) by wearing all-encompassing black burqas or covering their faces with the niqab?

Perhaps it is the tendency to walk around with a dog-eared copy of the Qur'an tucked under your arm into which you can dig in order to produce handy snippets to support your fallacious and specious argument that Islam is somehow 'a Religion of Peace'.

No doubt there will be someone out there all too ready to accuse me of Islamophobia for pointing out that Muslims are not the same as the rest of us when it comes to assimilation and integration, and that Muslim leaders at the time of writing (such as President Erdogan of Turkey) specifically encourage Muslims not to assimilate or integrate to Western democratic host countries in which they may find themselves.

Even our Assistant Commissioner of Police, Neil Basu, the most senior counter-terrorism officer in the UK at the time of writing (who is paid his lavish salary and even more impressive retirement package in order to protect the British people from the depredations of the hordes of swivel-eyed Islamic fanatics who roam the streets of our cities) is not immune from spouting the most semi-literate pseudo-academic drivel.

In August 2019, it was reported in the mainstream media that he had implied that assimilation for Muslims living in the West is an entirely negative process and that anyone who thinks or says otherwise is guilty of – wait for it, wait for it – yes, you guessed it, 'Islamophobia'. This was absolutely outrageous for a man in his position, who should have been expected to discharge his duties with absolute impartiality, rather than to pontificate on political matters outside of his domain in such an arrogant manner.

If you can't define the term 'Islamophobia' without defining the term 'Muslimness' and you can't define the term 'Muslimness' without defining (or being accused of) 'Islamophobia', then you find yourself in the same unenviable position as the Ouzelum bird – a legendary creature, beloved in British and Australian folklore, that flies in ever-decreasing circles until it completely disappears up its own backside.

It may *appear* to be in the interests of Muslims to ensure that the term 'Islamophobia' remains undefined, or alternatively defined in such woolly terms as to render the phrase completely meaningless – but it is definitely not in the interests of non-Muslims, who require a comprehensive, watertight definition that will be fit for purpose when legal tests under British and international law are applied, in order that criticism of the political ideology of Islam should not be sanctioned or criminalised.

Our goal should be maintain the ability to criticise every aspect of the political ideology of Islam and to subject it to the most ruthless examination – for if we are able to do so, openly, honestly and without fear of retribution from politically correct authorities, and if every single non-Muslim in the West realises the horror of what awaits them if Islam were ever to supplant our Judaeo-Christian Western civilisation, then in due course we will be able to take all the appropriate precautions, and that will mean that even Muslims themselves will eventually realise the error of their ways and discard their political ideology, consigning it to the dustbin of history. That will be a day worth fighting for.

For on that day, Islam will disappear in a puff of smoke, never to return, and all of mankind will be able to breathe a sincere, fervent and heartfelt sigh of relief.

Printed in Poland
by Amazon Fulfillment
Poland Sp. z o.o., Wrocław